Felicia Chan is a lecturer in Screen Studies at the University of Manchester where she researches the construction of national, cultural and cosmopolitan imaginaries in film. She is also co-editor of *Chinese Cinemas: International Perspectives* (2016) and founding member of the Chinese Film Forum UK.

'*Cosmopolitan Cinema* argues that "world" or transnational cinema is underwritten by the commodification of difference, and articulates a project of cinematic cosmopolitanism based on the critical experience and affective negotiation of linguistic and cultural limits. An admirable book.'

– Pheng Cheah, University of California, Berkeley

'As much of the world retreats behind national walls, *Cosmopolitan Cinema* turns to globally recognised East and Southeast Asian films. Its originality lies in the acknowledgement of the pitfalls that can make cosmopolitanism complicit with hubris and neglect of the local, together with a call for critically engaged cosmopolitanism that interrogates how local specificity is globally connected.'

– Chris Berry, King's College London

'Felicia Chan's book offers a critical reflection on the imperative of acknowledging and embracing difference and foreignness at the interface of cinema's textual and extra-textual levels. This call for critical cosmopolitanism – rooted in an ethos of "learning to live with paradox" – is especially urgent during these post-Brexit, Trump-triumphant times.'

– Song Hwee Lim, Chinese University of Hong Kong; author of *Tsai Ming-liang and a Cinema of Slowness*

TAURIS WORLD CINEMA SERIES

Series Editors:
Lúcia Nagib, *Professor of Film at the University of Reading*
Julian Ross, *Research Fellow at the University of Westminster*

Advisory Board: Laura Mulvey (UK), Robert Stam (USA), Ismail Xavier (Brazil), Dudley Andrew (USA)

The *Tauris World Cinema Series* aims to reveal and celebrate the richness and complexity of film art across the globe, exploring a wide variety of cinemas set within their own cultures and as they interconnect in a global context. The books in the series will represent innovative scholarship, in tune with the multicultural character of contemporary audiences. Drawing upon an international authorship, they will challenge outdated conceptions of world cinema, and provide new ways of understanding a field at the centre of film studies in an era of transnational networks.

Published and forthcoming in the World Cinema series:

Animation in the Middle East: Practice and Aesthetics from Baghdad to Casablanca
Edited by Stefanie Van de Peer

Basque Cinema: A Cultural and Political History
By Rob Stone and María Pilar Rodriguez

Brazil on Screen: Cinema Novo, New Cinema, Utopia
By Lúcia Nagib

The Cinema of Jia Zhangke: Realism and Memory in Chinese Film
By Cecília Mello

The Cinema of Sri Lanka: South Asian Film in Texts and Contexts
By Ian Conrich and Vilasnee Tampoe-Hautin

Contemporary New Zealand Cinema: From New Wave to Blockbuster
Edited by Ian Conrich and Stuart Murray

Contemporary Portuguese Cinema: Globalising the Nation
Edited by Mariana Liz

Cosmopolitan Cinema: Cross-cultural Encounters in East Asian Film
By Felicia Chan

Documentary Cinema: Contemporary Non-fiction Film and Video Worldwide
By Keith Beattie

East Asian Cinemas: Exploring Transnational Connections on Film
Edited by Leon Hunt and Leung Wing-Fai

East Asian Film Noir: Transnational Encounters and Intercultural Dialogue
Edited by Chi-Yun Shin and Mark Gallagher

Film Genres and African Cinema: Postcolonial Encounters
By Rachael Langford

Impure Cinema: Intermedial and Intercultural Approaches to Film
Edited by Lúcia Nagib and Anne Jerslev

Latin American Women Filmmakers: Production, Politics, Poetics
Edited by Deborah Martin and Deborah Shaw

Lebanese Cinema: Imagining the Civil War and Beyond
By Lina Khatib

New Argentine Cinema
By Jens Andermann

New Directions in German Cinema
Edited by Paul Cooke and Chris Homewood

New Turkish Cinema: Belonging, Identity and Memory
By Asuman Suner

On Cinema
By Glauber Rocha
Edited by Ismail Xavier

Palestinian Filmmaking in Israel: Narratives of Place and Identity
By Yael Freidman

Paulo Emílio Salles Gomes: On Brazil and Global Cinema
Edited by Maite Conde and Stephanie Dennison

Performing Authorship: Self-inscription and Corporeality in the Cinema
By Cecilia Sayad

Queer Masculinities in Latin American Cinema: Male Bodies and Narrative Representations
By Gustavo Subero

Realism in Greek Cinema: From the Post-war Period to the Present
By Vrasidas Karalis

Realism of the Senses in World Cinema: The Experience of Physical Reality
By Tiago de Luca

The Spanish Fantastic: Contemporary Filmmaking in Horror, Fantasy and Sci-fi
By Shelagh-Rowan Legg

Stars in World Cinema: Screen Icons and Star Systems Across Cultures
Edited by Andrea Bandhauer and Michelle Royer

Thai Cinema: The Complete Guide
Edited by Mary J. Ainslie and Katarzyna Ancuta

Theorizing World Cinema
Edited by Lúcia Nagib, Chris Perriam and Rajinder Dudrah

Viewing Film
By Donald Richie

Queries, ideas and submissions to:

Series Editor: Professor Lúcia Nagib – l.nagib@reading.ac.uk

Series Editor: Dr. Julian Ross – rossj@westminster.ac.uk

Cinema Editor at I.B.Tauris, Maddy Hamey-Thomas – mhamey-thomas@ibtauris.com

FELICIA CHAN

COSMOPOLITAN CINEMA

CROSS-CULTURAL ENCOUNTERS
IN EAST ASIAN FILM

Published in 2017 by
I.B.Tauris & Co. Ltd
London • New York
www.ibtauris.com

Copyright © 2017 Felicia Chan

Paperback edition published 2024

The right of Felicia Chan to be identified as the author of this work has been asserted by the author in accordance with the Copyright, Designs and Patents Act 1988.

All rights reserved. Except for brief quotations in a review, this book, or any part thereof, may not be reproduced, stored in or introduced into a retrieval system, or transmitted, in any form or by any means, electronic, mechanical, photocopying, recording or otherwise, without the prior written permission of the publisher.

Every attempt has been made to gain permission for the use of the images in this book. Any omissions will be rectified in future editions.

References to websites were correct at the time of writing.

Tauris World Cinema Series

ISBN: 978 1 78076 722 2
PB: 978 1 35050 572 8
eISBN: 978 1 78672 187 7
ePDF: 978 1 78673 187 6

A full CIP record for this book is available from the British Library
A full CIP record is available from the Library of Congress

Library of Congress Catalog Card Number: available

Contents

List of illustrations	viii
Foreword	ix
Acknowledgements	xvi
Introduction: Cosmopolitanism and the cinema	1
1 The cosmopolitan challenge of multilingual cinema	18
2 Cosmopolitan memory and self-reflexive cinema	55
3 Film festivals and cosmopolitan affect	92
4 Embodiment as (cosmopolitan) encounter	119
Postscript: Critical cosmopolitanism and comparative cinema	141
Notes	148
Bibliography	175
Filmography	190
Index	193

List of illustrations

1.1	*In the Mood for Love*: Silhouette of a coconut tree	33
1.2	*Whisper of the Heart*: 'Think I should've kept it in English?'	43
1.3	*Whisper of the Heart*: Shizuku's 'Country Roads'	45
1.4	*A City of Sadness*: Wen-ching in his photo studio	50
2.1	*24 City*: A factory being dismantled	60
2.2	*24 City*: Direct address of characters to the camera	62
2.3	*24 City*: Actress Joan Chen playing Xiaohua / Little Flower, who is said to resemble Joan Chen	66
2.4	*24 City*: Shot of TV set screening *Xiaohua / Little Flower* (1979) with a young Joan Chen in the starring role	67
2.5	*Lust, Caution*: Wang Chia-chih / Tang Wei performs 'The Wandering Songstress'	73
2.6	*Lust, Caution*: At the pictures in Shanghai	74
2.7	*Lust, Caution*: Wang Chia-chih in Western dress	75
2.8	*Millennium Actress*: Chiyoko on a bicycle	80
2.9	*Late Spring*: Noriko on a bicycle	81
2.10	*Millennium Actress*: Old lady with a spinning wheel	81
2.11	*Throne of Blood*: Spirit with a spinning wheel	82
2.12	*Millennium Actress*: Ida is hailed by arrows	82
2.13	*Throne of Blood*: Washizu is hailed by arrows	83
2.14	*Millennium Actress*: Chiyoko in a 'Machiko shawl'	84
2.15	*Millennium Actress*: Chiyoko rides through history	89
2.16	*Millennium Actress*: Chiyoko in European dress	89
2.17	*Millennium Actress*: Chiyoko being filmed by Ida	90
3.1	The Majestic theatre in Singapore, *c.* 1950s. Bels Collection, courtesy of the National Archives of Singapore	106
4.1	*Life of Imitation*. Courtesy of Ming Wong	124
4.2	*After Chinatown*. Courtesy of Ming Wong	131
4.3	Billboard of *Four Malay Stories*. Courtesy of Ming Wong	135

Foreword

The move towards rethinking questions of difference and otherness in such a way as to reveal the affective pull of political events and social processes has become ever more urgent. A renewed interest in looking to theories of cosmopolitanism to do this took a powerful grip on academic debates in a post-9/11 Western context. Two key ideas characterised the extensive discussions around this concept: first, the wish to engender a sense of belonging, or even citizenship, beyond the nation, and to generate the feeling of being 'at home in the world';[1] and, secondly, an affirmation of living easily with cultural diversity, or what Paul Gilroy has called 'convivial culture'.[2] These and many other cosmopolitan aspirations were discussed in order to try and find a critical vocabulary that spoke directly to the demands of that particular geo-political moment and its aftermath.

Fifteen years later, partly as a consequence of responses to 9/11, there continues to be a pressing need to find new languages to challenge xenophobia, racism and nostalgic monocultural nationalisms. Writing this foreword today,[3] I am struck again by the ongoing importance of cosmopolitan visions – even if these must always be tempered by an acknowledgement of the problems presented by their idealising imaginaries. Questions of borders, migration, asylum, displacement and exile in the context of war and violence are at the top of many of our intellectual agendas today. But these issues have never been separable from colonial and post-colonial histories whose globalising effects have repeatedly demonstrated the transnational implications of legacies of injustice and exploitation.

Many scholars have turned to art, literature and cinema to find imaginative spaces through which to explore the difficult questions of why difference continues to be so threatening and how the unfamiliar is transformed into otherness and 'foreignness' in ways that justify contempt and intolerance.[4] But whilst other disciplines in the humanities and social sciences have embraced cosmopolitan visions with considerable enthusiasm, film studies has engaged with them with a certain caution and scepticism. With its power to reach into our psyches and draw us into its imaginative worlds of strangers, the cinema might have held the promise of a cosmopolitan optimism, fulfilling our wishes to envision a better political futurity. We might have expected it to provide the focus of debates about how to stage the problem of seeing ourselves from the outside in ways that might engender a more generous hospitality towards strangers and a sense of belonging beyond the nation state. But instead film scholars have tested cosmopolitan debates and grounded its universalising claims and utopian tendencies in particular geo-political contexts.[5]

Cautious about the tempting move from cultural forms to political visions, and sceptical about the models of spectatorship that might underscore ideas of social transformation through the arts, film studies scholars have responded to cosmopolitan agendas through situated close readings of texts and locations. On the whole, these have demonstrated the difficulties and limits of cosmopolitan ideals and have located the points of friction that might halt fantasies of transnational legibility. This is not to argue that cosmopolitan aspirations have not been of interest to film studies; rather, it is to indicate that the field generally has tended to match the dependence of such aspirations upon universalising tendencies with a localising and grounding response.

One problem for scholars of cosmopolitanism has been the extent to which it might be mobilised beyond its Western origins and its original Western frameworks. In this book Felicia Chan takes this challenge into her study of East and Southeast Asian cinema with eloquence and precision. Holding onto the progressive potential of the expansive cosmopolitan promise, Chan's focus on uncertainty and ambiguity throughout this study counteracts any lingering idealisations of cross-cultural encounters. This emphasis on encountering others through linguistic, geographical, temporal and embodied differences holds us firmly within a cinematic framework of formal and structural constraints and yet also captures the nuanced incompletions of such encounters. If, on the one hand, we are presented with case studies of multilingualism, border crossing, transnational mobility and circulation, and cross-cultural comparison, we are rarely allowed to forget the particularities of located memory, experience and history, on the other.

This focus on the encounter as the route through debates about cosmopolitan cinema places an uncertainty of outcome centre-stage. As Jacques Derrida has argued, the ethical possibilities inscribed within cosmopolitanism in the encounter with the stranger also always holds the potential for its opposite.[6] And the assumption of shared ground in the exchanges that constitute hospitality is haunted by histories of hostility to foreigners and foreignness. To equate openness to others with a mutually legible ease would thus be mistaken. In the cinema, these affective contradictions are played out on a globalised stage through the uneven and unequal distribution and circulation of resources and representations. The ambivalence that, following Zygmunt Bauman,[7] interests Chan here shifts between the embodied aesthetics of screen encounters and the limits of legibilities that may not always travel smoothly across national, cultural and linguistic boundaries.

Chan's interest in the cosmopolitan contradictions of the cross-cultural encounter is always one that takes seriously the cultural imaginaries that cinema's image of itself has continued to generate. Approaching cinema through this lens locates it firmly within the project of modernity, whose hallmark has been the reflexivity of its own cultural forms. Less elaborated, though, are the ways in which such reflexive modes are transformed as they travel across national and linguistic boundaries. Taking cinema as a modern form concerned with its own aesthetic histories, Chan moves these into dialogue with the aspirations and limits of a cosmopolitanism that seeks to embrace diversity and enable generosity through a geographically located study with particular emphasis on practices of translation and mediation.

This book speaks to a number of unanswered questions about the place of East and Southeast Asian screen cultures in studies of cosmopolitanism. What kinds of challenges might be brought to the cosmopolitan project from these cinematic contexts? How might questions of language and location play out in particular ways in these transnational cinemas? If we turn our attention to cinemas across these regions, how might their configurations and histories present challenges to the universalisms of cosmopolitan aspirations? And, if these challenges run deep, is there still an intellectual and political purchase in this framework for scholars in the twenty-first century?

One key focus in this book is the challenge multilingual cinema presents to cosmopolitanism, revealing its paradox as *both* an appealing yet unrealisable ideal *and* the source of a necessary test of the limits of current notions of multiculturalism and hybridisation. Reconceptualising the cinema as a site of encounter with 'foreignness', Chan's readings trace the history of sound as a site of shifting discourses of the foreign as a 'matter of time and place'.[8] If proximity to foreignness is in part the appeal of what the cinema can bring to audiences, putting them 'in transit' as they consume the latest stories of elsewhere,[9] then the pleasures of such intimacy with otherness may also be interrupted or reconfigured through the mediating practices necessary for films to be legible in particular locations. Changing patterns of dubbing, subtitling and simultaneous dual-language shooting are mapped across the history of filmmaking in East and Southeast Asia in this book. The multiple uses of Chinese languages in Hong Kong cinema in general, and in Wong Kar-wai's arthouse films in particular, are taken as examples of the contradictions embedded within cross-cultural encounters. The history of the mediation of films to audiences by live narrators (*benshi*) in Japan is another route through which to explore the challenge of multilingual cinema to cosmopolitan imaginaries. Examples from the dubbing and subtitling of Japanese animation films for Western audiences offer another focus for tracing the processes of how the drawing of borders aesthetically brings audiences into proximity with imperfect translations. Each of these case studies is meticulously embedded within the longer history of cinematic forms and the wider context of geo-political hierarchies.

The question of cinematic forms has been central to an extensive debate about the place of film in trauma and memory studies.[10] Does cinema's self-reflexivity have a particular role to play in representing the trauma of violent experiences and histories? Often named as that which is beyond representation, trauma has been defined as the scene of which the subject is required to absent her/himself in order to survive. And yet, cinema has always promised its audiences an encounter with an affective presence unlike other art and media forms. If the problem of witnessing has been central to the study of trauma, then cinema's promise might appeal where other forms of encounter have failed. How might cinema afford the means to return to unspeakable acts of violence in ways that contribute to cosmopolitan visions? This is one of questions Chan asks in this book. Turning to formal questions of self-reflexivity in cinema, Chan explores what she calls cosmopolitan memory in the context of unnarratable events.[11] Close readings of *24 City*, *Lust, Caution* and *Millennium Actress* bring questions of memory and trauma into national and transnational frames, exploring the changing histories of Chinese labour, of China as a country under Japanese occupation and of cultural and political histories of Japan through a personalised lens. Situated within a consideration of cinema's interconnected styles of self-reflexivity, the readings here raise vital issues about the possibilities and limits of representational strategies in relation to violence and trauma. Exploring the extent to which cinema might operate as a space of public witnessing through the spaces opened up by reflecting upon its own formal histories, Chan leaves us with a sense of the potential of film not to resolve political questions but to hold incommensurate memories within the same frame.

One of the challenges of bringing together cosmopolitanism and cinema is to find ways to do so that speak to not only the production and formal dimensions of film but also to their contexts of consumption. Given the tendency for cosmopolitan debates to assume a universal address, this task can present methodological challenges that might feel overwhelming. One of Chan's responses to this is to anchor her discussion in the cosmopolitan affect of film festivals. This provides a way to explore questions of distribution and exhibition whilst locating the analysis within very particular times and places. Reading film festivals as cosmopolitan spaces, Chan suggests that their atmospheres or moods are generated both by the potential for unexpected encounters with strangers at the screenings and related events, and by the unpredictable affects circulating in response to particular films that shift the boundaries of inclusion and exclusion throughout the festival. Having established a reading of the festival as a genre governed by protocols and conventions, Chan takes her experiences with the Singapore International Film Festival as her focus in offering readings of the excitement and frustrations that constitute the fluid exchanges and shifting affective grounds of such events.

The so-called turn to affect in the last decade or so has carried with it a promise to move away from more structuralist modes of textual determinism in film studies and towards an understanding of the cinema as an embodied encounter. Critics like Vivian Sobchack and Laura Marks have elaborated approaches less dependent on theories of subjectivities and psyches and more orientated towards the senses.[12] As Mica Nava has suggested, we might conceptualise cosmopolitanism through a model of a visceral response to how differences are perceived and represented.[13] The gallery film here offers an exploration of these different modes of haptic spectatorship, and Chan finds the perfect cosmopolitan focus in the work of Singapore-born and Berlin-based artist Ming Wong.

If the concepts of masquerade[14] and mimicry[15] shaped theories of spectatorship in the 1970s and 1980s, drawing attention as they did to the artifice of femininity and the performativity of colonial subjects, then in Wong's work the misrecognitions in these theoretical interventions are literalised through artistic pastiche of cinema's racialised mythologies. Recreating and re-enacting classic films, such as *Chinatown* or *Death in Venice*, and yoking together *Imitation of Life* and *In the Mood for Love*, Wong presents well-known scenes and scenarios with 'miscast' actors, including himself, playing characters of different ethnic backgrounds. Playing all the original characters from one scene himself (crossing gender and ethnic differences), for example, Wong disturbs the conventional legibilities of difference that histories of spectatorship have relied upon. The encounters here are with an affective disturbance that mixes pastiche with political critique. Replacing the cinematic pleasures of voyeurism and fetishism with a spectatorship characterised by misrecognition and disidentification, the art of the mismatch is admired for its performance of imperfection. As Chan's close readings show so eloquently, this work speaks to a cosmopolitanism not as an idealised form of world citizenship or as an ease with the unfamiliar but rather as a place from which to reshuffle histories of difference with style and humour that also has a sharp political edge.

This book represents an important intervention into debates about cosmopolitanism and cinema. Central to its thesis is the claim that uncertainty and ambiguity not only have their place in the cosmopolitan imaginary but might also be considered constitutive of it. Mapping the ways in which this plays out across East and Southeast Asian screens, Chan demonstrates how questions of mobility, travel and displacement make it critical to reconceptualise cosmopolitanism with ambiguity at its heart. Taking examples from China, Hong Kong, Singapore, Japan and many other sites across the region, this book challenges debates about cosmopolitan cinema to develop methods flexible enough to track changing geo-political landscapes and nuanced enough to understand their affective modes of embodiment and engagement. It is a pleasure to read an account that delivers such attention to detail and location, as it speaks to debates about changing encounters with difference in a globalised world, with its new demands for shifting modes of citizenship and participation.

Jackie Stacey, Professor of Media and Cultural Studies,
University of Manchester

Acknowledgements

Book projects can accrue many debts, and mine may be tracked as far back as the early 2000s when I was working on my PhD and searching for a comparative framework under which I could discuss what was then known as 'transnational cinema'. While traces of the PhD thesis have found their way into this volume, it was not until my appointment as Research Councils UK (RCUK) Fellow in Film, Media and Transnational Cultures with the Research Institute for Cosmopolitan Cultures (RICC) at the University of Manchester between 2008 and 2013 that I found cosmopolitanism a particularly productive critical frame through which to explore my career-long interests in the politics of cultural translation, the formation of cultural imaginaries and the negotiation of self-identities in world cinemas. Among the RICC-ers, I would like to thank especially Heather Latimer, Madeleine Reeves, Atreyee Sen and Jackie Stacey for their unfailing support and encouragement in all the years I have endeavoured, in fits and starts, to complete this book.

The conception of this volume took more concrete shape during my term as a Visiting Senior Research Fellow at the Asia Research Institute (ARI), National University of Singapore, from April to July 2013. I am grateful to Professor Chua Beng Huat, leader of the Cultural Studies in Asia cluster within ARI, for his mentorship and example, whose work in inter-Asia cultural studies beyond a Euro-American frame has been influential on my own. Serendipitously, my time at ARI coincided with the visits of a number of professional associates and distinguished scholars, among whom were William Callahan, Pheng Cheah, Rada Iveković, Song Hwee Lim, Wendy Larson and Andrea Riemenschnitter, and with whom many memorable conversations and meals were shared. Growing up in Singapore, I had not appreciated how much its prevailing casual dining-out culture contributed to a group's sociality until I returned as a visitor myself. Thanks are owed to Pheng Cheah and Song Hwee Lim in particular for their professional friendship and sensible advice, the latter invariably dispensed over numerous cups of milky Southeast Asian tea.

Part of Chapter 3 was previously published as 'Film festivals and affective spaces: Singapore's Majestic Theatre', *Cinergie* 6 (November 2014), available at www.cinergie.it/?p=4905. Thanks to Roy Menarini, editor of *Cinergie*, for permission to reprint the selected material, as well as to Monia Acciari for her invitation to submit the piece originally. Friends and colleagues from my time with the Singapore International Film Festival who were credited in the original publication also deserve a place here: Philip Cheah, Dave Chua, Prisca Gan, Kong Kam Yoke, Lok Meng Chue, Mabelyn Ow, Teo Swee Leng, Sebastian Zeng and many others. Ideas in other sections of the book have been tested out at various conferences over the years and at where the feedback has been invaluable. These include events at the University of East London (*Parallax Views*, 2014), University of Leeds (*Language/Cinema*, 2012; *Impure Cinema: Interdisciplinary and Intercultural Approaches to World Cinema*, 2010), University of Glasgow (*Memory and the Witness in Chinese-Language Cinema*, 2012), Princeton University (*Cosmopolitanism in the Landscape of Modernity*, 2009), the National University of Singapore (*Perspectives on City Scales and Cosmopolitan Cultures*, 2008), and the University of Manchester (*Multiplicities: World Cinema, Globalised Media and Cosmopolitan Cultures*, 2008). Many of these ideas, especially of individual films, were also tested on both my undergraduate and postgraduate students over the past few years. To them I extend my gratitude not only for adding real value to my research but also for challenging me to communicate it more effectively. A round of thanks is owed to my editor at I.B.Tauris, Madeleine Hamey-Thomas, for her patience and understanding, as well as her persistence in pushing this project through its final stages, and to my freelance copy-editor, Paula Clarke Bain, for the meticulous care and speed with which she approached the manuscript.

For their fellowship, example, assistance and support in various capacities, further credit and appreciation must be extended to Hayley Bradley, Stacy Johnson, Robin Loon, Vicky Lowe, Fiona Nuttall, Sarah Perks, Tan Soo Yean, Tang Fu Kuen, Valentina Vitali, Darren Waldron, Timothy R. White, Andy Willis, Ming Wong, Yangwen Zheng and the late Paul

Acknowledgements

Willemen, as well as to my family in Singapore. And finally, the last gesture of gratitude in this list of acknowledgements is reserved for Richard Donlan, whose love for the cinema is a constant reminder never to abandon my own.

Felicia Chan

Introduction

Cosmopolitanism and the cinema

This book is an attempt to put in conversation two constructs of modern life – cosmopolitanism and cinema – both driven by idealism, fantasy and aspiration, and yet each also embodying within their own ideational conceptions internal contradictions which could serve to keep the worst ideological outcomes at bay. On the more optimistic end of the spectrum, cosmopolitanism encompasses visions of a universe united in difference. Yet, cosmopolitanism has also been viewed with scepticism, especially for what its critics see as a *de facto* imperialist project. David Miller, for instance, argues that the actions required of individuals to act with egalitarianism towards others require special 'obligations' conferred by a proximity of relations, which is premised on the idea that one feels more inclined to show consideration for people closer to us than those further away. This dynamic of proximity and distance becomes exponentially complicated when extended to groups, collectives, communities and nations,[1] the affiliations to which can shape one's sense of identity. Cosmopolitanism at its most optimistic invokes the notion of a global citizenship that can appear too abstracted to be effectual, and can complicate individual and collective obligations towards human rights and global justice. Pheng Cheah, writing about the 'cosmopolitical' in 1998, analyses the political efficacy of cosmopolitanism as a framework for understanding the increasingly complex relations between national communities (and imaginaries) and the rising impact of global capitalism, and asks: 'even if a popular global consciousness exists, is it or can it be sufficiently institutionalised to be a feasible political alternative to the nation-state form? Or is it merely a cultural consciousness without political effectivity?'[2]

The question of institutions is one that Robert Spencer explores in relation to cosmopolitan criticism and post-colonial literature, where cosmopolitanism operates 'both [as] a disposition – one characterised by self-awareness, by a penetrating sensitivity to the world beyond one's immediate milieu, and by an enlarged sense of moral and political responsibility to individuals and groups outside one's local or national community – and, it is very important to add, a set of economic structures and political institutions that correspond to this enlarged sense of community'.[3] For Spencer, the value of cosmopolitanism lies in its function as a critical framework for reading literature (and by that extension works of art) rather than as a theme or an outlook expressed within the work. A cosmopolitan critical framework would allow for contradictions and conflicts within a work to surface: 'They [cosmopolitan works] each incite a desire for cosmopolitanism at the same time as they arouse indignation at the way in which the structures and attitudes of the present frustrate cosmopolitanism's realisation'.[4] In other words, cosmopolitan texts are self-conscious, self-reflexive texts. They encourage a mode of reading (and perhaps even writing) out of which an equal measure of self-consciousness could lend itself to political critique. The power of cosmopolitan texts, then, can be said to lie not in their expression within the art form but in their ability to acknowledge their own limits. As Spencer puts it: 'cosmopolitanism cannot by definition be realised in works of art; it can only be pointed to as a possibility. [...] it is important that texts lend emphasis to their own failure in this respect'.[5] It is in this spirit that I address the notion of a cosmopolitan cinema in the course of this volume.

The visions proffered by cosmopolitanism and cinema are both highly seductive. Popularly, cosmopolitanism is especially attractive to those constitutive of a class which prides itself on its mobility and adaptability to new cultures. To be cosmopolitan, to be a *cosmopolite*, is often understood to be 'a citizen of the world', and one who is perhaps more importantly assumed to be *at ease* in the world. Appadurai delineates this understanding of

Introduction: Cosmopolitanism and the cinema

cosmopolitanism as one which assumes 'a certain cultivated knowledge of the world beyond one's immediate horizons, and is the product of deliberate activities associated with literacy, the freedom to travel, and the luxury of expanding the boundaries of one's own self by expanding its experiences'.[6] One could easily include within this class the cine-literate, the self-professed cultural consumers of 'world cinema', with whom I self-identify, though not without reservation. This form of cosmopolitanism has frequently suffered the charge of elitism, as it appears to celebrate a life of privilege reserved for those with sufficient financial and social capital to exploit it. Gyan Prakash notes that the history of a 'subaltern cosmopolitanism', encompassing the histories of those who paid the price for 'colonialism and empire, slavery and capitalist exploitation, the world wars and the Holocaust and other such inhumanities', 'remains to be fully appreciated and written'.[7] Yet, he also acknowledges the continued attraction of an aspirational and critical cosmopolitan politics that could be mobilised with some attention to 'ethicopolitical processes and work'.[8] In spite of reservations about its practice, practicalities and politics, it is thus worth noting that cosmopolitanism remains attractive as an *aspiration*, both consumptive and critical. Nina Glick Schiller and Andrew Irving, editors of *Whose Cosmopolitanism?* (2015), observe in their introduction that contributors to the volume (of whom I am one) devoted to the 'critical perspectives, relationalities and discontents' of cosmopolitanism nevertheless 'note that partial, fleeting, uncertain and fragile domains of commonality, expressed as empathy, recognition and sociability, can be found in disparate locations and situations [...] [from which] springs the search for moments, expressions and relations of openness that express human aspirations for justice and equality'.[9]

Equally, there is something magical about the cinema that speaks to our fantasies and desires. In spite of the occasional proclamation of its 'death' under the pressures of smaller screen technologies like television and digital formats, narrative film endures. In fact, cinema is celebrated on the small screen regularly by various retrospectives, especially within holiday programming and frequent Top 50 or 100 countdown series. Although these are largely clip shows, their emphasis on personal recollection nonetheless signals a preoccupation with cinema's capacity to trigger personal memories and reminiscence. When people recall films, they recall older histories and imagined younger selves; as Jackie Stacey's research on female spectators uncovered, 'Hollywood memories' of stars from the 1940s and 1950s bring out a 'nostalgic desire for a lost past, for imagined former identities, and for a time "when stars were really stars"'.[10] Film scholars themselves are not exempt from the pull of nostalgia. Many draw on that love of the cinema in their pursuit of broader and more theoretical questions of self and identity, culture and context in their work. In the preface to his historical study of the cinemas of Shanghai and Hong Kong, Poshek Fu recalls a personal passion for cinema growing up in the 1950s and 1960s:

> Every once in a while, always on Sundays, my parents took us to see new Shaw Brothers Mandarin (and occasionally Hollywood) pictures at movie palaces in the Central District. It took us more than an hour by boat and bus to get there, which only added to the thrill of these infrequent trips. These were the paramount events in my childhood, as important as Chinese New Year celebrations. Sitting in the quiet, cool darkness of a movie theater watching the unfolding of a modern, urbane life so fascinatingly different from mine, I could not make out what the figures on the screen said to each other, even though they looked as 'Chinese' as I was.[11]

Thus, the act of going to the cinema itself builds and draws on memories of previous experiences at the movies, and shapes one's encounter with the medium on screen. (The sense of a 'foreign' encounter the younger Fu experiences at the cinema is a notion I shall return to shortly.) It could be said that cinema's role as a textual and technological medium has been to reflect, refract and continually reframe the aspirations and contradictions inherent in modern life back onto the screen for consumption. Reflecting on the early years of cinema at the turn of the twenty-first century, Laura Mulvey writes that '[c]inema gathered together and streamlined its prehistory of illusion and deception by means of "natural magic", giving modernity a perfect site on which to play out the continuing dramas of reality, the unconscious and the imagination'.[12]

It is on this site of the cinematic text that I explore some of the inherent tensions within cosmopolitanism, the inherent tensions between its ideals and the reality of its limits. While cosmopolitanism may speak to aspirations of affiliation and belonging, it cannot always be reconciled with cultures and consequences of exclusion and exile. Galin Tihanov warns against valorising the 'enforced cosmopolitanism' of the exilic experience, arguing that the 'liberal consensus' which has chosen to see 'the cross-border experience of migrant workers, worshippers or writers [as] always a source of cultural enrichment and a display of personal energy and endurance [...] glosses over – or simply fails to see and acknowledge – the attendant manifestations of inequality and disempowerment'.[13] What is left out are 'other essential aspects: the need to circumscribe one's experience in the constraints of a new cultural framework, the imperative to begin to translate that experience in languages that are often not yet one's own, and to grope one's way through the loss and trauma intrinsic in this process of transition' and '[w]hen this work of translating and accommodating one's experience and lifeworld fails, when the participation in a new polis proves beyond reach, the spectre of rupture, deprivation and disenfranchisement makes a numbing appearance'.[14] To give the exilic experience full political and ethical consideration, Tihanov argues that it is necessary to 'deromanticize' and 'deliberalize' the exile from the grip of 'methodological individualism'[15] and to reinscribe the individual 'into *collectivities* that are no longer necessarily nation-bound, and as such help us envisage for the first time a genuinely different border crosser: neither an exile (or even a refugee) nor, for that matter, a consummately proficient individual doer and getter'.[16] Likewise stripped from its liberal romanticisation, cosmopolitanism, according to Tihanov, can help us reimagine that state of border crossing, one 'not [...] exclusively centred on individual agency and a humanistic recognition of uniqueness'.[17] Cosmopolitanism, Tihanov argues, may offer us a different 'methodological tool that would assist us in addressing the open wounds of transition, the ruptures and apertures of difference channelled through the experiences of border crossing'.[18] It is within this frame that I offer a way of thinking about cinema that gives voice to the experience of border crossing, often by crossing multiple borders as a cultural form.

Thus while it may be possible to discuss a cosmopolitan cinema as one which displays various features of cosmopolitanism within its narrative and thematic concerns, such as its expression of multiculturalism, openness to difference, its depiction of global communities and linguistic cultures, and so on, doing so – that is, prescribing onto cosmopolitanism modes of diversity – restricts its potential, I believe. For me, a cosmopolitan cinema does its best work when it enables us to talk and think of cosmopolitanism as a critical mode of understanding cultural practices and relations – what Tihanov calls 'collectivities' above – especially when we consider cinema's own historical cosmopolitan aspirations. The inception of cinema in Europe in the late nineteenth century fed into cosmopolitan aspirations of modern life, during a period of growing industrialisation and increasing desire for travel. Those desires and aspirations have not abated, and in the twenty-first century, cinema continues to operate as a cultural formation that mediates and is mediated by encounters from travel to and experience of foreign cultures. In *Cinematic Journeys* (2010), Dimitris Eleftheriotis addresses mobility and travel as dominant modalities in cinema. Although writing specifically here about 'travel films' in the late nineteenth century, Eleftheriotis' observations can well be applied to cinema more broadly: 'Travelling becomes instrumental in the construction and actualisation of this peculiarly Western modern subjectivity: as an essential tool of scientific discovery and the extension of metropolitan imperial power on a macro level, as a way to complete one's education and acquire valuable cultural capital on a personal level'.[19]

My excursion through cosmopolitan cinema in the course of this book begins not with *how* cinema travels or crosses borders: there is already an extensive body of work on the subject, including Eleftheriotis' and others' work on the transnational, transcultural, even global nature of various cinemas. Instead, my own cinematic journeys assume *a priori* cinema's imperative for travel and seek to explore what occurs *where* and *when* cinema crosses borders. Questions that shape the explorations to follow include: Does cinema offer a safer space through which border-crossings and foreign encounters may take place? Or does it, in so doing, reinforce the domination of institutional structures of power? Can cinema perhaps offer imaginative possibilities and new dimensions for how different social, cultural and critical relationalities may be advanced? My approach to a 'cosmopolitan cinema' is thus not intended as a semantic substitute for 'transnational' or 'world' cinemas or, more recently in the literature, 'global' cinema,[20] but as one which enables an articulation of encounters with difference that simultaneously resist fragmentation (into endless proliferations of difference) and coalescence (eradicating difference altogether). In other words, I see a cosmopolitan cinema as neither one which

Introduction: Cosmopolitanism and the cinema

simply champions a one-world fantasy where we can all 'get along', nor as one which simply encourages the proliferation of difference beyond practical limits. The former concern belies a neo-imperialist project for which I have many reservations. The latter concern, however, shares in particular Tihanov's scepticism of a methodological individualism that places individual subjectivity and experience at the centre of cultural analysis. Cinema is as much a practice and a process as it is a product; it is also an affective experience that can hold in tension a multiplicity of perspectives, and consequently allow it to speak to the multiplicities of cosmopolitan debate.

How can the medium do this? When we study the textuality of the cinema – its visual and aural dynamics, its rhythms of editing, its sequencing of events – we are also always confronted by its historiography. When we look at a film critically, we are also looking at its modes of production, presentation, distribution, exhibition and reception. We are looking at how we, as spectators, readers and consumers, are textually and contextually produced, and how these textual productions may be resisted or embraced. Through aesthetic techniques that produce various modes of identification and distancing, films invite us to adopt a position in relation to the narrative, whether that position is to empathise with a character, to distance ourselves from the action, or to complicate that positioning by reflecting on the camera's own act of looking, by negotiating with and playing on spectators' levels of knowledge, be it historical, cultural or otherwise. The chapters in this book explore the relationship between cosmopolitanism and the cinema by addressing the degrees of cultural proximity and distance to the text encountered in films. It draws from Zygmunt Bauman's idea of the stranger, who is neither an enemy nor a friend, but rather an unknown entity, and considers what it means to be produced as a stranger in film. The stranger, according to Bauman, is different from an enemy, and occupies that space of ambivalence inherent to modernity. While friends vs. enemies are oppositional and mutually defining positionalities, the stranger introduces an aspect of the unknown and the unknowable into human sociation. According to Bauman, the presence of the stranger produces ambivalence in our response because of our inability to place him on the friend–enemy spectrum, 'because the stranger is neither friend nor enemy; and because he may be both. And because we do not know, and have no way of knowing, which is the case'.[21] 'Strangeness' then, in

Bauman's configuration, is less about difference than about being uncertain of, or uneasy with, difference. Strangers could seem 'like us' inasmuch as they are 'not like us'. The stranger is both ambiguous and ambivalent: we do not know to what extent they share our values and world views, and for the most part the 'not-knowing' is what constitutes our relationship to them. My analyses of the films in the following chapters draw on the dynamic between the ambiguous and the ambivalent produced by what I will identify as cosmopolitan 'encounters' confronted by and in the films. These encounters take place through questions of text, via multilingualism, translation and self-reflexivity, and questions of context, via festivals, histories, marketplaces, performances and critical approaches.

At the core of the chapters that follow is an exploration of the state of 'not-knowing' that the encounter with cinema affords, especially in what I would call the politics of the 'foreign film'. As I am writing in English, and operate in an English-speaking milieu, my definition of 'foreign film' refers to non-English-language film in the sense that the film industry and English language trade magazines like *Variety* and *Screen International* employ the term. In these circles, 'foreign film' is frequently synonymous with 'world cinema', as Dimitris Eleftheriotis notes: ' "world cinema" implies a position of foreignness. A film is a "world film" for some not all its spectators: one assumes that Chinese cinema can only be a "world cinema" to non-Chinese audiences. Thus "world cinema" is a discursive space occupied de facto by foreigners, foreign films and foreign spectators, as they meet each other in encounters made possible by journeys of cultural products'.[22] However, questions and degrees of foreignness are a matter of nuance depending on the conditions and contexts in which these encounters occur. Chinese audiences may well be aware that in the global film industry dominated by Hollywood, Chinese cinema is perceived as a 'world cinema', and is frequently marketed as such even by domestic industries: that Johnnie To's action cinema produced within Hong Kong's commercial industry has entered the European festival circuit as an 'auteur's cinema' is one such example; or that middle-class English-educated Chinese audiences in Singapore literate in Anglo-European commercial and art cinemas may well also view 'Chinese cinemas' as a 'world cinema' is another. 'World cinema' implies a position of foreignness, but it is a position that can be selectively applied to different cultural contexts and positions, which are also shifting all the time.[23] Hence, my use of these terms as the market understands them in my analyses of the films is not intended to reproduce or reinforce their institutional power; rather, inherent to my approach is the questioning of these norms through the exploration of the spaces and subjectivities that fall beyond or between those boundaries. Not all films expose or exploit those liminal spaces, but those that do encourage us to inhabit those liminal spaces by turning us into 'strangers' as we negotiate our own 'foreignness' against the 'foreignness' of the films before us. And while such encounters and negotiations entail some form of translation, they are not necessarily always in linguistic terms. As Naoki Sakai writes:

> If the foreign is unambiguously incomprehensible, unknowable, and unfamiliar, then translation simply cannot be done. If, conversely, the foreign is comprehensible, knowable and familiar, translation is unnecessary. Thus, the status of the foreign is ambiguous in translation. The foreign is incomprehensible and comprehensible, unknowable and knowable, unfamiliar and familiar at the same time. This foundational ambiguity of translation is derived from the positionality occupied by the translator. The translator is summoned only when two kinds of audiences are postulated with regard to the source text, one for whom the text is comprehensible at least to some degree, and the other for whom it is incomprehensible. The translator's work consists in dealing with the difference between the two audiences. The translator encroaches on both and stands in the midst of this difference.[24]

The 'foreign(er)' in Sakai's framework is akin to Bauman's 'stranger', occupying the liminal space between the knowable and the unknowable, the familiar and the unfamiliar. The role of the translator in this instance is both necessary, yet unfulfilled.

Issues of cultural translation are thus central to my attempt to conceptualise a cosmopolitan cinema. Any cultural text that travels necessitates some form of translation, and historically the film industry has adapted a number of translative processes to reach its audiences. The most widely experienced processes of translation, and perhaps the most practical solutions to the problem, are those of dubbing and subtitling. Despite their widespread practice, relatively little discursive attention has been paid to the cultural politics of these practices beyond their practicalities. Most often, linguistic encounters in cinema are explored via their efficacies, and the process is placed on a relatively linear continuum extending from 'domestication' (dubbing) to 'foreignisation' (subtitling).[25] In practice, not all translative efforts in the cinema can be placed neatly on this continuum. The use of subtitles in Woody Allen's *Annie Hall* (1977) translates not what the characters are saying from one language to another, but what they are thinking in the same language as is spoken in the dialogue, and the ironic mode disrupts the conventional function of subtitles as translative devices. In *Film Socialisme* (2010), Jean-Luc Godard intentionally truncates the English subtitles in the film, reducing the subtitled dialogue 'to nutty fragments of what Godard calls "Navajo English," stereotypical grunts more than anything'.[26] In this instance, *Film Socialisme* acknowledges, and even rewards, the one who does not fully understand, for if one understood the French dialogue without the need for subtitles, the game between the film and the spectator remains incomplete. To fully participate in the puzzle is to acknowledge that access to the text is limited, and to acknowledge that comprehension is incomplete is part of the puzzle of the game of the text itself. This poses the next question: to whom is the film – the game – addressed? I am interested in these moments of disruption produced by such encounters of mis- and in-comprehension. These are moments of disruption that indicate the text's possible reflection on its own act of translation as an incomplete transaction, as Walter Benjamin describes it (by way of Steven Rendall's translation): 'this representation of the intended object by means of an incomplete form or seed of its production'.[27] Translation, for Benjamin, is not an end process but a 'mode',[28] an ongoing dynamic among languages, 'a preliminary way of coming to terms with the foreignness of languages to each other'.[29] Cosmopolitan, multilingual films bring this dynamic to the fore. When we watch these films we are watching these dynamics play out, including the dynamics of our own limited access to the text. An example of these dynamics can be seen in Poshek Fu's experience cited above, where he recalls, as a Cantonese speaker, his 'foreign encounter' with the Mandarin cinema as a young child. Both Cantonese and Mandarin are identified as Chinese languages, yet are entirely dissimilar. Out of such specific encounters, I explore broader questions of translatability and comprehension. The key question remains not so much what we need to understand, but what happens when we do not? How do we articulate the positionality of the spectator for whom the act of translation can only deliver partial comprehension? Does it matter if one fails to distinguish between one 'foreign' language and another? What are the cultural and political implications of not being able to hear or grasp the differences between Cantonese and Mandarin? Or Québecois and French? Or Catalan and Spanish? Or various other regional dialects and accents within a national culture? What would be the (useful) function of English subtitles in these instances, if at all?

Even more important to my study is how this dynamic may be read to operate on the level of *cinematic language*. In the chapters that follow, I look at how certain films negotiate narrative storytelling with a level of intertextual self-referencing that enables them to circulate in markets beyond local and domestic cultural milieus. I explore cinema's capacity for self-reflexivity beyond post-modern ideas of 'play' which is important for what it can tell us about how films operate and circulate as cultural forms by engaging not only with genre, style and context, but also with cultural memory. These films enact a historicity of cinema, the identification for which is important in how we understand what is at stake when stories and histories are enacted in a certain way, use technologies in a particular way, and when some of these stories 'grab' mass audiences and others do not. For instance, what are the ethics of telling the story of the historical tragedy of the Titanic via the romance of a fictional 'Hollywood' couple (played by Kate Winslet and Leonardo di Caprio) when there are two thousand 'real' stories waiting to be told? To what extent is history honoured and to what extent is it erased? Does cinema even have a responsibility to history? The answer is mostly individual and would have to depend on one's politics and expectations of the medium. Indeed James Cameron's *Titanic* (1997) engendered much scholarly debate following its unprecedented success at the box office and Academy Awards, and some of these questions are explored in the 'Titanica' special issue of the journal, *Interdisciplinary Literary Studies* (2003) 5.1,[30] and in Tim Bergfelder and Sarah Street's edited collection on *The Titanic in Myth and Memory* (2004).[31]

The fact remains that *Titanic* garnered US$200 million at the point of its initial release in 1997 and earned another US$345 million upon its re-release in 3D format in 2012; the latter's opening weekend in China alone grossed US$58 million.³² In this sense, the film has a social and cultural impact regardless of whether one subscribes to its politics or not. The extreme case of *Titanic* exemplifies the two levels of fantasy operating in film that Paul Willemen distinguishes: one is the fantasy of the story and the draw of the illusion; and the other is the fantasy implicit in the mode of storytelling itself, a mode which, in the case of popular film, marshals vast amounts of capital and labour. A more 'honest' film politically, as Willemen would describe it, is one where the two sets of fantasies are more closely aligned.³³ For him, *Titanic* would not be such a film, simply because its conspicuous repression of its own storytelling devices within the 'classical' mode³⁴ sits at odds with its fetishisation of the technology employed (initially the IMAX special effects in 1997, and later 3D, and so on) to mobilise that very mode of repression. For Willemen, and as I shall argue throughout most of this book, the very presence of the technology of the cinema always already politicises the act of visual (and aural) capture.

Cosmopolitan Cinema attempts to re-engage discussions of the cinematic text with a fresh understanding of its worldliness. Cosmopolitanism implies a disposition and mode of engaging with the world, yet what constitutes 'the world' is always already contentious, and contingent on contexts and cultures. Empires created 'worlds', as do ideologies and social practices, and these can sometimes reshape 'the world' as we understand it. Post-colonialism emerged from a set of world-making practices to re-constitute another's world, as has neoliberal capitalism. A 'world view' is perceived to originate from specific socio-historical circumstances. Yet, a 'world' also exists in the realm of the imagination: fictional worlds, imagined pasts, reconstructed memories, all constitute worlds of a sort, along with conglomerations of people, societies, institutions and environments. It is this realm of the imagination that art, literature and cinema invokes. In his book, *Cosmopolitanism and Culture* (2012), Nikos Papastergiadis offers a reading of 'cosmopolitan agency'³⁵ in contemporary art as a strategy for coping with the politics of fear that appear to have been ushered in by the new century, arguing that art has played a role 'in re-evaluating the function of imagination in the construction of reality. In particular, […] the artistic combination of a critical attitude towards the forces of globalisation and a creative engagement with the forms of spatial belonging ushers forth a cosmopolitan imaginary'.³⁶ For him, 'the creative function of art' serves two functions, both 'as a reflector of emergent forms of global change and as a generator of new modes of being and action in the world'.³⁷ In his book, *Ways of Worldmaking* (1978), Nelson Goodman argues that imagined worlds in art and fiction are no more randomly constructed out of symbols 'than a carpenter makes a chair by putting pieces of wood together at random';³⁸ they always possess referents to the 'real' world, however that realism is construed. In other words, the act of world-making in fiction, art and film is therefore already a relational one. It is both an act of border-creation (in the sense of defining a realm) and an act of border-crossing (if only the border between the imagined and the 'real') – and thus, in a manner of speaking, a cosmopolitan endeavour. Writing of world literature, Pheng Cheah describes 'the imaginative process' of literature as one 'that generates cosmopolitan feeling'.³⁹ Reading Goethe, Cheah posits the 'world' in world literature as 'an active space of transaction and interrelation': 'The content of ideas that are exchanged matters little; what is of greatest worth is the ethos generated by the transaction. The world is only to be found and arises in these intervals or mediating processes. It is constituted by and, indeed, is nothing but exchange and transaction'.⁴⁰ For Cheah, such a conception of the world resists the totalising forces of globalisation and guards against 'reducing it to a superstructure of an economic base'.⁴¹ Central to Cheah's conception of world literature as cosmopolitan is literature's capacity to exceed its material environs. He writes:

> As something that is structurally detached from its putative origin and that permits and even solicits an infinite number of interpretations, literature is an exemplary modality of the undecidability that opens a world. It is not merely a product of the human imagination or something that is derived from, represents, or duplicates material reality. Literature is the force of a passage, an experience through which we are given and receive any determinable reality.⁴²

For Cheah, literature operates within a 'structure of opening through which one receives a world and through which another world can appear. This structure is prior to and subtends any social forms of mediation as well as any sense of public space [...] because it is nothing other than the force of giving and receiving a world'.⁴³

In contrast, while cinema's affective qualities may offer entry points into imaginative worlds, the omnipresence of the *apparatus* binds it to a material structure that cannot be avoided; rather, to elide the structure is to repress its cultural politics. In a critique of Bordwell, Staiger and Thompson's now-ubiquitous conception of *The Classical Hollywood Cinema* (1985), a methodological framework for reading American films that subsume aesthetics and style for narrative coherence and clarity, Miriam Hansen challenges 'the totalizing account of classical cinema', noting that 'what is left out, marginalized or repressed' include genres lending themselves to phenomenological readings, such as 'comedy, horror, and pornography that involve the viewer's body and sensory-affective responses in ways that may not exactly conform to classical ideals'. She notes also the repression of 'the role of genre in general, specifically the affective-aesthetic division of labor among genres in structuring the consumption of Hollywood films', as well as that of the role 'granted to stars and stardom, which cannot be reduced to the narrative function of character and, like genre but even more so, involve the spheres of distribution, exhibition practices, and reception'.[44] In other words, cinema cannot be taken out of the material contexts that produce and sustain it. To do so is to uncover only half the story.

In his essay *The World, the Text and the Critic* (1983), Edward Said explores the notion of the worldliness of the text in terms of the relationship between the text and 'circumstantial reality',[45] or put in different words, the affiliations that locate a text in the world, both as clusters of ideas and material artefacts. Cinema engages the relationship between text and world in specific ways. Cinema as textual practice enables real and imaginative worlds to be constructed through narrative, visual and auditory means. As a textual practice, it is also embedded within specific contextual conditions, which include the conditions and cultures of production, presentation, distribution, exhibition and reception. Dubbed the 'seventh art' by Italian film theorist Ricciotto Canudo, after architecture, sculpture, painting, music, poetry and dance, cinema was conceived of by Canudo as a synthesis of the rhythms of space and time embodied by the other arts.[46] Yet, it should be noted that unlike all the other arts with premodern roots, cinema is very much a product of late modernity and of industrial-capitalism. Like photography before it, it is a technological art form, only one whose technical investment both in pre- and post-production stages are far higher than its precedent. To produce a complete film – and there are many projects that never see completion due to lack of investment – there are costs for cast and crew, actors, writers, directors, sound editors, grips, as well as publicity and marketing; and then there are the investments in technology, cameras, projection equipment, sound systems, distribution networks, and so on. Cinema as an art form developed hand in hand with technological modernity, and also with the development of the idea of the modern nation-state and psychosocial subject. Murray Pomerance sees modernity as 'the era of public illumination [that] brought a new sense of exteriority: what had once been privately imagined was now dramatically depicted, broadcast, systematized for all to read and know'. Cinema was central to this development as it 'offered a vision of ongoing and unfolding eventuality, instantaneous linkage [...] [in] action and gesture as such', that enabled it to reflect 'modernity's contraction of experience from the timeless to the momentary'.[47] Social relations changed in this new era, altering 'the field of engagement though which people came to meet and work with one another. Talents and abilities separated themselves from personalities. Intentions could be guarded and hidden. Identity could be fabricated'.[48] Cinema both reflected and contributed to this change:

> What film could reflect was all the rich confusion of: light and electric stimulation (thus, scientific development), temporary and impenetrable relationship (thus, social mobility and the omnipresence of strangers), alienation of labor from biography and history (thus, the pervasive organization of capitalism and its form of exploitation), and the onwardly rushing movement (movement in many directions at once, so that collision, and then war, were inevitable) – the hallmarks of the modern world.[49]

Thus, while reading film for its psychosocial insights into society's self-representation and engagement with the world may be valuable, it is worth remembering that, by and large, the industry and nation states that support the medium see themselves primarily as doing *business*. UNESCO's Institute for Statistics compiles large amounts of production, distribution and attendance data for each member nation, over any other cultural form, citing cinema as 'the world's most lucrative cultural industry and one of the most popular cultural practices'.[50] The site produces no comparable data for theatres, concert halls or art galleries. These economies of power, and their shadow economies, then have psychosocial impacts on individuals, if not whole communities. On one end of the spectrum, Aida Hozic explores in *Hollyworld: Space, Power, and Fantasy in the American Economy* (2001) how the intricate relationship between the power of Hollywood's capital and the American economy has shaped the movie industry's production of fantasy;[51] whilst on the other, Ramon Lobato explores in *Shadow Economies of Cinema: Mapping Informal Film Distribution* (2012) how the shadow economies of illegal distribution, piracy and informal exhibition circuits constitute not a marginal aspect of cinematic culture but one that has to be as actively engaged as their more formalised counterparts.[52] Therefore, when films tell particular stories about particular communities or national histories, it is always worth asking who might have a stake in these stories and why. Exploring the relationship between texts and contexts can tell us something about the stories 'we' as a society, or imagined community, tell about ourselves, in the past and the present, including aspects we sometimes do not openly admit to. Hence, it is also always worth investigating why some stories are never told and even actively repressed, erased or forgotten. It is equally important to articulate the processes we mobilise (industry, history, politics) in order to create these stories (or maintain their absences). As Said put it, 'Texts are a system of forces institutionalized by the reigning culture at some human cost to its various components. [...] the critic is responsible to a degree for articulating those voices dominated, displaced, or silenced by the textuality of texts'.[53]

This book is thus concerned with how the tripartite relationship between world, text and critic – between the cinematic form, its contexts of production and cultures of critical reception – can help us understand how cosmopolitanism's ideals and contradictions may be mediated through the form of the cinema in ways that allow us to reflect on those ideals and contradictions. Likewise, viewing cinema through a cosmopolitan lens may also encourage us to rethink aspects of cinema studies, which may have themselves been bound by conventions and undisputed ways of knowledge- and world-making. So while the chapters in this volume collectively investigate the conditions and contexts necessary for cinema to be understood as 'cosmopolitan', they do not set out to delineate 'cosmopolitan cinema' as a categorical term with a stable typology and this

Introduction: Cosmopolitanism and the cinema

volume makes no definitive claim to how a cosmopolitan cinema may be constituted as a singular entity. Instead the chapters are framed as a series of explorations across four types of filmic encounters – as varied as multilingualism, self-reflexivity, affect and embodiment – that approach the relationship between cosmopolitanism and the cinema as one that emerges out of the dynamic, and productive, tension between the two.

As a postscript to this introduction, it is necessary to explain that my choice of examples is drawn mainly from a range of East and Southeast Asian cinemas, only because these constitute the cultural cinemas that have been at the foreground of my research in recent years. Other cultural and national cinemas, and indeed individual films, may pose similar or different questions to the ones I raise here, depending on their own cultural and historical specificities.[54] Nonetheless, it is hoped that the questions raised may sufficiently form the basis from which to take the investigation of a critical cosmopolitan framework further thereafter. To an extent my choice of East and Southeast Asian cinemas as objects of study enact the dual sense of cultural ownership and alienation I feel from them, as a post-colonial Southeast Asian subject working in English and in England. Yet this sense of knowing and not knowing, belonging and not belonging, and perhaps even the *attraction* of what Rey Chow has phrased in different circumstances an 'ontological conflict'[55] could also be described as that which constitutes the experience of cosmopolitanism within an 'everyday' context, an experience Mica Nava has termed 'visceral'. Nava articulates this relational aspect of cosmopolitanism as 'a structure of *feeling*: as an empathetic and inclusive set of identifications; to focus on its vernacular, everyday, domestic expressions; to isolate some of its national and class specificities; and to trace its development from an oppositional culture at the beginning of the twentieth century'.[56] Nava explores the psychic dimension of cosmopolitanism within the fractiousness of modernity, where the cosmopolitan allure of the foreign and foreign travel may equally be read as 'a psychic revolt against the parents and the parental culture – not only, therefore, in a sense of not-belonging, of no-home, no-country, but also in a desire to escape *from* family, home and country'.[57] Beyond biography, this 'parental culture' may also be substituted for any hegemonic culture – imperialist, patriarchal, colonial – and reading cosmopolitanism through the cinema may help us revisit some of its epistemic norms.

1

The cosmopolitan challenge of multilingual cinema

Cosmopolitanism is sometimes popularly signified by the presence of multiple cultures and languages within a society. However, it is not synonymous with multiculturalism as a political doctrine and practice. The discursive differences between cosmopolitanism and multiculturalism can be said to lie in the approaches and attitudes to 'difference'. Multiculturalism advocates the co-existence of and mutual respect for different cultures,[1] while cosmopolitanism intimates a more overt, if not always entirely comfortable, embrace of difference. While multiculturalism need not presume the co-interaction of cultures and is predicated on tolerance, cosmopolitan multiculturalism, in a manner of speaking, gestures beyond tolerance towards a more open mode of sociality. This desired openness is not without its tensions.

Jackie Stacey worries that a kind of 'common sense' celebration of cosmopolitan openness presents its own hegemony, and closure. She argues that the 'idea of an "openness to difference" posits a self that is transparent, accessible and fully intelligible to ourselves and others, and a "consciousness of world citizenship" assumes that the world is somehow graspable as a totality with which we can straightforwardly identify'.[2] 'What if,' she asks, 'the projection of world citizenship is a blended panhumanity that violently erases difference instead of recognizing it?'[3] David Chandler identifies the 'cosmopolitan paradox' as one where 'the gap between universal aspiration and hierarchical practice [...] is rooted in the essence of the cosmopolitan thesis itself' and cautions that 'there is a real danger that the cosmopolitan impulse will legitimize a much more hierarchical set of international relationships'.[4] Yet, it is *because* there is such a danger, not in spite of it, that this conversation is worth having. Bruce Robbins writes:

> The interest of the term cosmopolitanism is located, then, not in its full theoretical extension, where it becomes a paranoid fantasy of ubiquity and omniscience, but rather (paradoxically) in its local applications, where the *unrealizable ideal* produces normative pressure against such alternatives as, say, the fashionable 'hybridization.' Its provocative association with privilege is perhaps better understood, in this context, as the normative edge that cosmopolitanism tries to add to the inclusiveness and diversity of multiculturalism – *as an attempt to name a necessary but difficult normativeness.*[5]

In this chapter, I look at how multilingual films enable us to attempt to name 'the difficult normativeness' of language, universalism and translation in the cinema.

My definition of 'multilingual cinema' goes beyond the use of two or more languages within a film, although I also look at some examples of this. I include, in my definition, films which engage with the need for translation between languages, but which, for production and exhibition reasons, do not necessarily replicate those linguistic differences within the film. This definition takes into account practices of reshooting films in different languages (not just dubbing over the dialogue), such as in the early Laurel and Hardy films where the two comedians would reprise their original roles in Spanish, Italian, German or French, by speaking their lines phonetically while shooting with a local crew. This definition also includes dual-lingual shooting, such as in the Norwegian English venture, *Kon-Tiki* (2012), where each scene in the film was shot twice concurrently: once in Norwegian and once in English, to cater to different markets, the latter primarily for the American market. For Joachim Ronning, one of the two directors, 'the decision was a practical one', a choice between 'making "Kon-Tiki" this way or not making it at all'.[6] The questions posed by these processes allow for a more nuanced reflection on the encounter with 'strangeness', of which the foreign is partly constituted, beyond concerns about translative accuracy and linguistic authenticity.

Even before the advent of synchronised sound in cinema exhibition from the 1930s, multilingualism was already implicated within the form of the silent cinema, which employed written inter-titles to convey dialogue and narrative context. For exhibition in different linguistic communities, these inter-titles were easily substituted in the target language of the intended audience. In so doing, linguistic differences, and often national and cultural identities, were readily effaced, at least for Anglo-European audiences. The widespread adoption of synchronised sound in the inter-war period exposed this repression, as audiences' perception of silent actors' voices, accents and personae did not necessarily correspond with how they imagined stars and characters to speak. Although this practice purportedly ended several silent star careers, it also made substantial profits for the studios and was very quickly normalised as a production practice.[7] Politically and practically, the coming of sound transformed the cultural function of cinema in two ways. Firstly, it foregrounded cultural difference through linguistic difference. Once dialogue could be spoken and recorded, films became identified with linguistic identities that not only brought to the fore issues of comprehension and translation, but also highlighted the dissonances of accent and aurality. In so doing, the coming of sound transformed the notion of an 'imagined universality into nationality and language' in Anglo-European cinema.[8] Secondly, the coming of sound was also instrumental in reconfiguring cinematic production and reception in alignment with national film histories. Once films could be identified according to linguistic identities, they invariably became intertwined with the politics of language as they play out in the politics of national identities and formations. Correspondingly, the development of sound cinema coincided with the rise of European nationalisms during the inter-war period and contributed substantially to the formation of what we have now come to understand as 'national cinemas'. Cinema in the twenty-first century continues to bear this legacy, as cultural distinctiveness denoted by language remains one of the organising principles behind 'foreign language film' categories within the industry, as well as 'world cinema' entries at international film festivals.[9]

Beyond the geo-cultural boundaries of Anglo-European cinemas, however, the politics of language and cultural difference played out somewhat differently in other territories. It is worth noting that as Anglo-European films were exported to other parts of the world during the silent era, the presence of the foreign in these non-European markets could not have been as easily suppressed. For early East Asian audiences, for example, not only was the technology that brought the cinema to them also accompanied by the foreign ownership of distribution and exhibition channels, but their markets were also flooded by a stream of foreign films depicting unfamiliar scenes from America and Europe.[10] Unlike American or European audiences, East Asian audiences did not recognise themselves or their milieux in the films. As Pang Laikwan notes in her study of China's earliest encounters with the cinema, including a detailed account of early film screenings in public gardens, audiences related to the 'space of foreignness' rather differently.[11] Pang notes that the lack of extant materials notwithstanding, enough of her research on the introduction of early Anglo-European cinema to Chinese audiences indicates that

> While people in the West reexperienced their own everyday life in these actuality films, the Chinese might have received western-made images in profoundly different ways. According to the 'cinema of attractions' theory, what captured an American audience watching a view of an American street in film was not the images as such but the cinematic apparatus. However, most Chinese viewers were not familiar with the foreign images they saw onscreen.[12]

She goes on to cite a news report from 1897 where the reviewer of these strange foreign images describes his experience as such: 'The electric lights are like tall candles. The cars moving along the street combine to become a swimming dragon. So many people walk around it looks as if cloth is being woven [...] Viewers were so elated that their eyebrows rose and their faces rapidly changed colour'.[13] For the Chinese viewer at this time, 'what impressed him [...] was as much the representational process as the referent itself'.[14]

In Japan, the foreignness of film was mediated by the presence of live narrators (most widely known to English readers by their Japanese nomenclature, the *benshi*) who translated these foreign films aurally for local audiences. These *benshi* were often stars in their own right and their popularity, it is often cited, accounted for their persistence well into the sound era in the 1930s.[15] Hideaki Fujiki offers a snapshot of a *benshi* performance at the height of their popularity. It is important to note here that the *benshi*'s performance was often 'autonomous from the film on the screen':

> In the early 1900s, before multiple-reel films began to circulate, the *benshi* typically offered a preliminary demonstration prior to the screening (*maesetsu*) that emphasized the marvel of the moving image or that provided background on the film's story. Initially, the *benshi*'s performance did not hold as much commercial appeal as the novelty of the film technology and the unfamiliar foreign stories. By 1903, however, [...] the *benshi* were performing a variety of feats, so that seeing them became a prime reason audiences attended movies.[16]

As multi-reel cinema became more prevalent and narratives more complex, the *benshi*'s vocal performance 'became more nuanced and sophisticated', manipulating their voices and performative skills 'to create an interplay between their speech and the screened images', to the extent that they sometimes 'created narratives that were distinct from the film's plot, or made the projectionist adjust the projecting speed so that they could speak more'.[17] Within these contexts of reception, there can be no pretence, nor even a suspension of disbelief, that events and characters on the screen were anything *but* foreign. If anything, the encounter with the foreign seemed to be an intrinsic, and inextricable, part of the receptive pleasure of cinema itself.

The persistence of the *benshi*, several years after Japanese cinema exhibition had already transitioned to sound, is often read as a phenomenon that is 'uniquely' Japanese. Both Joseph Andersen and Donald Richie, two authors who produced one of the earliest accounts of Japanese film history in the English language, take pains to stress the particular Japanese character of *benshi* practice, even if they sometimes acknowledge that live narration occurred in early cinema elsewhere, including in Europe and the Middle East.[18] In his 'second and third thoughts about the Japanese film' addition to the expanded edition of the seminal text he co-wrote with Donald Richie, Joseph Andersen draws a close connection between the *benshi* and earlier oral narrative traditions in Japanese literary and theatrical art and culture, such as Noh, Kabuki and doll drama, as well as 'less appreciated but still fundamental double modes in such literary forms as *ezoshi*, *ekotoba*, and *kibyoshi* which integrate picture and word' and a 'wide range of solo performer storyteller traditions of Japan', which he outlines in some detail.[19] According to Andersen it was the 'cosmopolitan reformers of the Japanese film who appeared after 1917 [who] frequently sought to make films that could play independent of live performance' and he notes with some satisfaction that '[t]hey absolutely failed to get their way in the movie theaters'.[20] In contrast, Fujiki revisits the history of the *benshi* and locates their success precisely within the modernisation that was taking place within Japan in this period, arguing that while 'the *benshi*'s stardom embraced some traditional theatrical exhibition practices, [...] it was also upheld by the newly emerging corporate business model'.[21] The *benshi* were stars within a system where their 'identities, names, and/or image [...] enticed people into playhouses and circulated via advertising and publicity to promote fan culture'.[22] Reformists, Fujiki notes, campaigned for the *benshi* to serve a more explanatory function in film than one whose performances superseded it.[23] According to Fujiki, these 'reformers' whom Andersen had called 'cosmopolitan' sought in some ways to make the multi-reel film, whose storytelling modalities were becoming increasing complex, more readily understood to audiences. The reform movement, it could be said, attempted to democratise the cinema for audiences by wresting control of the narrative from the *benshi*. Fujiki concludes that, in the end, it was a combination of factors, including 'the subordination of the *benshi* to the film industry and Japanese government [regulation] [that] made them more easily replaceable by the talkie', where 'combined with the prevailing ideology that in cinema a character's image and voice must be unified into one body, the talkie was accepted as more natural and effective than the *benshi*'.[24]

I employ the extended example of the *benshi* here as an indication of how the processes of domestication and foreignisation are more complex than simple explanations of border crossings and cultural assimilation or rejection will allow. What is of interest to my conception of a cosmopolitan cinema is not simply how the *benshi* mediated the foreign in film but also how the historicisation of the *benshi* itself as 'uniquely' Japanese is then singularly held up as a practice foreign to Western cinema. 'Foreignness',

I argue, must always be taken as a matter of time and place. Consider, for instance, the importation of *benshi* practice for film screenings to Japanese American audiences during the silent era in Los Angeles, in a period where 'many Japanese Americans were faced with anti-Japanese sentiments everywhere except Little Tokyo'.[25] Japanese *benshi* 'on tour in the West Coast'[26] were employed to perform with the films and even proved lucrative for Fuji-kan, the theatre that supported them: 'This traditional Japanese way of screening took less money and less time than making title cards'.[27] In Little Tokyo, Los Angeles, *benshi* practice was not so much the domestication of a foreign cultural form, but one that reminded Japanese American audiences of a distant 'home', not so different from the reminders of home that early European immigrants to America saw in the cinema of the silent period.

While the *benshi* may have offered a form of sound cinema for their audiences, the advent of synchronised sound soon became a global standard, even in Japan, and to a degree standardised not just forms of storytelling in film but also introduced the standardisation of language within national cinemas. As Bourdieu argues, the standardisation of language is central to any nation-building project: 'The official language is bound up with the state, both in its genesis and its social uses. It is in the process of state formation that the conditions are created for the constitution of a unified linguistic market, dominated by the official language'.[28] If cinema allowed for the projection of national imaginaries, the coming of sound merely intensified this relationship, as state mechanisms, and sometimes even audience preferences, sought to impose further cultural uniformity and standardisation through the symbolic power of language. In the struggle for national representation and for the inclusion in the national voice of local and regional politics, cinema can form the site on which these struggles take place. In the case of Chinese cinemas, as I shall argue below, multiple dialect and regional language cinemas have always had to negotiate with the state-mandated Mandarin in mainland China as well as in Taiwan and Hong Kong where historical struggles over what constituted 'legitimate' Chinese linguistic identities have raged.

These questions are not easily resolved by practices of dubbing and subtitling, though those are the solutions employed by the industry today. For instance, American films dubbed in French for audiences in France are sometimes also 'double-dubbed' in Canada for Québecois audiences in order to conform to local accents and regional expressions. Luise von Flotow cites the vociferous objection by a Québec politician to the Franco-French dubbing of Dreamworks' *Shrek the Third* (2007), who claimed that 'his and many other Québec children could not understand the Franco-French put in the mouths of Hollywood creatures'.[29] Von Flotow observes that, aside from the use of French slang, 'many other aspects of Franco-French dubbing tend to irritate Québec audiences: regional French expressions, French syntax, French pronunciation, and the pitch of the actors' voice which is much higher and more "pointu," more hectic'.[30]

Linguistic and national identifications can be internally or externally imposed. For instance, although a relatively minor category at the Academy Awards, the Best Foreign Language Film category remains an important avenue by which non-English-language cinema can gain a foothold in the lucrative American market and obtaining one of the five nominations is highly desirable. Awarded to films produced outside of the United States with a predominantly non-English dialogue track, this award category stands alone amongst the other Academy Awards by being conferred on the submitting *country* rather than individual filmmaker or producer. As a result, selections, nominations and disqualifications occasionally throw into relief complex issues of national identity and identification, particularly when that identification is also linguistically determined. Until 2006, the film submitted for consideration had to contain dialogue in the 'official language' of the submitting country. This disqualified minority languages without official national status, including many aboriginal languages: for example, despite being awarded a Caméra d'Or at Cannes, and Best Canadian Film by both the Toronto Film Critics Association and the Toronto International Film Festival, *Atanarjuat: The Fast Runner* (Zacharias Kunuk, Canada 2001) was disqualified as it was in Inuktitut, an Inuit language, and not one of Canada's official national languages. Other similar examples include *Private* (Saverio Costanzo, Italy 2004), a film made by an Italian director about Israel–Palestinian conflict which was disqualified on account of being shot in Arabic and Hebrew, rather than Italian; and *Be With Me* (Eric Khoo, Singapore 2005) which was disqualified on account of being mostly in English, which, though an official language of Singapore, was not considered a foreign language to the US. The award's regulations appear even more arbitrary when the irony of the latter is pointed out: that the 93-minute film is, in effect, mostly silent, containing only about two and a half minutes of dialogue (in English and Chinese).[31] Yet, *Le Bal* (Ettore Scola, Italy/France/Algeria 1983), a film set in France and without any dialogue at all, was nominated as an *Algerian* entry. Such anomalies pepper the history of the Award, and while on the one level the ceremony may be dismissed as no more than a bit of fodder for celebrity magazines, on another level there are real political and economic consequences. The visibility that even a nomination at the Oscars affords many of these 'foreign-language' films can impact their global distribution and exhibition prospects and should not be underestimated.[32]

Multilingual cinema therefore presents us with a cosmopolitan challenge. On the one hand, linguistic pluralism in film signals an openness to difference and the space for multiple voices to exist; on the other, it can also call attention to the inherent contradictions and multiplicities embedded within the cross-cultural encounter. In this chapter, I approach some of these questions via three case studies: the first explores the cultural politics of the multiple use of Chinese languages in Hong Kong cinema, and in Wong Kar-wai's arthouse cinema in particular; the second explores the cultural politics of dubbing and subtitling through a little-known Japanese animated feature; and the third explores the implications for the (multi-)linguistic encounter when silence, or muteness, is an inherent part of the vocal mix.

Multilingual Chineseness in Hong Kong cinema

Hong Kong cinema is sometimes discussed in English-language scholarship under the general category of 'Chinese' or 'Chinese-language' cinema. However, Kwai-cheung Lo notes that Hong Kong's geographical proximity to mainland China and its historical legacy as a British colonial city in effect enabled it to negotiate variations of 'Chineseness' to different audiences:

> To many foreign visitors, Hong Kong already appears to be a very 'Chinese' city. It was used to exhibit Chineseness when the 'real' China could not be accessed. In fact, the returned Hong Kong may serve as an exemplar of Chineseness not because the colonial city disassociated from Chinese culture in order to

produce a Hong Kong identity, but because it has been producing and reshaping Chineseness since the early colonial era.[33]

As a former British colony operating close to the Chinese mainland, Hong Kong has long had to negotiate both with Chineseness as a cultural and ethnic marker of identity, and with Chineseness as a political signifier against the geo-political domination of the mainland. Stephen Teo refers to this self-consciousness as Hong Kong's 'China syndrome',[34] borne out by the Hong Kong 'new wave' cinema that emerged in the 1980s. Unlike the European new waves in the postwar period, the Hong Kong new wave cinema occurred within its commercial industry. Rather than introduce a new modernist aesthetic, the Hong Kong new wave was marked by a resurgence in Cantonese-language cinema. This emerged from a new Cantonese-language cultural consciousness that was responding to the domination of Mandarin-language cinema in Hong Kong up until this period.[35] A 'Second Wave' soon followed from the late 1980s, and marked not a separate cultural movement, but one which took the Hong Kong-Cantonese cultural consciousness further as the deadline for the 1997 handover of Hong Kong by Britain to China approached. Films from this movement are characterised by having placed Hong Kong's identity at the core of their thematic and narrative concerns, concerns that ran across both its commercial and independent cinemas. Along with Fruit Chan, Peter Chan, Mabel Cheung and Stanley Kwan, among others, Hong Kong filmmaker, now also international auteur, Wong Kar-wai is considered among this group.

In this section, I explore how Wong's calculated employment of Chinese languages, notably Mandarin and Cantonese, in many of his films offers a way of thinking about multilingualism in cinema as I have denoted above. It should be noted that this form of bilingualism is common in mainstream Hong Kong cinema as well; however, while Wong's films have continued to be the subject of critical attention within film scholarship, many volumes tend to be devoted to the study of aesthetics, for example, the auteur's recurrent use of setting and music to evoke themes of love and loss, as well as affects of nostalgia and the romance of time.[36]

Since *Chungking Express* (1994) propelled Wong onto the international film festival circuit as a celebrated auteur, Wong's reputation for producing stylish arthouse films has been firmly established, especially when *In the Mood for Love* (2000) reached beyond the arthouse to mainstream audiences worldwide. While the sumptuous visual aesthetic of the films has enabled them to cross into different international markets, less attention has been paid to their use of language, especially when, as is the case with *In the Mood for Love*, the dialogue is superseded by the sheer visuality of the film. In this chapter, I explore the multilingual properties of Wong's films in terms of their implications for international reception and a comparative cultural studies framework in the study of film. Given that cinema circulates globally and across cultural and linguistic borders, questions of translation are always at the forefront of their reception, practically (in terms of markets) and discursively (in terms of cultural comprehension). Markets respond to the practical needs of translation via established practices such as subtitling and dubbing. However, discursively, these practices have implications on how meaning is constructed within the text and to whom it is directed.

Wong's 'Hong Kong' films – that is, films that have been noted to focus on Hong Kong's subjectivity as shaped by its history and politics – have tended to employ a polyphony of Asian languages, whose mutual incomprehensibility creates different relationships between the characters, between the film and audiences within and outside of East Asia. In several of these films, characters frequently switch from one language to another, or speak in one language while the other replies in a different one without acknowledging their mutual incomprehensibility. For example, within a short sequence in *Chungking Express*, the character of Cop 223 / He Qiwu[37] (Takeshi Kaneshiro) attempts to ring a number of old girlfriends from a public phone, switching effortlessly between Mandarin, Cantonese and Japanese, and reflects on the actor's own polyglot background. In other parts of the film, a smattering of Urdu can also be heard, a language spoken by the Indian migrant community in the busy, multicultural area of Chungking Mansions in Hong Kong, an area Gordon Mathews refers to as a 'ghetto at the center of the world'.[38] In the follow-up film to *Chungking Express*, *Fallen Angels* (1995), He Qiwu's father also speaks in Hokkien, a dialect from southern China and also one of the main languages of Taiwan. In *In the Mood for Love*, Wong's best known feature to date, Mrs Suen (Rebecca Pan) speaks in Shanghainese, while Mrs Chan (Maggie

Cheung) replies in Cantonese. Wong has used Pan in a similar role in *Days of Being Wild* (1990) as a signifier for the community of Shanghainese people who migrated to Hong Kong during the turbulent period of the Cultural Revolution (1966-76) on the mainland. This use of multilingual Chineseness in Wong's films does more than simply denote linguistic and cultural diversities within the territory – rather the highly formal and stylised ways in which the dialogic relationships between languages are set up operate as particularly studied *performances of difference*.

The multilingualism in the films portrays Hong Kong at the crossroads of Asia, a cosmopolitan city in which many cultures interact and intersect. In that respect, not many spectators would come to Wong's films understanding 'every' language, and it is the fissures of linguistic identity construction that dramatise Lo's description of Hong Kong: 'Hong Kong's Chineseness is a site of performative contradictions. It is like a crack in the edifice of Chineseness. Its existence is simply a living and contingent contradiction, in the sense that the city's culture both exaggerates and negates Chineseness in the vicissitudes of its sociopolitical milieux'.[39] Many Hong Kong residents inhabit multilingual spheres: Lo notes that the myth of Hong Kong as 'essentially a monoethnic, monolingual Cantonese-speaking community' is belied by the use of 'Hakka [*kejia*], Hoklo [*fulao*], Chiu Chau [*chaozhou*], Fukien [*fujian*], Sze Yap [*siyi*], and Shanghainese together with Mandarin/Putonghua [...] in many Hong Kong families'.[40] These dialects or language systems are by and large mutually incomprehensible without some form of mediation or translation between them. Sheldon Lu goes as far as to say that 'the use of a specific [Chinese] dialect in a film pertains to nothing less than the symbolic construction of the modern Chinese nation-state', and notes the 'parallel cinemas' that have sprung up in Taiwan (between 'Taiwanese (Hokkienese)-language cinema and Mandarin cinema') and in Hong Kong (between Cantonese-language cinema and Mandarin cinema).[41] Writing with a measure of theoretical distance about her own childhood in Hong Kong, Rey Chow describes the complex cultural and linguistic negotiations a schoolchild in Hong Kong would have to navigate, especially when the writing of standard Chinese did not always correspond with the Cantonese vernacular. These negotiations she intimates are not only particularly onerous but also distinctly artificial.[42] Add to this process the imposition of a colonial education, where the privileging of English as the language of value over Chinese 'became, for the colonized, a lesson in none other than the continual, disciplined *objectification* of an intimate part of themselves',[43] and the instability of the ontological conflict she identifies is compounded. Rather than leading to the replacement of one language by another, Chow writes, the confrontation between languages 'in fact positions the colonized subject in an interesting, if perpetually conflicted, ontological situation in which there can be no pure linguistic practice because the use of one language is habitually interfered with by the vying availability of others'.[44]

Just to take one example from the films, this 'vying availability' of both Cantonese and Mandarin is played out in an especially exaggerated and stylised fashion through the relationship between Chow Mo-wan (Tony Leung Chiu-wai) and Bai Ling (Zhang Ziyi) in *2046* (2004). Throughout their tempestuous relationship, the fact that Chow speaks exclusively in Cantonese and Bai Ling exclusively in Mandarin connotes the mutual lack of communication and compatibility between them, even though they respond to each other within the diegesis as if they understood what the other was saying. The structure and sounds of Cantonese and Mandarin are sufficiently different for the languages to be mutually incomprehensible, unless one were versed to some extent in both languages. A more common scenario in Hong Kong would be, as Ackbar Abbas finds, to hear a more hybrid, even patois, form of Cantonese, 'sprinkled with snatches of Mandarin, English, and barbarous sounding words and phrases', a linguistic form he refers to as 'a hybrid language coming out of a hybrid space'.[45] The issue is not one of linguistic competence on the part of the characters, but on the part of the spectator. While the characters could be presumed to have working knowledges of both Mandarin and Cantonese, there is no evidence for this presumption within the diegesis. Instead, each character's exclusive use of one language over the other in the film *without any attempt to bridge the divide* points to a formal decision made by the filmmaker to maintain their mutual exclusion.

In doing so in such a self-conscious fashion, *2046* does not only allude to the politics of language within the history of Hong Kong, as I have outlined above, but also the linguistic and cultural politics that have played out within the history of Hong Kong cinema itself, where until the 1970s, there was a divide between the higher-budget Mandarin-language films and the lower-budget Cantonese-language films,[46] until the latter's resurgence in the 1980s. Yingjin Zhang divides the history of Hong Kong cinema prior to the 1980s into three main phases: the first phase spans 1945 to 1955, the second 1956 to 1965, and the third 1966 to 1978.[47] The first phase involved the migration of large numbers of artists and producers from Shanghai, 'many of whom expected their sojourn to be temporary'.[48] This group left Shanghai after the end of World War II, when the civil war breaking out in China 'took a spiritual toll' on them.[49] These emigrants 'initiated a trend of Mandarin cinema in postwar Hong Kong that rivaled its Shanghai counterparts in both critical realism and genre innovations while exhibiting a strong nostalgic ambience'.[50] This development evolved alongside the Cantonese film industry already present in Hong Kong at the time.[51] However, rather than blending into a pan-Chinese hybrid, as already noted above, 'the Cantonese and Mandarin cinemas remained parallel film cultures',[52] with the Shanghainese made-in-Hong-Kong films depicting the city as 'an abstract, cardboard city, using Hong Kong locations dressed up as the streets and quarters of Shanghai [...]. The styles, themes and content of Hong Kong's Mandarin films evoked the classics of Shanghai cinema of the 30s'.[53] Yingjin Zhang notes how even 'their respective production staff rarely mixed', to the extent that 'they served two separate audiences in Hong Kong and overseas, and their characteristics could be contrasted in opposite terms [...]: for Cantonese cinema, cheap, simple, unpretentious, folk roots, southern, energetic, whereas for Mandarin cinema, expensive, arty, pretentious, urban roots, northern and stiff'.[54] The rivalry between the Mandarin and Cantonese-language cinemas intensified during the second phase of the 'competing studios' era,[55] where the two main studios, Cathay and Shaw Brothers, were in 'cut-throat competition', and 'kept luring each other's top artists and outpacing each other's production plans'.[56] They competed in both the Cantonese and Mandarin-language markets and in similar genres. During this era, a form of linguistic hybridity would emerge, which Yingjin Zhang argues reflects 'the convergence in Hong Kong cinema', that is 'the mixing of Cantonese- and Mandarin-speaking casts in the same films', which Zhang interprets as pointing to a 'self-confidence' with which Hong Kong filmmakers chose 'by confronting rather than evading the hybridity of their cultural identity'.[57]

Towards the mid-1960s, however, the Shaw Brothers would dominate, especially in Mandarin-language productions, 'because a Mandarin title could be sold at a higher price than a Cantonese one'.[58] The decline of Cantonese-language cinema was in part due to its inability to meet audience expectations (note the 'cheap' descriptor above), an audience which was already able to consume Mandarin and foreign films.[59] The rise of Mandarin cinema during this period was also supported by the importation of films from Taiwan, mainly martial arts fantasies, romances and melodramas.[60] During this period, the Southeast Asian market also grew in importance because the mainland government had banned Cantonese-language films,[61] accelerating the Hong Kong film industry's desire to expand its market share in other territories, especially to overseas Chinese communities around the world.

The revival of Cantonese Hong Kong cinema in the third phase after 1966 marks the entry of Golden Harvest, the new studio who founded superstars Bruce Lee and Jackie Chan and consolidated Hong Kong's reputation for the madcap kinetic cinema it is today most well known for. Mandarin-language cinema, in the style of the old costume fantasy dramas, would experience a severe decline in this era[62] to be revived only in the late twentieth century with *Crouching Tiger, Hidden Dragon*, which I have discussed elsewhere.[63] Following the three phases outlined by Zhang, there was, in the 1980s, the Hong Kong 'new wave' cinema, which is noted for its diversity of styles and genres but bound by a common concern with search for identity in Hong Kong.[64]

On these textual traces of history the films also include traces of other cultural geographies and imaginaries as well, which are rarely explored in accounts of Wong's films. These include the history and migration of Chinese peoples through Southeast Asia via Hong Kong that is frequently gestured to in Wong's films. For instance, in *In the Mood for Love*, following the unconsummated relationship with Mrs Chan (Maggie Cheung), Mr Chow (Tony Leung) leaves for Singapore. The narrative transition is marked by a shot transition to the silhouette of a single coconut tree against the sky, accompanied by the epigraphic text signalling its location, 'Singapore, 1963' (Figure 1.1). The shot is introduced along with the strains of the melody of the Javanese folk song, 'Bengawan Solo', the title of which refers to the name of an ancient river, its nostalgic tune

The cosmopolitan challenge of multilingual cinema

Figure 1.1 *In the Mood for Love*: Silhouette of a coconut tree

and lyrics recalling the enduring nature of the river and the culture that sprang up around it. In the film, however, the song is sung in *English* by the Shanghainese actress and singer, Rebecca Pan Di-hua (b. 1931), who also has a role in the film as the gregarious landlady, Mrs Suen. Thus, in *In the Mood for Love*, the song refers not specifically to the location of Indonesia but to the cultural space and time in which the song had been popularised in Hong Kong by popular singers of the day.[65] Writing on Wong's trilogy, *Days of Being Wild*, *In the Mood for Love* and *2046*, architectural historian Lai Chee Kien analyses 'corollary constructions of the Southeast Asian Chinese diaspora in the 1960s', arguing that 'the three movies co-inscribed the spaces and circulations of the region together with Hong Kong for a specific duration of its colonial history', underscoring 'the inextricability of Southeast Asia and Hong Kong for the Chinese diaspora of that period'.[66] For Lai, Wong's use of tropical signifiers (such as coconut trees, plantations, jungles, the consumption of tropical fruit and so on) echoes the use of similar images from Hong Kong cinema of the 1950s, showing 'for urban Hong Kong audiences, what differentiated their cinematic spaces from Nanyang [or Southeast Asia, literally 'south seas']'.[67] The citation of these tropical images in Wong's films thus looks beyond their exoticism, even though they may still be read as such by Western audiences, and instead inscribes them very specifically within a history of regional and colonial politics:

> With China largely absent, Southeast Asia became the de facto space for Hong Kong's correlated identity formations. Hong Kong not only served as a space for cosmopolitan travel and migration for Nanyang, it also actively co-produced that constitutive network of relationships through print, musical and other media, including cinematic ones. The initial stereotyping and subsequent familiarization of objects, people, landscapes and the food of Nanyang graduated the degrees of these encounters and identities. The reappearance of Southeast Asian spaces in Wong's trilogy is thus his memory and portrayal of those constructed proximities and endearments. The eventual loss of cinematic connections from the 1970s onwards, concomitant with the decline of the textual, aural and corporeal networks among the Chinese diaspora, led to the gradual isolation of Hong Kong from the region's social and economic spheres.[68]

Out of this instability of linguistic relationships and cultural politics within Chinese cinemas in Hong Kong have emerged some idiosyncratic dubbing and subtitling practices. By the 1980s, the parallel Mandarin and Cantonese film cultures had become far less distinct, and Hong Kong cinema, as a relentlessly commercial industry, adopted both dubbing and subtitling practices in order to respond to the needs of their different markets. For the mainland Chinese and some overseas markets, Cantonese films from Hong Kong were frequently dubbed into Mandarin, losing, as many argue, much of the nuance and wordplay of the original Cantonese. At the same time, English and Chinese subtitles are also employed on both the Cantonese and Mandarin versions. The presence of English subtitles is owed to British colonial law which made them mandatory, and the functionary nature of the exercise has produced unintended consequences. Quirky expressions and syntactical anomalies in Hong Kong English subtitling have long been the subject of mirth in cult fandom. Lo explains: 'Hong Kong cinema is famous for its slipshod English subtitling. The subtitlers of Hong Kong films, who are typically not well educated, are paid poorly and must translate an entire film in two or three days'.[69] The experience of the subtitled Hong Kong film 'in the West', he adds, 'produces a residual irrationality that fascinates its hardcore fans', especially when 'the distortion is written into the very essence of Hong Kong films and is one of the major appeals for Western fans'.[70] He cites Julian Stringer's 'disorientation' with the arcane subtitling of John Woo's *A Better Tomorrow* (1986), in which the impenetrable babble of phrases such as 'Learning. That's what you've to learn!' and 'Don't trust those cunny!' left Stringer 'lost and linguistically floundering, adrift on "an alien sea of undecipherable phonic substance".[71] Meaghan Morris recalls with dismay her initial experiences with Hong Kong cinema in the 1970s:

> I'm embarrassed because I remember what it was like to see a 'Hong Kong film,' any Hong Kong film, in that blankly Orientalist way – unable to distinguish one film from another let alone kung fu from swordplay (or, indeed, from karate and then from chambara), wholly ignorant of Chinese genres, and believing in response to the famously bad English dubbing that the films were uniformly so terrible they were funny – a camp reception of Hong Kong films that survives in some Western fan subcultures today.[72]

Although this bilingual subtitling, 'irrational' as the phrases may sound in English, became 'the norm of Hong Kong cinema'[73] and enabled its products to reach into overseas markets, for audiences in Hong Kong and Southeast Asia accustomed to such a practice, subtitling is a part of the film, not something in addition to it. The presence of at least two sets of subtitles (in English and Chinese) in every film means that viewers are constantly reminded, even if they have learned to ignore the presence of the words onscreen, 'of the others' existence',[74] and there is thus little or no resistance to subtitling for which the American and UK mainstream markets are notorious.

The presence of Chinese subtitles in Hong Kong films is usually understood to be an acknowledgement to the heteroglossia of Chinese vernacular languages/dialects, which may differ considerably in spoken form but share a degree of uniformity in written form. These enable Chinese speakers not versed in either Mandarin or Cantonese to follow the dialogue. Even so, meaning can still be lost in translation as the Chinese subtitles are sometimes rendered in idiomatic Cantonese, which is an aural rather than a written language, and not in 'standard' Chinese.[75] As Chua Beng Huat notes, 'Chinese languages can be phonologically strange to each other' and the written form, although assumed to be shared across Chinese dialects, does not always facilitate comprehension because 'the meaning of a written word is nevertheless not always assured'.[76] This is because written Cantonese frequently employs characters only as transliterations of its spoken sound, rather than for its written meaning, and, read literally, would then be incomprehensible. This curious phenomenon produces 'an interesting disjuncture when a Chinese audience is watching a film or a television programme that is dubbed in one Chinese language while carrying scripted Chinese subtitles in another, when one simultaneously listens to and reads the dialogue'.[77] A kind of dynamic tension is produced by one set of literacies rubbed up against another, an effect that Lo notes 'creates a doubleness within the original text – not by juxtaposing two mutually incomprehensible national languages, as other subtitled films do, but by reinforcing the split between the spoken and written languages, thereby destroying the possibility of any easy identification'.[78] Foreignness in these instances becomes a question of degree and a matter of interweaving layers of meaning-making; the lines between languages, between source and target, are not clearly demarcated. To acknowledge the act of subtitling only as an act of 'violence' on the text or a 'corruption' of meaning,[79] as Nornes puts it, is to reinforce the value of the 'original' even if it is noted to be 'lost', transcendent or infinitely deferred.

Given the political nature of language, there are further implications when the dialogue is uniformly dubbed into Mandarin as is most likely the case for exhibition in mainland China or in Singapore, where since the 1970s, in order not to undermine the state's 'Speak Mandarin Campaign', all non-Mandarin Chinese languages in the public media (that is, film and television) are required by the state authorities to be dubbed into Mandarin,[80] even though, paradoxically, all other 'foreign' films – such as French, Iranian, Japanese, among others – may be screened in their original languages with subtitles. In this context, the cultural politics shifts to a different domain. Returning to Wong's *2046*, if all the Cantonese in Chow Mo-wan's dialogue is dubbed into Mandarin, the friction between the characters, Chow and Bai Ling, is played out as a lovers' spat, rather than also a *textual trace* of the history of a territory played out through the history of the medium as I have argued. At the same time, subtitling demands a level of literacy in the language of its audiences. As film scholars or cinephiles, it is sometimes too easy to dismiss mainstream America's or Britain's aversion to subtitled films; but in Singapore, for example, even though a version of local colloquial English is widely spoken, reading comprehension is not always of a high level; likewise audiences may find written Chinese equally difficult to understand. To these audiences, subtitles can be obstacles rather than vehicles of cultural access.

Yet in multilingual societies, it is entirely plausible that such linguistic dissonances resonate at different levels for audiences with different levels of literacy, and could perhaps be more widely studied in cross-cultural interpretations of cinema. Speaking anecdotally, the idiosyncratic English subtitles in Hong Kong films operate at different levels in Singapore, for example, where because the local patois – 'Singlish' or Singapore Colloquial English – is already a non-standard form of English,[81] one is conditioned to read beyond the explicit meaning of the words and to decipher meaning from the mode of address and from the contexts from which the distortions might arise. In this context, Hong Kong English subtitles, funny though they may be, are not really that 'foreign' to me. In a sense, this negotiation of distance and proximity can be described as a form of 'double interdict', as Derrida describes it in his treatise on the 'monolingual other'. He writes: 'When I said that the only language I speak is not mine, I did not say it was foreign to me. There is a difference. It is not entirely the same thing [...]'.[82] The difference lies with the 'double interdict' experienced by the monolingual other, in which both the assumed 'mother tongue' and the learned language of the subject is 'interdicted', leaving the subject at a loss for words and yet not speechless: 'In what language does one write memoirs when there has been no authorized mother tongue? How does one utter a worthwhile "I recall" when it is necessary to invent both one's language and one's "I," to invent them at the same time, beyond this surging wave of amnesia that the double interdict has unleashed?'[83] This double interdict occurs when the assumed mother tongue is displaced, or 'interdicted', by the learned language (in Derrida's case, French, in mine, English), and the learned language is then displaced by the prosthetic point, or culture, of origin.[84] Rey Chow explores

Derrida's 'rhetorical turns' as 'a way of confronting us with the problem of language as *legacy*':

> What does it mean to have a language – when we believe that a language has been left or delegated to us? Does having a language mean coming into possession of it like a bequest from bona fide ancestors and/or being able to control the language's future by handing it down to the proper heirs? Is such ownership through belonging, descent, or posterity a privilege that is exclusive to native speakers?[85]

Hence, the experience of translation may be encountered entirely differently by a 'native' Cantonese speaker like Lo, and a non-Cantonese-speaking, limited-Chinese-reading, English-speaking, ethnic Chinese Singaporean, like me. Lo writes that 'subtitles undermine the primacy and immediacy of the voice and alienate the aural from the visual', especially since '[m]ost Hong Kong movies are shot postsynch in order to save time and money. The soundtrack is added to the film only after the entire film is shot. Therefore the visual is never intimately tied to the aural'.[86] As Lo is from Hong Kong and is fluent in Cantonese, his experience of the film needs no mediation via the subtitles; he admits to just ignoring them.[87] As one who is reliant only partially on aural recognition, and partially on subtitles (along with their dissonance), my experience is more one of a re-suturing of the film's component parts – the visuals, the spoken dialogue and the written subtitles – separated initially by the gaps in my fluency. The translation that I put together in my mind is both conscious of and conditioned by the awareness that I am not able to translate fully, and thus am not able to know, everything that is being translated. As I have discussed, the multilingualism of Wong's films underscore rather than undermine, the impossibility of spectatorial omniscience.

Dubbing and subtitling in Japanese animation

Not all film cultures foreground these tensions consciously or willingly, especially mainstream commercial film cultures, from which various practices of dubbing, subtitling and remaking have emerged as means of negotiating with, if not suppressing entirely, aspects of the foreign. Hollywood's preference for remakes over foreign imports as a form of domestication of foreign texts is well known and often attributed to US audiences' persistent resistance to subtitles. This attitude creates a conundrum for international distributors trying to market foreign-language cinema to the US. US distributors intent on marketing foreign films outside of the arthouse 'ghetto'[88] have been noted to resort to extraordinary lengths to get the films noticed and, where they can, perhaps even to shape audience tastes. B. Ruby Rich writes of the concerted effort by the US film distributors in the mid-1980s to 'bait' audiences into 'switching' to foreign cinema. She notes a particular memorable example of how audiences were 'duped' into sitting through Zhang Yimou's Chinese-language *Raise the Red Lantern* (1991), and how this deception involved the screening of advertising trailers of the film without any dialogue or subtitles. Rich recalls: 'The audience settled contentedly in their seats until the opening credit sequence ended and the talking – and subtitles – began. Then [...] a sudden burst of groaning was audible. The audience was face-to-face with the ruse and realized it had been duped. But people stayed. And the film became another hit'.[89] The strategy here is not restricted to Chinese-language films as a similar practice also succeeded earlier with Pedro Almodóvar's *Women on the Verge of a Nervous Breakdown* (1988).

Although subtitling in comparison calls more attention to the 'foreignness' of the text than dubbing, there is nonetheless the concern in the professional practice with minimising any disjunctures and dissonances in the effort to negotiate with diverse histories and cultural geographies. Henri Béhar reflects on his work as a professional translator and subtitler, calling subtitling 'a form of cultural ventriloquism', where 'the focus must remain on the puppet, not the puppeteer': 'Our task as subtitlers is to create subliminal subtitles so in sync with the mood and rhythm of the movie that the audience isn't even aware that it is reading. We want not to be noticed. If a subtitle is inadequate, clumsy, or distracting, it makes everyone look bad, but first and foremost the actors and the filmmakers. It can impact the film's potential career'.[90] Within Béhar's view, the cultural labour of subtitling must remain invisible for it to retain its cultural value. Lawrence Venuti describes this process as an 'eclipse of the translator's labor'.[91] In order for the subtitles to remain unobtrusive, any kinks in the text and awkward spots in the translation have to be smoothed over. In other words, the foreignness of the encounter should attempt to efface itself, even as the subtitles on the screen continually signal their presence. Abe Mark Nornes describes this practice as one that is far from benign; for him, subtitling is a 'practice of translation that smooths over its textual violence and domesticates all otherness while it pretends to bring the audience to an experience of the foreign'.[92] Subtitles, according to this model, allow audiences to feel as if we have linguistic, and thus cultural, access to the diegesis, to the world of the film, but in reality as discussed above, our access may be limited.

Scholarship on the politics and practices of dubbing and subtitling is more prevalent within the fields of linguistics and translation studies rather than in film studies. Notable exceptions include the whimsical anthology, *Subtitles: On the Foreignness of Film* (2004), edited by Ian Balfour and Atom Egoyan, Abé Mark Nornes' *Cinema Babel* (2007) and Carol O'Sullivan's *Translating Popular Film* (2011). If, as Venuti asserts, 'any attempt to make translation visible today is necessarily a political gesture',[93] my interest here is less in what happens when translation breaks down, but what happens when we are not supposed to notice? In this section, I explore the dubbing and subtitling of a Japanese animated feature as a kind of multilingual encounter, beyond linguistic and translative 'accuracies', and discuss the cultural implications for its international circulation.

Japanese animation is popular in the US and the UK and, due to its association with cartoons and children's entertainment, tends to be dubbed into English for the youth market. However, as the popular Japanese animation house Studio Ghibli gains more visibility and popularity in the US and the UK, it is also attracting a growing adult market, and frequently programmed by independent cinemas as part of its 'specialist film' fare.[94] Indeed, Studio Ghibli can be said to have successfully straddled the high-brow/low-brow divide, reaching out to family as well as foreign cinema audiences, and thus circumvented some of the traditional restrictions subtitled films have faced in the exhibition market. In the US and the UK, Studio Ghibli films are also regularly featured on cable channels such as Turner Classic Movies and Film Four, and their season programmes often feature both the Japanese-language (with English subtitles) and English-dubbed versions of the films, a practice not usually employed with other subtitled or dubbed films.

Writing about 'the absolute exigency of the subtitled print' in the independent and arthouse circuit, Mark Betz notes that 'clearly these rules do not apply for popular or low genres',[95] genres which include spaghetti westerns, Hong Kong *kung fu* comedies and *anime*. Betz attributes this to a cultural bias conflating film auteurs with their national cinemas, in spite of the prevalence of co-productions, noting that the 'name of the auteur and the purity of his or her intentions, the need to hear the "original" sound track in its "original" language – both of these mutually determining notions are invoked as proof of the superiority of subtitling over dubbing, yet few find these issues of any relevance to popular cinemas'.[96] Within this frame, Japanese animated films count as a 'popular cinema'. However, what is interesting about the transnational popularity of Studio Ghibli is that its founder and chief creative force, Hayao Miyazaki is now also widely perceived as a film auteur. In a career profile of Miyazaki, *The New Yorker* magazine describes the filmmaker as 'The Auteur of Anime'.[97] By association, the films released by Studio Ghibli are regularly received as auteurist works in the international market.

The film I focus on in this section, *Whisper of the Heart* (1995), is a lesser-known work released by Studio Ghibli, directed by one of the studio's key animators, Yoshifumi Kondo. Before his untimely death in 1998, Kondo was touted to be Miyazaki's successor. Unlike Ghibli's many international hits, *Princess Mononoke* (1997), *Spirited Away* (2001), *Howl's Moving Castle* (2004) and *The Wind Rises* (2013), which were released theatrically and mainly dubbed in English with American voice actors, *Whisper of the Heart* was released in the US only on cable television and directly on DVD. These formats allowed, unusually, both dubbed and subtitled versions of the film to circulate simultaneously, and for audience interest and awareness to build up gradually by word of mouth. In 2006, as part of a Studio Ghibli season, *Whisper of the Heart* was released on the American cable channel, Turner Classic Movies, both in the English-subtitled Japanese-language version and the English-dubbed concurrently. Film Four in the UK programmed a similar season in 2015. In her study on the cross-cultural acceptance of Japanese animation, Anne Cooper-Chen notes that the kinds of Japanese animated films and television series that are popular in the US tend to be from science fiction and fantasy genres, whereas more realistic, 'slice of life' features are popular in Asian markets.[98] *Whisper of the Heart* falls into the latter.

Whisper of the Heart is a low-key, whimsical coming-of-age story centred on a 15-year-old girl, Shizuku Tsukushima in her last year of middle school. There is very little dramatic tension, action or jeopardy in the film beyond charting Shizuku's own immature attempts to write her *magnum opus*, translate a well-known American song into Japanese and establish a (very chaste) relationship with a schoolmate, Seiji Amasawa, who harbours his own ambitions of becoming a violin maker in Cremona, Italy. The overarching themes within the film are of the pull towards the safety of home and the need to leave home in search of individual self-realisation, themes echoing the spirit of the *bildungsroman*. It is Shizuku's attempts at translation that I wish to focus on here. Throughout the film, we see Shizuku attempt to translate the lyrics of John Denver's 'Take Me Home, Country Roads' (1971) into Japanese as part of a class graduation project. Throughout, we see her struggle, not only to convey the meaning of the verses, but also inform the translation in a way that would make it relevant to her graduating class. There are at least five versions of the song in the diegesis, and each one furthers the plot, cements relationships, and comments on the film's themes of home and self-realisation. In this analysis, I focus on two of those translations: the first is an early translation of the song's lyrics which Shizuku tests out on her friend, Yuko; and the second is a full-length version of the song she sings at an impromptu jam session, which also constitutes the musical and narrative climaxes of the film. My comparisons are conducted between the English subtitles employed in the Japanese DVD release (with the English subtitle track) and the American dialogue in the US DVD release, made for the American market. My focus is not on the 'accuracy' of the translations as such but on the questions raised by each process, questions such as: What cultural processes are at work when an American song about the longing for the American mid-West ('Country Roads') is translated into Japanese, which is then re-translated into English subtitles for an Anglophone audience? What processes are further at work when it is dubbed compared with when it is subtitled?

In the first translative encounter, Shizuku admits her difficulties with the translation process and offers her friend, Yuko, a parody of her own efforts instead: 'Country Roads' becomes 'Concrete Road' in a self-reflexive moment acknowledging the geographical and cultural gulf between the girls' experience of urban Tokyo and John Denver's idyllic West Virginian mountains. The subtitled and dubbed versions of this encounter produce markedly different cultural effects. In the English subtitled version, Shizuku and Yuko sing the following in Japanese to the tune of Denver's song:

> *Concrete Road*
>   (Transcribed from the English subtitled,
>   Japanese edition DVD)

> Concrete road, wherever you go
> Forests give rise to valleys far away
> Western Tokyo, on Mount Tama
> My hometown lies on concrete road

The meaning of Shizuku's Japanese lyrics is offered in translation by the subtitles. Immediately following the song, the girls laugh at the comic irony of the lyrics with Yuko remarking: 'What is this?', while Shizuku adds, significantly: 'Think I should've kept it in English?' (Figure 1.2).

This line of dialogue is completely omitted in the US dub. In the dubbed version, Shizuku and Yuko already speak in (American) English, and when they sing Shizuku's 'Concrete Road', they are merely putting new (English) words to the already familiar tune of Denver's song. They sing the following version in English:

> *Concrete Road*
> (US dubbed version)

> Concrete road, everywhere I go
> Discovering West Tokyo
> Chopped down forests, buried valleys
> My hometown, down concrete road

Figure 1.2 *Whisper of the Heart*: 'Think I should've kept it in English?'

Diegetically and logically, asking the question 'Think I should've kept it in English?' in English would make no sense at all, and the remark is appropriately omitted. Shizuku's lyrics also lose something of their comic irony from her original act of wilful mistranslation from the English to the Japanese. When Yuko remarks afterwards, 'What is this?', we can indeed ask ourselves, 'What is the point of this?' What *is* this act of rewriting the lyrics of what is already revered as an American classic about the American mid-West?

While the subtitled version of the film maintains a consciousness throughout of the cultural gap between Denver's 'Country Roads' and contemporary Japan, the US dubbed version of *Whisper of the Heart* effaces the Japanese social context and effectively turns the characters into American teenagers, whose voice actors all speak with a standardised American accent, sometimes known as 'General American'. However, no cultural explanation is further given for the Japanese uniforms, cultural norms and mannerisms (like Shizuku and Yuko bowing to their teachers). Thus in the US dubbed version, Shizuku's efforts at translation are rendered largely redundant. Mark Betz is critical of valorising the subtitled print above the dubbed one, arguing that '[f]rom an archival standpoint, there is really no version of a film "as originally produced" to preserve or, as is more often the case, conserve, except perhaps for the unviewable in-camera negative', and that screening a dubbed print can be 'archivally sound as a practice'.[99] To an extent, I agree. Reception contexts are important and English-dubbed dialogue will guarantee a Ghibli film's wide release. However, in the case of *Whisper of the Heart*, I would argue that the subtitled version works 'better' than the dubbed one, not so much because of the perceived cultural value of the 'original' and 'authentic' Japanese language, but because the effacement of the struggle of translation defuses the entire narrative thrust of the film itself, as well as alters the nuances in the characterisation and relationships in the film. Shizuku, the translator, albeit inexperienced, is only able to find her own voice via the effort and process of translating a song from a particular culture and historical period into her own. It is this process of self-discovery, *enabled by the encounter with the foreign*, that forms the emotional core of the film. Removing Shizuku's (and our) struggle to translate removes much of the narrative power of the film.

The narrative trajectory of the film culminates in an impromptu musical jam session near the end when Shizuku sings her final, completed

The cosmopolitan challenge of multilingual cinema

Figure 1.3 *Whisper of the Heart*: Shizuku's 'Country Roads'

translation of 'Country Roads' (Figure 1.3). In this version, Shizuku seems to have come to terms with herself and her ambitions. The following are extracts from the opening verse of the two versions of the song:

> *Country Roads*
> (Shizuku's final version, English subtitled,
> Japanese edition DVD)
>
> No one is with me
> Going fearlessly
> That's the way I live in the dream I saw
> I must put my loneliness away
> And protect myself and I'll learn to be strong
>
> *Country Roads*
> (Shizuku's final version, US dubbed edition)
>
> I've dreams of living alone but fearless
> Secret longing to be courageous
> Loneliness kept bottled up inside
> Just reveal your brave face
> They'll never know you lied

In the subtitled version, where she sings the song in Japanese, the lyrics suggest that she chooses to reject the rural nostalgia of Denver's original. Instead, with a translator's prerogative, she opts to personalise the song for herself and her schoolmates, teenagers in urban Tokyo on the cusp of young adulthood. The call is to go 'fearlessly' into the future. So while the melody of Denver's song is familiar and nostalgic, the lyrics in translation emphasise a *farewell* to 'Country Roads' and the need to resist its pull towards the past ('I must put my loneliness away / And protect myself and I'll learn to be strong'). In this version, the message is clear: it is time for the kids to grow up and face their futures. In contrast, while the US dubbed version retains the theme of looking ahead rather than backwards into the past, it also emphasises the ruse necessary to move forward. It speaks of secrecy ('Secret longing to be courageous'), repression ('Loneliness kept bottled up inside') and deception ('They'll never know you lied'). The differences between the two versions are subtle, yet important to note for their cultural and political implications. In the subtitled version, a cultural distance is maintained that allows for some of the Japanese context to the narrative and the characters' attitudes to seep through, including the context of the downturn of the Japanese economy in the mid-1990s, beginning a decade-long recession, and disrupting the security of a working population accustomed to a generation of full and lifetime employment. This provides a cultural and historical backdrop to Shizuku's eventual realisation that 'just wanting to write is not enough'. In her pursuit of her novel, she neglects much of her schooling and her family life. When the novel fails to manifest as the *magnum opus* of her dreams, we (through Shizuku's experience) are made aware that singular ambition alone is nothing without developing other aspects of one's self and delivering on one's social responsibilities. In other words, for Shizuku self-realisation is not achieved simply with the resolute courage to pursue one's ideals but also the honesty to acknowledge one's limits. It is possible to read a Japanese cultural ethos here which, while it does not disavow a drive for individual ambition, warns of the possible pitfalls of failure. Although her creative efforts are supported by her parents – her mother is also pursuing a degree at night school – Shizuku is told in no uncertain terms by her father that if she chooses to make her own way in life, she will have *no one to blame* if she fails. Such advice reads in counterpoint to the pioneering ethos embedded in many American narratives, where protagonists are encouraged to pursue their dreams in spite of possible failure and societal disregard.

At this point, I should stress again that what I am concerned with is not the 'accuracy' of the dubbing or subtitling as such, but that the cultural proximity each process negotiates with the text has different implications for reception. In the US dubbed version, the American expressions sometimes jar with the Japanese body language and mannerisms of the characters, as well as *shoujo* (loosely translated as 'girls') manga conventions. In the subtitled version, something akin to 'parallel tracks' run in my head during the different renditions of 'Country Roads'. Because of the familiarity of Denver's song, the original of which is covered by Olivia Newton-John in the opening sequence of the same film, when I watch and hear Shizuku sing her translated version, both Denver's and Newton-John's renditions run along inside my head even as I am hearing the voice actors (Youko Honna / Brittany Snow) sing the words, with and without subtitles, in what I can only describe as an *intertextual echo chamber*[100] where the various versions of 'Country Roads' reverberate off each other and collectively constitute a text that constantly demands 'translating'.

As Naoki Sakai argues, translation then is 'not only a border crossing but also and preliminarily an act of drawing a border'.[101] The question that the drawing of these borders by the dubbing and subtitling processes I have outlined puts to cosmopolitan debates is not whether one version is translated more 'authentically' or travels more easily than the other, but what forms of cultural negotiation and literacy cinema can demand of us on these occasions. The invisibility of the translator that is prized in both dubbing and subtitling practices is disrupted at different moments in the different versions of *Whisper of the Heart* as I have discussed. It is by confronting these moments of disruption, rather than looking to their seamless integration, that we may explore the complex trajectories of how and where texts travel across territories and temporalities, in order to chart where we stand among them.

Must cosmopolitanism speak?

If multilingual cinema is as I have argued the result of dynamic encounters with language and difference, with partial comprehension and imperfect translations, then the question of inarticulacy must have a place in the conversation. Ironically, with the advent of the sound cinema, silence in film, or perhaps more accurately muteness, can now be brought to the fore. Memorable mute characters range from comedy icons like Charlie Chaplin's The Tramp and Harpo Marx; to tragic heroines, like Sarah Norman (Marlee Matlin) in *Children of a Lesser God* (1986) and Ada McGrath (Holly Hunter) in *The Piano* (1993); to ambivalent anti-heroes, like the recurring Hsiao-kang (Lee Kang-sheng) character in nearly all of Tsai Ming-liang's films.

In East Asian cinema, especially the auteurist, festival cinema influenced by European new wave movements, muteness can sometimes signify, or symbolise, a more collective inarticulacy. For example, the muteness of Tony Leung Chiu-wai's character, Wen-ching, in *A City of Sadness* (Hou Hsiao-Hsien, Taiwan 1989) has been read as symptomatic of the unspeakable horror and trauma of what is known in Taiwan history as the 2.28 incident – 2.28 referring to the tumultuous events of 28 February 1947 when an anti-government uprising was brutally suppressed by the state resulting in thousands of civilian casualties. The bloody incident launched over three decades of martial law and authoritarian rule in Taiwan known as the 'White Terror' period.[102] Sylvia Lin writes of how the film garnered both praise and criticism in Taiwan. Although *A City of Sadness* was the first Taiwanese film to win the Golden Lion award at Venice that year, 'the film and its director came under scathing attack by critics from the entire range of Taiwan's political spectrum'.[103] Lin summarises its detractors' views thus: 'At the core of the criticism is the representation of history or, to be exact, of the 2/28 Incident, but it also entails larger issues that have loomed over Taiwan's political and cultural landscapes since the lifting of martial law. That is, who owns this part of Taiwanese history, who is legitimate to speak for Taiwan and recapture its past on screen, and by what means?'[104] As with Hong Kong cinema, the polyphony of languages and dialects found in recent cinema from Taiwan can reflect the cacophony of voices competing for attention over the struggle for historical legitimacy. Alongside the Japanese, Minnan (native Taiwanese), Shanghainese and Mandarin heard in the film, Leo Chanjen Chen notes the different tonal, and gendered, quality of other sounds within the diegetic space of the film:

> Above this hubbub of tongues, there is an overarching contrast between male and female tones. Menacing male voices with undecipherable accents, issuing public announcements – the broadcasts of Chen Yi, the military governor of Taiwan responsible for the massacres, crackle harshly across the screen – are counterbalanced by the gentle feminine voice-over of Hiromi's diary and letters, the refuge of private feelings and reflections.[105]

Significantly, *A City of Sadness* is Taiwan cinema's first film to be shot with synchronised sound, as post-production dubbing had been the industry norm previously. It is also acknowledged as one of the first films to address what Chen has deemed to be '[h]istorically, the most forbidden of all subjects […] the founding crime of the KMT [Kuomintang] regime in Taiwan, which had led to the imposition of martial law in the first place'.[106] Although the film tells the story of the rise and fall of a family's fortunes through the experiences of four brothers, my analysis focuses on Wen-ching, the youngest brother of the four, who is deaf and mute. I offer a reading of the character's (and actor's) performance of muteness as one that is not only doubly significant within national and historical contexts, but also within the film's production and reception contexts as well.

According to Chen, 'Wen-ching's inability to speak stands for the island itself, his fate as the sign of what it has silently endured from others',[107] although it is evident within the diegesis that Wen-ching's inability to speak is not equated with an inability to communicate. He communicates with his family by writing on pieces of paper as well as through photography (Figure 1.4). However, the performance of muteness by the central character in the film reminds us of the importance of *speech acts*; so much of the discourse and politics of identity are fought solely on grounds of visibility and visuality. Indeed, muteness in the film is a speech act inasmuch as the spoken dialogue is and the film itself mimics these mute forms of speech acts on a formal level through the use of titles and intertitles. The dynamics of the film's play on articulation and speech suppression extends to metatextual domains, dynamics etched onto, but not always visible on, the body of the text as it negotiates different encounters with foreignness. It is these interweaving dynamics that constitute the cosmopolitanism of Hou's film beyond its transnational, festival and arthouse circulation.

Figure 1.4 *A City of Sadness*: Wen-ching in his photo studio

The casting of Hong Kong actor Tony Leung Chiu-wai in *A City of Sadness* is one nodal point on which these dynamics play out. Today, Tony Leung is acknowledged to have reached the pinnacle of his career as the star of Wong Kar-wai's *In the Mood for Love* (for which he became the first Asian male to win the Best Actor award at the Cannes Film Festival in 2000), *2046* and *The Grandmaster* (2013). At the time *A City of Sadness* was released, however, Tony Leung was only beginning to emerge from a career in TV and just on the cusp of a movie career in Hong Kong, and not yet the superstar he is today. He gained mainstream visibility with John Woo's *Bullet in the Head* (1990), and by the mid-1990s, Leung would become a recognisable face among Hong Kong cinema's stable of stars, alongside Leslie Cheung, Maggie Cheung and Andy Lau among others. In an interview on Taiwanese TV, director Hou reveals that Leung was cast in *A City of Sadness* primarily to capture the Hong Kong market.[108] In another interview, Hou also reveals that Leung was cast for the expressiveness of his 'eyes',[109] an expressiveness constituted by a mix of melancholy and mournfulness frequently commented on in countless media profiles across his career.[110] However, Leung's suitability for the role as Wen-ching ended with his visual profile, as the Hong Kong Cantonese-speaking actor was not able to speak Minnan, the native Taiwanese vernacular many Taiwanese films of the period employed as a gesture of political defiance against the state-enforced national language, Mandarin.[111] The decision to cast Leung as deaf and mute was an expedient, and elegant, solution to the problem, yet embedded in the decision may be located traces of other struggles in Chinese cultural history. As Chen further notes: 'Part of the reason the film was attacked [by critics] when it came out was that it implied [...] Wen-ching is about to be beaten up because his muteness is mistaken for a mainlander inability to speak Minnan'.[112] As with the films of Wong Kar-wai discussed earlier in this chapter, the dialogics and politics of Chinese languages and histories are here transposed onto the diegesis and enter into the cultural dynamics of the textual form if one were predisposed to look for these instances.

The context of the reception of *A City of Sadness* also speaks pertinently to the dynamics of speech and silence as the film travels through international markets. Although nearly every anthology of Taiwan cinema and Chinese cinemas in general mention this film, often with much reverence, as a landmark in global film history, the film is nearly impossible to obtain on DVD. The film was seen at European film festivals on first release, and continues to be available for theatrical retrospectives; however, to date no official English-subtitled DVD exists and the VHS release by Artificial Eye in 1996 has long since become a rare commodity. Informal online distribution circuits exist on YouTube and other filesharing sites and some online versions have been fansubbed, another translative phenomenon to be accounted for when addressing issues of cross-border circulation.[113] The relative lack of availability has prompted Valentina Vitali to consider Hou's presence in Europe as an auteur 'in absentia'. Researching a number of British, French and American film magazines of the 1980s, Vitali notes a conspicuous absence, that while Hou's films were extensively written about, the proliferation of the discourse on Hou's work was characterised by a glaring absence: 'that of the films themselves'.[114] Vitali indicts the European critical community, in their writing of the films without a sense of historical location, for reproducing readings 'hollowed out of any sense of historicity and reduced to a cluster of ostensibly universal formal devices'.[115] She argues that this focus on aesthetics and the lack of historicity permitted the reification of a mode of relating to film in general,[116] here pointing to the mode of relating that characterises a European arthouse response to non-European 'world cinema'. By Vitali's assessment, 'Hou's famous long-take and ellipses tend to be presented as formal devices that create a distance (between the events dictated and the spectator) which is to be appreciated and savoured as distance per se, rather than as a way of opening up an aesthetic field and a strategy of greater intellectual and sensorial understanding'.[117]

So we are no longer talking here about what happens to a film when it crosses borders, and how it translates to different audiences. Instead, the contention must be: *under what terms* does translation take place in the absence of a source text? If Hou's films have been read thematically and stylistically as a kind of cinema of ellipsis – or perhaps even of 'absentia' to adopt Vitali's term – where historical events take place off-screen, where long sequence shots pause meditatively on landscapes and objects instead of action, *A City of Sadness* may be said to be emblematic of the very ellipsis itself on several contextual levels. To read a film like *A City of Sadness* transnationally and cross-culturally necessitates an equal reading of what the text does not articulate, not just in the diegesis, but also in the modes of production, presentation and reception that constitutes its (non-)existence in the world.

Concluding remarks

In the introduction to their whimsical anthology on *Subtitles: On the Foreignness of Film* (2005), Balfour and Egoyan write: 'Every film is a foreign film, foreign to some audience somewhere – and not simply in terms of language'.[118] Although the films I have discussed call to the problem of translation textually, the context for translation is never a matter for the text alone. There are several discursive, and also practical, contexts to consider, which I have attempted to put in dialogue. Practical limits can often shape the discursive, but discursive contexts can also help us make sense of the structures of the power that operate within those limits. Much of the scholarship on dubbing and subtitling in films therefore tends to emphasise the practicalities and pragmatics of the process and the implications for the 'accuracy' of the translation.[119] Many accounts note some kind of 'loss' in the translation, and several cite this as an inevitable consequence of the process, most of them working from the premise that translation is both necessary and useful. On one level it is. As an avid consumer of world cinema, I am grateful for the work translators do to make these texts available to me. On another level, I seek to think through the argument Shohat and Stam introduce in their article, 'The cinema after Babel: language, difference, power' (1985), where they note that the study of language and film tends to be weighted in favour of 'the abstract system of langue' compared to 'the concrete heterogeneity of parole'.[120] Nearly three decades since the article was published, the balance has not shifted towards the latter, towards the study of multiple language use in film, except for the occasional volume such as Carol O'Sullivan's *Translating Popular Film* (2011).[121]

Part of the challenge of studying bilingualism and multilingualism in film is the question of methodology. In writing about 'foreign' films, John Mowitt has ventured the suggestion of a linguistic shift and thus the reframing of their conception. He calls it a 'spoonerism', one that writes not of 'foreign language films' but of 'foreign film languages', and goes as far as to argue not for a bilingualism of spoken languages, but a bilingualism in film languages. 'Bilingualism', he writes, 'embodies a mode of foreignness that is far from simply relative. Only from the standpoint of an imperceptible "monolingualism," in other words, from within a film culture where a certain enunciative tendency or stance has become normalized, is "bilingualism" intelligible as foreign'.[122] Consequently, if we drop the concept of 'monolingualism' in cultural production, that is to say that there is only one way of conceptualising culture or cultural texts, and that this way of conceptualising is dependent on the monolithic and essentialised, then 'bilingualism', or alternative modes of reading, will cease to be 'foreign'.

Rey Chow's notion of 'languaging' as a way of understanding linguistic practice within the context of post-colonial cultural politics may help us move away from these binaries. In her book, *Not Like a Native Speaker: On Languaging as a Postcolonial Experience* (2014), Chow writes of the importance of theorising 'intercultural equivalence'[123] as we search for ways to talk about translation beyond linguistic commensurability and compatibility. She writes:

> I want to suggest that the equivalence and coevalness between cultures, however dissimilar those cultures might seem, ought to be a type of potentiality we seek and explore – that is, *regardless of the number of languages involved and even if only one language appears in use* [...] Such equality – the signal that the partners in interaction are peers – however, is precisely what intercultural translation can endeavor to enunciate even as it apprehends, as it must, the undeniable existence of cultural limits and incompatibilities.[124]

This approach is particularly relevant at this juncture as English continues to spread as a global language.[125]

Rada Iveković calls for an 'epistemological revolution', a reconceptualisation of the terms by which we understand how boundaries are created and crossed, and how we speak about translations in culture, as we attempt to 'to converse and translate from one episteme to another, in a postcolonial and post-Cold War situation and under conditions of utter inequality of languages'.[126] Cautioning against the 'normativity' of 'political contexts and frames of mind', which are 'highly dependent on historic conditions, times and forms of instituted, and sometimes constituting, power', Iveković argues that translation must be understood beyond language into 'epistemological contexts',[127] to avoid simply reproducing 'transnational elites', whose social and cultural capital allow them to travel and sell their labour across national borders, while 'other niche temporalities and alternative sub-citizenships [are] created for the migrant workers or women – underpaid and no-rights no-benefit workers in those same places'.[128] Iveković's offer of a 'new political economy' involves not the perpetual reconfiguration of borders creating new 'identities' and sub-groups, but a different way of perceiving how knowledge is constructed.

This look into the cosmopolitan challenge of multilingual cinema is in part a call for an acceptance of, and a working-with (rather than a working-out-of) partial translation and comprehension not as a 'problem' to be solved, but as an opportunity to interrogate where the boundaries in our disciplines and modes of enquiry lie. The goal is not to erase those boundaries as such, but to open up new epistemological frameworks for understanding more intimately how cinema operates as a socio-cultural formation within fairly complex times.

2

Cosmopolitan memory and self-reflexive cinema

All cinema manifests, to a degree, the tension between formalism and realism. Accounts of early cinema often juxtapose the naturalism of Lumière's early films with the whimsical, illusionist tricks of Georges Méliès. Today, cinema continues to be celebrated for its capacity to capture, and equally manipulate, 'reality'. Occasionally, a film can display, even perform, an awareness of its own textual devices by pointing to its own modes of articulation and enunciation. In this chapter, I explore self-reflexivity in cinema as one modality by which the cinematic text comes to terms with some of its inner tensions, tensions which as I have argued in the previous chapter open up the space to critical cosmopolitan debate. 'Self-reflexive cinema', an epithet I have employed in the title of this chapter, is not a genre in cinema studies. Instead, it could be considered a modernist mode of practice that operates across genres and aesthetic styles, in which films are positioned in relation to their own process of memorialisation and historiography.

A useful way of thinking about the relationship between cinema and memory is through Freud's notion of 'screen memory', 'as one that owes its value as a memory not to its intrinsic content but to the relation obtaining between this content and some other, which has been suppressed'.[1] Although Freud was not speaking of the cinema specifically but of how traumatic memories are displaced onto different images and narratives, it is nonetheless interesting that he uses the notion of the screen as an overarching metaphor. After all, Freud was writing at a time when the cinema was being birthed (1899), and it is perhaps no surprise that the language of the screen has become intertwined with the language of the psyche and with the language of memory. As Susannah Radstone puts it:

> The cinema's long-standing and intimate relationship with memory is revealed in cinema language's adoption of terms associated with memory – the 'flashback' and the 'fade,' for instance – to describe cinematic dissolves between a film narrative's present and its past. The routinized deployment of these terms has rendered them unremarkable, suggesting an apparently automatic, involuntary, and mechanical relationship between cinema and memory'.[2]

Radstone goes as far as to argue that memory may even be constituted 'as cinema', and not in the way it has been historically 'conceived of by analogy with cinema'.[3] As noted above, the way we talk about the cinema employs a similar lexicon to the way we attempt to describe memory. However, as cinema continues to capture and produce cultural memory, the boundary between the two has become increasingly porous, and cinema has also been seen to possess the 'capacity to discipline, enhance, supplement, or substitute for memory'.[4] Radstone notes three ways in which the relationship between cinema and memory may be constituted: the first is 'memory as cinema',[5] the second is 'cinema as memory',[6] and the third a 'transition or hybrid' formulation she calls 'cinema/memory'.[7] The first refers to how we envision and speak of our memories in cinematic terms; the second refers to how cinema itself produces memories; and the third conflates the two as a kind of 'transitional or hybrid world':

> This is a world constituted of images, sequences, and their associated effects. Situated within the mind, yet positioned between the personal and the cultural, cinema/memory melds images remembered from the cinema with the inner world's constitutive 'scenes' or scenarios. […] In place of formulations that give primacy to the cinema or to memory, what emerges is a liminal conception of cinema/memory, this strand of film theory dissolves conceptual boundaries between the inside and the

outside, the personal and the social, the individual and the cultural, and the true and the false.[8]

In other words, it is not always possible to demarcate the two, and indeed, it is this inability to identify where cinema and memory begin and end that offers self-reflexive cinema its creative possibilities.

By looking at how certain films reflect upon their own processes of filmmaking, I explore not so much how films reconstruct people's memories (although they also do this) but how the act of reconstruction itself involves evoking other memories, not least of which are the memories of the history of the medium itself. Historical representation remains popular in cinema partly as a way of looking back into the past, but also as a means of engaging the present through the past. When the past is radically traumatic, it can be difficult to re-enact and even harder to re-examine. Writing on the relationship between melodrama and 'cultural trauma', E. Ann Kaplan argues that 'personal and social traumas caused by political and social transition were displaced into fictional melodrama forms where they could be more safely approached or remembered but also forgotten'.[9] However, she further notes that as the psychic impact of trauma is ultimately unrepresentable, films tend to focus on 'traumatic cultural symptoms' instead: 'independent cinematic techniques show paralysis, repetition, circularity – all aspects of the non-representability of trauma and yet of the search to figure its pain'.[10] If as Kaplan argues, '[t]rauma is narration without narrativity',[11] I explore how some of this paralysis, repetition and circularity are enacted through a film's reflexive exploration of its form, and its own culpability or inability to narrate what are in effect unnarratable events. In so doing, I hope to speak also to how notions of 'cosmopolitan memory' (and thus history) are enacted, and enabled, by the cinematic text.

Writing about the Holocaust, Levy and Sznaider present the notion of 'cosmopolitan memory' as a frame through which 'memory politics' may be understood;[12] that is, the politics positing the question of who and what structures have the power to shape collective and national memories. They argue that 'the cosmopolitanization of memories refers to practices that shift attention away from the territorialized nation-state and the ethnically bound frameworks that are commonly associated with the notion of collective memory [...] Rather than presuppose the congruity of nation, territory and polity, cosmopolitanized memories are based on and contribute to nation-transcending idioms, spanning territorial and national boundaries'.[13] Within this framework, Levy and Sznaider analyse how memories of the Holocaust have been 'cosmopolitanized' in the sense that they have moved away from the actual people who experienced those events in a particular time and place, and into a cultural and collective process of memorialisation.[14] This chapter addresses the role cinema may be able to play in understanding the processes of memorialisation and the politics of memory, through its function as an act of witness and of performance, as well as its form, via the following films: *24 City* (Jia Zhangke 2008), *Lust, Caution* (Ang Lee 2007) and *Millennium Actress* (Satoshi Kon 2001).

Self-reflexive memory and witness

Biographies of Chinese filmmaker Jia Zhangke often trace his career from an underground and dissident filmmaker to arthouse festival favourite, who is known for engaging social reality through the use of a particular style of 'fictionalised documentary'.[15] Zhang Xudong has described this artistic ethos and practice as a 'poetics of vanishing',[16] in that Jia's films have been known to document with artful slowness the voracity of China's rapid economic change. The success of his fourth feature film, *The World* (2004), which unlike the previous films received approval from the Chinese authorities, allowed Jia to emerge from the world of underground filmmaking. Valerie Jaffee, writing in July 2004, reported that 'the Film Bureau of the People's Republic of China announced that Jia Zhangke's "credentials as a director" had been "restored"' and that Jia was being 'welcomed back into the fold of legitimate Chinese cinema'.[17] Since then, Jia has gained a reputation for making films that are able to walk the fine line between critiquing China's social and political practices (thus gaining him much attention in the international press and festival circuit) and avoiding the authorities' disfavour. This balancing act is necessitated by the pragmatic demands of the industry (for example, a Jia Zhangke film as a product desired by the international arthouse and festival market) and the arcane censorship practices of the Chinese authorities, where the boundaries of transgression, and thus sanction, are never clear. Jaffee, keen to dismantle the 'myth' of Chinese underground filmmaking, notes that 'the act of making a film outside the official system may have all along represented more a procedural or tactical decision than a moral, political or aesthetic one', and 'banned in China' became something of a brand in its own right among festival circles.[18] Jaffee describes the haziness of the picture as such:

> The fact that scholars and reviewers both in China and abroad often have a hard time saying for sure whether a given film was banned or not – understandably so, as a certain number of non-banned films get tiny releases and often eventually become unavailable in China, while plenty of bans on particular films are eventually lifted – offers further defense for the assertion that the line between the underground and the state-sanctioned surface is blurry and, perhaps, not all that significant. Particularly now that certain banned films can be purchased on pirated DVD and VCD in China's major cities, the difference to urban, educated domestic audiences who know how to look for these films can seem slight indeed. Be all that as it may, the catch-phrase "banned in China" almost certainly helped certain films gain an audience outside of China.[19]

Jaffee concludes that the term 'underground filmmaking' denotes an 'administrative status and nothing more', noting from a survey of Chinese independent films released in the 1990s that the 'underground' status was merely 'a convenient way to get a debut film made with a reduced number of hassles and hurdles'.[20] Nonetheless, emerging from the underground has allowed Jia to tap into a greater pool of resources: *The World* was jointly produced by the state-supported Shanghai Film Group, Hong Kong's Xinghui Productions and Japan's Office Kitano. It has also allowed him to take his films out of Shanxi province, and his hometown of Fenyang, where his first three underground films were set, into Beijing, China's capital, in which *The World* is set, and thus literally take them into the wider 'world'.

Jia's reputation as international auteur was consolidated with *Still Life* (2006), which won a number of festival awards, including the prestigious Golden Lion at Venice in 2006. *Still Life* is one such 'fictionalised documentary' for which he is now known. It is shot contemporaneously with the building of China's Three Gorges dam and its imminent impact on life in a city situated below the floodline. My analysis focuses mainly on *24 City*, Jia's next feature film after *Still Life*, which continues with this aesthetic mode but within the frame of self-reflexive filmmaking. This may sound counter-intuitive at first – how can a film be realist and self-reflexive at the same time? I argue that while the film's realism presents a meditative take on impact of rapid social and economic change on modern China, the high degree of formal reflexivity forces us to engage with the medium's own role in its accounting of past and present. The result is a look into China's socialist past without nostalgia even as it offers us a glimpse into its hollow consumerist present without explicit censure.

The film *24 City* is constructed around nine interviews with former employees, and children of former employees, of a factory that is being decommissioned to make way for new luxury apartments in the city of Chengdu, the capital of Sichuan province in southwest China. Typical of Jia's other work, the dismantling of the physical apparatus of the factory seems to take place in real time as the cameras roll (Figure 2.1); Chris Berry has translated the Chinese phrase for this practice of contemporaneous shooting *jishizhuyi* as 'on-the-spot realism'.[21] The scenes of this dismantling of the factory are interspersed between the interviews, alongside still or tracking shots of what is left of the crumbling structure – the peeling paint and suspended cables set to melancholic musical strains imbue what is essentially a grim and ugly structure with a strange ethereal quality that forms the backdrop to the each interviewee's memories. Thomas Austin

Figure 2.1 *24 City*: A factory being dismantled

describes the film as 'a selfconscious intervention into the constitution of cultural memory',[22] which is achieved through 'self-reflexive textuality and repeated citations of other cultural texts: poetry, music and films'.[23] However, as these citations require certain prior knowledges, memories and cultural literacies, the film's intertextual references do not necessarily resonate in the same way with different audiences and, perhaps unsurprisingly, critics had a number of varied responses to the film.

For example, the reviewer for the *San Francisco Chronicle* makes this objection to the film: 'The trouble is, Jia does not indicate which is documentary and which is acting [...] In other words, half of this movie – four of the nine people interviewed are actors – is a big lie'.[24] This criticism of Jia's methods is interesting for the assumptions it makes about what films – especially films purporting to be 'documentaries' – ought to be doing, that is, presumably, telling us the 'truth'. In this instance, Johnson assumes that, because some of the interviews are scripted and performed by actors, the film is necessarily a 'lie', yet presumably he has few issues with biopics and other fictional narratives. Furthermore, such a practice is not entirely alien to the performing arts: in fact, verbatim theatre is a form of theatre-making where the script is derived from interviews with research participants, and often delivered 'verbatim' in the final performance by actors. What bothers Johnson, however, is not that part of Jia's film is fictionalised but that *the audience is not taken into its confidence*: the film has excluded him from its address. In contrast, Manohla Dargis of *The New York Times* seems more predisposed to being placed at a distance to the text: 'There's something slightly disorienting about a work that doesn't have the usual markers that assure you that now you're watching a fiction, now you're watching a documentary, which, as I realized on second viewing, can work beautifully for a movie about profound dislocation'.[25] Austin has explored the indexicality and intertextuality employed in the film, and argues for how the film's 'aesthetic strategies offer their own pleasures, but they also enable an inquiry and an intervention into the discursive production of memory, a move that has particular resonance in postsocialist China'.[26] Following this, my discussion of *24 City* explores how the film makes its interventions via the form of cinema as witness to individual and collective memories. As the stories unfold, these memories of individual lives coalesce into national histories, fragmenting and dissolving while recombining anew via the medium of the cinema. In other words, the witnessing camera is not just there to record and to observe, but actively participates in the very act of recollection itself.

In *Death 24x a Second* (2006), Laura Mulvey writes of the maturation of cinema as a cultural form and its increasing awareness of its own temporality, or perhaps even our own increasing awareness of cinema's temporality. In *24 City*, the gradual tracking of the camera through the dilapidated space juxtaposed against the enforced stillness of the shots where the subjects are made to stand and look directly into the camera (Figure 2.2) create a curious sense of what Mulvey, quoting Freud, describes as 'the uncanny'.[27] There is a kind of 'death' in the haunting scenes in *24 City*: as the film unfolds, we become increasingly aware of having participated in a kind of elegy for... what, really? Certainly not for the excesses of Maoism in twentieth-century Chinese history, nor the real hardships that many of these individuals have endured through Factory 420's various incarnations, both for civilian and military purposes. In a footnote to his analysis of one of these still shots, Austin remarks: 'Here and elsewhere the film invites curiosity and speculation about the untold stories of those who face the camera in silent video portraits, and whose portrayals are thus presented as incomplete',[28] echoing Mulvey's uncovering of the poetry in the stillness and movement of cinema:

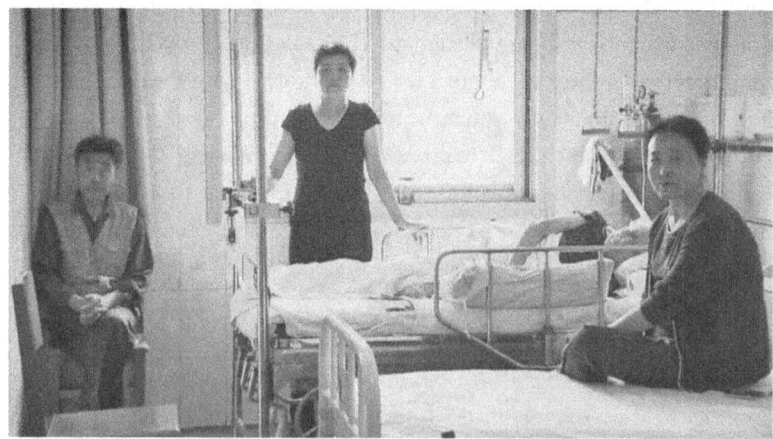

Figure 2.2 *24 City*: Direct address of characters to the camera

Although the projector reconciles the opposition and the still frames come to life, this underlying stillness provides the cinema with a secret, with a hidden past that might or might not find its way to the surface. The inanimate frames come to life, the unglamorous mechanics are covered over and the entrancing illusion fills the screen. But like the beautiful automaton, a residual trace of stillness, or a hint of stillness within movement, survives, sometimes enhancing, sometimes threatening.[29]

There is some of this quality in the cinematography of these scenes of stillness in *24 City* – what is the secret, or this hidden past behind the crumbling concrete, behind the impassive faces of the people made to hold still and look into the camera? What do they seek from us?

Jiwei Xiao notes that 'despite its strong documentary quality, *24 City* has the feel of a past event – objects and people appear as if they were remembered, not perceived. A die-hard realist, Jia Zhangke is also a dreamer trying to use memory to battle the world in transience: he must act as if his camera could outstrip the fleeing present by gazing at it hard and long enough and by registering its minute-by-minute change, as if reality were always on the cusp of disappearance'.[30] In the face of such 'disappearance', we naturally search for the narrative drive and impetus within the interviews with the various characters, perhaps with the hope that somehow what these individuals tell us might help make sense of its ephemeral histories. What is the story we seek behind the dismantling of this factory and the building of these sleek, modern apartments? We have a vague sense it is a commentary on China's relentless modernisation, that much is evident – as Austin notes, 'This reconfiguration of urban space comes to stand for wider social transformations in the PRC'.[31] We also have a vague sense that we are being given snapshot glimpses into history as the interviewees speak of their experiences, which span the Korean War, the fallen ideals of state-imposed socialism and Maoism in China after World War II, and the changing aspirations of the generations of workers who have passed through the factory doors since then. However, what do all these recollections amount to? A nostalgia for simpler times, a regret for lost youth or a dispassionate acceptance of inevitable change in modern China? Austin invokes

Vivian Sobchack's 'charge of the real' here, which he reads alongside the film's reflexive drive:

> The film is in part, then, an oral history; but it also acknowledges itself as a fabrication, overtly deploying artifice in its staging, framing and soundtrack, and in the four out of nine interviews that are scripted and professionally performed. While *24 City* tries to capture the factory complex on the point of disappearance, and so to mitigate its loss in collective amnesia, the film never assumes its own transparency as a means of salvage.[32]

The film disavows its own transparency by refusing to reconstruct the past in flashback, a device that most narrative cinema and documentaries rely on. Instead, what we are asked to witness is the *performance* of the filmed interview as a mode of narration. In the absence of dramatic reconstructions, what we watch for, as the subjects speak, are tonal inflections and facial expressions, and it is through these that we are compelled to engage with their stories. In that sense, the interviews in *24 City* do not function as part of a show-and-tell operation; rather, *it is the act of telling that is the show itself.*

For this reason, it is possible to commiserate, if not to agree, with Johnson's indignation at being duped. In more conventional documentaries, operating according to what I have just referred to as a 'show-and-tell' formulation, any emotion we are required to invest is frequently directed at the story, whether it is the story of the event, or the story of the individual. In the fictionalised realism of *24 City*, we are being asked to invest ourselves in the act of memory-making itself, through the medium of cinema. It is a process that may well be experienced, as I discuss later, as inherently traumatic. The trauma of history in *24 City* is located not in the reconstruction of any singular event, but in their very absence, in the silences that punctuate the monologues, which are sometimes filled with new music, 1980s pop songs, and lines of Yeats' poetry inscribed on the screen. In his own interviews with the former employees of the factory, Jia notes their many silences: he recalls that the ' "more extraordinary stories of memory must have submerged into the silence, into the moments when these people finished telling their stories" and [that] probably "those silences are the most important".³³ As Xiao notes, in '[p]uncturing the cinema's surface with little holes of silence here and there, Jia drills into the depth of the repressed memory of socialist idealism'.³⁴

What surfaces from those 'holes of silence' are questions of how cinema itself operates as a repository for cultural memory, especially when a film like *24 City* enters the international festival circuit as part of an auteurist cinema. In addition amidst the neo-realist form, there is an internationally famous face among the cast, that of the Chinese American actress, Joan Chen. In preparation ahead of the making of the film, it was reported that Jia conducted over 130 interviews with former factory employees before distilling or condensing them into the nine we encounter in the film. Out of the nine individuals, five were actual former employees of the factory, and four are actors. Aside from Joan Chen, the other three professionals are Chen Jianbin, Zhao Tao and Lü Liping. While Joan Chen is known both internationally and within China, the other three are less well known to audiences outside of China. Zhao Tao, Jia Zhangke's wife, may be more recognisable within festival circles as she has appeared in nearly all his films. Chen Jianbin and Lü Liping, however, are barely known outside of China although they are familiar faces in Chinese films and television. Unless one recognised the actors, the interviews are more or less indistinguishable, raising questions of cultural translation and competency.³⁵

In *24 City*, Joan Chen appears as a fictional character, Gu Minhua, a former factory worker who recalls being described by colleagues as 'looking like Joan Chen' (Figure 2.3). Her character is nicknamed Xiaohua, or 'Little Flower', who is also the eponymous character the actress herself played in a 1979 film by Chang Tseng. Credited in her Chinese name as Chen Chong, Joan Chen won the coveted Hundred Flowers Award for Best Actress for her role as Xiaohua. Despite being crowned China's 'best-loved actress' at the time, Hollywood soon beckoned and Chen was cast in a few bit parts in popular American series of the time, such as *Knight Rider* (1984), *Miami Vice* (1985) and *MacGyver* (1985). She made her first Hollywood film appearance in the unabashedly orientalist film, *Tai-Pan* (1986), but it was the pivotal role of the flower-eating empress in Bertolucci's *The Last Emperor* (1987) that catapulted her into

Figure 2.3 *24 City*: Actress Joan Chen playing Xiaohua / Little Flower, who is said to resemble Joan Chen

international stardom. Her casting as Josie Packard in David Lynch's cult series, *Twin Peaks* (1990–1), cemented her presence within American popular culture, and it is unlikely that many viewers of *Twin Peaks* at the time would have been aware of her earlier contribution to Chinese socialist filmmaking.

24 City not only brings Joan Chen back to the Chinese screen, but as the character of Gu Minhua reflects on her Shanghai roots, the character also echoes the actress's own Shanghai roots, and the point where the character articulates her own uncanny similarity to the actress 'Joan Chen' is the point where history, memory and cinema fold back onto themselves in a kind of infinite loop or, in keeping with the Chinese theme, a mystical knot. This form of cinematic illusion returns us to the beginnings of cinema, within which is embedded the twin dialectic of both 'natural magic and the art of deception'.[36] From its early days as *camera obscura* through to photography and celluloid and now into the digital age, cinema's equal capacity to capture and transform reality continues to be a subject of fascination. Following the interview with Gu Minhua, also nicknamed 'Xiaohua', the camera in *24 City* draws our attention to a television set running a portion of the 1979 film, *Little Flower / Xiaohua*, initially in the background then in close up, with no comment or apparent explanation (Figure 2.4). The image is simply there, a material artefact, not occupying

Cosmopolitan memory and self-reflexive cinema

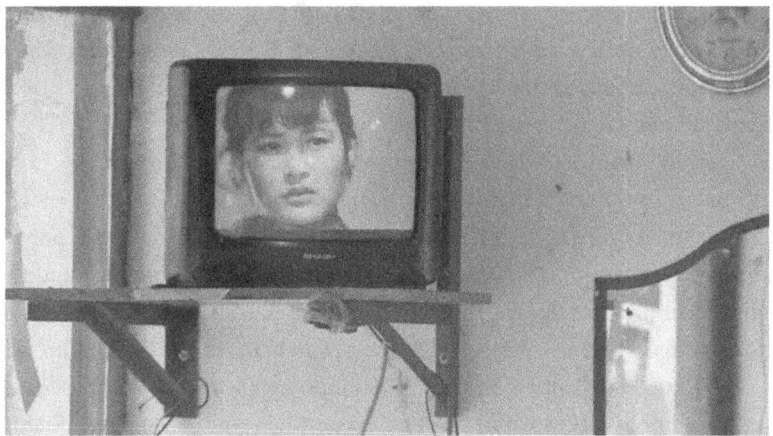

Figure 2.4 *24 City*: Shot of TV set screening *Xiaohua / Little Flower* (1979) with a young Joan Chen in the starring role

the whole filmic space of *24 City* but encased within that other material artefact, the old cathode-ray television set, an instrument of broadcast media that is itself rapidly being confined to history. In looking at Joan Chen playing someone who looks like Joan Chen and then watching a partial screening of a film where Joan Chen was a young actress, we are in effect looking into the annals of history, the layers of which we are encouraged to tease out like the layers in an archaeological dig. That is, if we even knew where to look.

Layered on top of all these layers are the memories of Jia, the filmmaker himself, such as the green hue that 'was deliberately mixed into the colour palette of the film during postproduction'.[37] It seems that when Jia 'was a small child growing up in northern China in the late 1970s and 1980s, he saw the green colour everyday and everywhere, often painted one metre high on walls of both private homes and public places – hospitals, offices, classrooms, and state-run factories. For Jia, green is apparently a very personal memory; yet instead of using the colour to express an individual sentiment, he "exhibits" it rather matter-of-factly by integrating it into the film texture'.[38] This idea of weaving a memory, as a glimpse, a flavour, or a palimpsest takes the film beyond questions of historical 'representation'. The past is not 'represented' or even recalled as such, but rather *recalled to memory*, in the same way that the opening images of *24 City*, in which streams of factory workers pour out of the building, call to memory images of that first Lumière short, *Workers Exiting the Lumière Factory*, identified today by textbooks as the very first commercial film to be screened in 1895. There are many other intertextual echoes besides.

Through this interweaving, what we are being invited to witness in *24 City* are not so much individual memories, or even collective memories as such, as the act, or the art, of memory-making itself. To add further poignancy to these acts of memorialisation, filming was also completed and the finished film then released shortly after the Great Sichuan Earthquake of 2008, a disaster which destroyed much of Chengdu in which the film was shot, killing 69,000 and rendering 4.8 million people homeless; thus locating our acts of witness within the film even more resolutely on that boundary between life and death, history and memory, reality and imagination. I close this section with a return to Laura Mulvey once again who writes:

> To look back into the reality of that lost world by means of the cinema is to have the sensation of looking into a time machine [...] However, the presence of the past in the cinema is also the presence of the body resurrected and these images can trigger, if only by association, questions that still seem imponderable: the nature of time, the fragility of human life and the boundary between life and death.[39]

I would add to this list further questions raised by *24 City*'s self-reflexive encounters, questions of the nature of cinema's ability to even record, or ameliorate, any of those concerns.

Self-reflexive memory and performance

Cosmopolitan memories are travelling memories.[40] Like the cinema, they are memories that cross borders, take on different forms and speak to different audiences. Reading Levy and Sznaider, Rapson argues that 'cosmopolitanism foregrounds the way in which specific atrocities become de- and re-territorialised from their original locations via related mediatory, commemorative and social processes, generating new global trajectories'.[41] Although it could be argued that all memories are mediated to some degree, once these memories relocate geographically and historically, the politics fought over their legitimacy, feasibility and authenticity are even further displaced onto the politics of mediatory processes.

Adapted from a short story by Chinese author, Eileen Chang, Ang Lee's *Lust, Caution* addresses not just the cultural and political memories of China under Japanese occupation but the constitution of those memories through a self-reflexive mode of address that sets up several other imperatives, one of which has been noted as 'interrogating Chineseness from [Ang Lee's] Taiwanese / diasporic Chinese position'.[42] The performative element in the film is something the essays in Peng and Crothers Dilley's 2014 anthology on Chang's short story and Lee's film return to frequently, particularly through readings of the ill-fated protagonist's performance as both an actress and an undercover agent. In this section, I explore the performativity of the *film* whose reflexivity is enacted via intertextual quotation and allusion. In so doing, I argue that the film locates itself not only within the history of modern China (and debates about 'Chineseness'), but also within that of Chinese-language and global cinemas as well. I explore how the theme of performance is addressed within the diegesis, as well as how the film performs its own mediation of Chinese film history, that is, the histories of Shanghai and Hong Kong as historic – and cosmopolitan – centres of Chinese-language cinematic production.

The film opens with the female protagonist, Wang Chia-chih[43] (Tang Wei), already immersed in her role as a spy. She is dressed in a fedora and Western-style trenchcoat worn over a Chinese dress, and makes a coded call in Chinese (switching between Mandarin and Cantonese at various points) from a European-style cafe located in Shanghai. Following this establishing sequence, we are taken into a flashback to the time when Wang is still a student at university and, while there, becomes an actress in a student play performed in support of the nationalist cause in China. It is the overwhelming success of Wang's debut performance that incites her fellow students to launch their reckless plan to assassinate the Japanese collaborator, Mr Yee (Tony Leung Chiu-wai), a plan which situates Wang at the centre of the film's plot. In his *boundary 2* essay on the reception of *Lust, Caution*, Leo Ou-fan Lee notes the apparently undue emphasis given in the film to Wang's performance in the university play prior to her recruitment as an undercover agent. He wonders: 'Why this repeated reference to her acting background as a student?'[44] James Schamus, Ang Lee's long-time collaborator, offers an indirect answer to this question in his introductory notes to the film's published screenplay:

> *Why did she do it?*
> The question is itself an admission of the impossibility of ever really answering it.
> And yet we ask.
> Another, more specific, way of asking:
> What act, exactly, does Wang Chia-chih perform at that fateful moment in the jeweler's shop when she decides whether or not to go through with the murder of her lover?
> And here, two words – *act and perform* – indicate the troubling question Zhang Ailing (Eileen Chang) asks us: for at the crucial moment when we *choose*, when we *decide*, when we *exercise our free will*, are we not also *performing*?[45]

There are many different layers of performance enacted in the film by the different characters, which speak to broader themes of nationhood and history,[46] and Peng and Crothers Dilley go as far as to say that '[q]uestions of acting and performance have been profoundly linked to the political history of twentieth-century China, especially after the issue of performance and subjectivity became politicized under Mao in early 1948'.[47]

I am interested in how the film mobilises these questions of performance and engages with its own ability, and resistance, to 'performing' its function, as a film 'about' self, nationhood and history. In his 1955 lecture series, which was later collected and published as *How to Do Things with Words* (1962), J. L. Austin introduced the idea of a 'performative utterance'.[48] A performative utterance, according to Austin, does not describe an action or a performance as such, but rather performs the very action through the act of uttering it. Examples he gives are: 'I do (sc. take this woman to be my lawful wedded wife)' and 'I name this ship *Queen Elizabeth*'.[49] However, he qualifies that 'the utterance, […] is far from being usually, even if it is ever, the *sole* thing necessary if the act is to be deemed to have been performed', and that 'it is always necessary that the *circumstances* in which the words are uttered should be in some way, or ways, *appropriate*'.[50] Poststructuralist, deconstructive, and queer readings of Austin have critiqued the unchallenged cultural frame under which those utterances are performed. Parker and Sedgwick, referring to the example of the marriage vow, note 'the dynamic of compulsory witness that the marriage ceremony invokes':

> It is the constitution of a community of witness that makes the marriage; the silence of witness (we don't speak now, we forever hold our peace) that permits it; the bare, negative, potent but undiscretionary speech act of our physical presence – maybe even *especially* the presence of those people whom the institution of marriage defines itself by excluding – that ratifies and recruits the legitimacy of its privilege.[51]

This tension embedded within any performance, of what is enacted and what is withheld, occurs in *Lust, Caution* within the diegesis and without.

Hsien-hao Sebastian Liao cites the scene in the geisha house as one where the antagonist, Yee, first reveals an apparent moment of vulnerability, signalled by the instance of his confession to Wang – 'I know better than you do about how to be a whore'. This utterance, for Liao, seems 'to serve as the tipping point where "lust" transforms into "love"'. However, as Liao later concludes, 'far from interacting with Wang on the personal level, [Yee] is *performing* all the time'.[52] In Liao's Lacanian reading of the film, 'what seems to be a moment of real contact […] turns out to be a moment of profound misunderstanding'.[53] However, the scene, pivotal as it is, is more than simply one of a confession of love, and more than simply reiterates that old connection between acting and whoring. Wang's performance that leads up to Yee's confessional performance, and thus the 'tipping point' in the narrative, also makes a *direct reference* to the Shanghainese film culture of the period. The geisha house is located in the Japanese district of war-time Shanghai, and the song Wang sings for Yee is 'The Wandering Songstress / Tianya Genü' from a 1937 film, *Street Angel / Malu Tianshi*, directed by Yuan Muzhi. *Street Angel* made an overnight star of its lead actress, Zhou Xuan, whose career spanned 1935 to 1953. The film tells the story of two sisters who fled the Japanese invasion of northeast China for Shanghai, one of whom is forced into prostitution and the other becomes a singer in a teahouse. Zhou Xuan plays the latter, and even in the 1937 film the song, singing of lost love and separation, was already presented as sentimental and nostalgic for more innocent times. If Liao's reading of *Lust, Caution* maps the sexual politics of the film onto the politics of Chinese nationhood, then the intertextual quotation of *Street Angel* in *Lust, Caution* may be thus seen as a kind of cinematic short-hand referring to political developments not just in history but also in the film industry during that time and the relationship between cinema and politics in war-time Shanghai, during which the city was occupied by Japanese imperial forces from 1937 to 1945.

Because of its wide reach across audiences, cinema is sometimes expected to be mobilised in times of national need. Indeed, filmmakers in Shanghai during the war were often faced with criticism by the nationalist fighters for not contributing to the resistance against the Japanese occupation. For instance, in January 1940, in Chongqing (the centre of nationalist resistance), there was a mob burning of *Mulan Joins the Army / Mulan Congjun* (Bu Wancang, China, 1939), a runaway hit at the time, simply because it had been made in Shanghai. It did not matter that the film, dramatising a sixth-century Chinese ballad of a young girl who disguises herself as a boy in order to join the army in her father's place, was in fact a public expression of patriotism.[54] Wang's performance of 'The Wandering Songstress' ties Lee's film intimately into a network of cinematic intertexts. *Lust, Caution* is set in the period between 1938 and 1942, during which the film *Street Angel* would have been contemporary, but in 2007, both 'The Wandering Songstress' and *Street Angel* have become 'golden oldies' within Chinese popular culture. When Wang performs the song for Yee, her lover, the actress (Tang Wei) is also performing *for contemporary audiences* a classic from the past (Figure 2.5), enacted in the film as if it were already past, but can only be recalled as such because it continues to have a contemporary presence in CD compilations, television re-runs (in parts of East Asia), and now on YouTube and other filesharing platforms.

The layering of these multiple temporalities extends to the meticulous reconstruction of Shanghai on the set of *Lust, Caution*, although it must be noted that the film creates less of a fantasy of old Shanghai than a fantasy for old *cinematic* Shanghai, the Shanghai that was not just once the centre of Chinese cinematic production, but also the key exhibition venue for many Hollywood classics of the Golden Age. Shanghai was the proverbial modern Chinese city during the 1930s and central to this experience of modernity in Shanghai was the cinema, as Poshek Fu recalls:

Cosmopolitan memory and self-reflexive cinema

Figure 2.5 *Lust, Caution*: Wang Chia-chih / Tang Wei performs 'The Wandering Songstress'

To be modern in Shanghai was to participate in its expanding culture of leisure and consumption: watching movies at downtown picture palaces, dancing in fancy clothes to jazz tunes in splendiferous dance halls, or shopping for modern (i.e. Western) luxury items at the four big department stores on Nanjing Road. [...] To see and be seen at these places of commercial enjoyment [including restaurants, cafes, hotels, and amusement halls] epitomized modernity in everyday life. In fact pre-war Shanghai had become associated with modern life in the eyes of the Chinese in the hinterland and Southeast Asia, who, when they had a chance to visit the city, sought a taste of it by joyfully participating in its ritual of going to a Hollywood film or shopping on Nanjing Road.[55]

Thus, *Lust, Caution*'s multiple references to Hollywood equally should not be overlooked. There is a moment in the film when Wang manages to eke out some time to herself and goes to the cinema hall. There, it is to see Ingrid Bergman's first Hollywood venture, *Intermezzo: A Love Story* (Gregory Ratoff, USA, 1939), which was released in the UK as *Escape to Happiness*. Outside the theatre, and inside the lobby, there are posters of *Suspicion* (Alfred Hitchcock, USA, 1941) and *Penny Serenade* (George Stevens, USA, 1941), both starring Cary Grant (Figure 2.6). Off-screen, *Lust, Caution* has been compared with another Hitchcock–Grant film,

Figure 2.6 *Lust, Caution*: At the pictures in Shanghai

Notorious (Alfred Hitchcock, USA, 1946), as well as with Bernardo Bertolucci's *The Conformist* (1970).

These allusions to Hollywood's golden past reflect on Shanghai's own home-grown culture of glamour, modelled both on Hollywood as well as traditional Chinese notions of femininity, and whose female stars were looked upon to be 'the very embodiment of modernity'.[56] The clothing of Wang in traditional Chinese dress that is at once displayed as modest and alluring testifies to the duality of this image: at one point in the film Wang and Yee go shopping for a dress which she models for him and for the camera's gaze. In a fascinating review of the national and cultural iconography of traditional Chinese dress, known as the *qipao* in Mandarin or the *cheongsam* in Cantonese, Matthew Chew explores how although the dress had 'ceased to be worn for everyday occasions after the 1950s in the People's Republic of China (PRC) and the late 1960s in Hong Kong, Taiwan and Singapore [...] it has powerfully re-emerged in the last few years'.[57] Part of the impetus for its popular revival in the early 2000s is its re-emergence in films showcasing its glamour. Despite this renewed interest, Chew notes that the *qipao* has not returned to everyday wear in contemporary life, except to be adapted by global designers for the international catwalk and the film industries' red carpet events.[58] Thus what recent films appear to evoke through the historical representation of this Chinese dress is to establish it even 'more firmly than before as an ethnic dress and a cultural representation of Chineseness'.⁵⁹ Significantly, then, in *Lust, Caution* when Wang wears the *qipao* in her impersonation of a rich businessman's wife, it could be said that her figuration cites the many images of female stars from the Golden Age of Chinese cinema in 1930s Shanghai, such as Ruan Lingyu, Hu Die and Zhou Xuan. Yet as Wang's Chinese dress is also often paired with a Western trenchcoat and fedora reminiscent of Ingrid Bergman and Golden Age Hollywood glamour (Figure 2.7), what she encapsulates on screen is a dual iconography not just of a historical time and an age, but also the cinemas of a certain time and age.

The cinematic recreation of old Shanghai in *Lust, Caution* also enacts the close relationship the city had to Hong Kong, not least of which because it was to the British-ruled territory that many Shanghai filmmakers fled during the war.⁶⁰ By the mid-1930s, Hong Kong was the regional centre for Cantonese film production.⁶¹ Some of its advantages included being a key nodal point in a transnational, pan-Chinese cultural network, which included Shanghai, Canton (Guangzhou), Singapore, Penang, San Francisco and Los Angeles.⁶² From the turbulent history of Hong Kong and Shanghai emerged a rivalry between the Mandarin-language and Cantonese-language cinemas,⁶³ as outlined in the previous chapter, both of which competed for the same markets and genres, as they did for economic and political dominance.⁶⁴ These cultural tensions are reiterated several times in *Lust, Caution*, again through the use of

Figure 2.7 *Lust, Caution*: Wang Chia-chih in Western dress

different Chinese dialects and languages, when the characters move and meet between Shanghai and Hong Kong. Wang often speaks to the servants of the Yee household in Shanghainese, switching to Mandarin when she speaks to the other wives, and occasionally in Cantonese as well. This linguistic switching may quite easily be overlooked as a plot point, except for the fact that the film keeps drawing our attention to it. In numerous instances, Wang's multilingual abilities are constantly commented on by other, usually minor, characters, and while these remarks and instances add nothing to the plot, they appear to gesture to wider cultural and historical contexts beyond the diegesis. For instance, when Wang is driven through the streets of Shanghai masquerading as the wife of a rich businessman, the driver remarks that her Shanghainese is reasonably fluent, and she explains that her mother was from Shanghai and that her family had fled to Hong Kong when the Japanese invaded. Is she fulfilling the demands of the part, explaining away her background in order to maintain her cover? Or is it this lived cultural experience that enables her to play the part successfully? The film leaves the question open. On another occasion, one of the wives comments on Wang's ability to understand the dialect of the opera being staged, and Wang again remarks that she had grown up with the form. On a third occasion, when the women are in Hong Kong and playing mahjong, one of the wives complains to the others that their cook has run away. Mrs Yee (Joan Chen) remarks exasperatedly in Shanghainese, 'You can't trust any of them here. And these Cantonese. I don't understand a word they say.' The irony of course is that the wayward Cantonese cook who ran away is then lamented by the women as the best Shanghainese cook they ever had.

What *Lust, Caution* performs, then, is a reconstitution of its own historicity, mobilising not so much the authenticity of representation as the historical legacy from which it comes, a historical legacy that embraces not just the fraught history of modern China, but also the manifold history of modern Chinese cinemas. It may thus be argued that it is cinema that 'cosmopolitanises' memories, in the sense that as film travels and takes the story of history beyond its geographical and historical points of origin, it offers the capacity to engage not just with new audiences, but also ways of engaging with the complexities of the present.

Self-reflexivity and (animated) form

The tension, or the dialogue if you like, between formalism and realism in animated films take place not on the level of the film's photographic capacity to capture reality but on the level of its formal manipulation, what Cubitt refers to as *techne*.[65] In this section, I am interested in animation's formalism, not only as a matter of the technology and techniques of the medium, but also in its dialogue with cinematic realism, or the perception of the realist drive in cinema.[66] Beyond Lumière's shorts, cinema's roots have been traced to earlier forms of animation, such as the flip book, the magic lantern and the zoetrope, and indeed, it may be argued that cinema, on traditional celluloid at least, running from a series of stills on a celluloid strip, is in effect no more than animation itself. In this section, I focus on cel animation, a form of profilmic animation (where drawings are filmed and set into motion), whose aesthetic Cubitt notes 'lent itself to the modern factory mode of production, with artists placed in a larger production machine in which their individual part was synchronised with others in the chain'.[67] Cubitt argues:

> Profilmic animation, orientating the viewer towards the object placed in front of the lens rather than the subject behind it, depends upon differentiating subject from object, and objects from one another. It is characteristically engaged in the motion of figures against grounds, and constructs its typical sequence as a set of causal relations distinguishing before from after. These distinctions may respect the normal laws of physics and social norms, or they may rebel against them, for example in the magic cinema of Méliès or the anarchy of Felix the Cat, but they operate constantly in the differentiation of the film strip from what it portrays.[68]

This form of animation sealed its place in popular cultural history largely through the work of Disney studios and Japanese *anime* which has become increasingly popular in the Anglophone world.[69]

That master of Soviet formalism, Sergei Eisenstein, described Disney as 'the great consoler' who brought a riot of colour to a grey world,[70] and Disney's works as a 'drop of comfort, an instant of relief, a fleeting touch of lips in the hell of social burdens, injustices and torments, in which the circle of his American viewers is forever trapped'.[71] The formal appeal of Disney's animation, Eisenstein argued, was its capacity for what he called 'plasmaticness' of the animated form, which he described as 'a being represented in drawing, a being of a definite form, a being which has attained a definite appearance, and which behaves like the primal protoplasm, not yet possessing a "stable" form, but capable of assuming any form and which, skipping along the rungs of the evolutionary ladder, attaches itself to any and all forms of animal existence'.[72] However, beyond pictorial representation, what fascinates in animation is the malleability of the form and its capacity for movement, or as Thomas Lamarre puts it, 'drawing movements and moving drawings'.[73] It is Lamarre's analysis of the form and aesthetic style of Japanese *anime* that I wish to explore with regard to *Millennium Actress*, and its construction of screen memories – screen memories which are also cosmopolitanised by virtue of their references to much of Japanese film and cultural history, some of which has also travelled outside Japan. My analysis of *Millennium Actress* centres on its use of cel animation as a cinematic aesthetic, rather than as a subgenre of cinema utilising drawings instead of photography. As such, I argue that its reference to Japan's cinematic history is not simply a 'cartoon' animated representation of that history, but one which, *by virtue of being animated*, situates itself within that lineage, perhaps even looking to extending it.

The narrative of *Millennium Actress* charts the personal history of Chiyoko Fujiwara, a fictional character and an actress whose life spans key historical moments in Japanese history over the twentieth century: beginning with the Great Kanto Earthquake in 1923 which devastated nearly all of Tokyo through the age of Japanese militarism in the mid-twentieth century, to the present moment of late capitalism, where old movie studios that had withstood the most powerful earthquakes, as one character notes, have succumbed to the unrelenting advance of bulldozers and demolition works. We revisit some of these events with Chiyoko as she narrates them in flashback for two documentary filmmakers, Tachibana and Ida, who have come to visit her in order to chronicle her life. As Chiyoko takes us through her memories, it becomes increasingly evident that Chiyoko's life is not so much marked by history as consists of one single event being played over and over across time, to which history functions simply as a backdrop. Chiyoko's life story is recounted as a perpetual search for a lost first love, a mysterious fugitive whom she had met fleetingly as a child, and for whom she continues to carry a torch right to her death bed. There is a level of banality to the fact that Chiyoko never grows from her experience, nor learns the truth of her imaginary lover's death before the end of the film. Instead she seems to replay the incident and her search over and over in her own mind through each film that she makes for the studio. However, what is compelling about the film is the self-reflexive device of inserting the two documentary filmmakers directly into Chiyoko's flashbacks, as they also constitute our points of entry into Chiyoko's memories. Tachibana is presented as her lifelong fan, and Ida as Tachibana's long-suffering assistant. The two arrive to interview the retired actress, now in her seventies, and find themselves drawn – quite literally – into her memories. The 'plasmaticness' of cel animation renders their presence in the diegesis entirely plausible: the two men can be thrown out of rocking trains one minute, shot by flaming arrows in the next, or pursued by nimble ninjas on another occasion, as these scenes are seamlessly joined by montage conventions. Tachibana is depicted as having a particular emotional attachment to Chiyoko because he had worked in the studio on one of her films as a young man and had been smitten by her. This affective attachment enables, perhaps empowers, Tachibana to take up a role within Chiyoko's present narrative, intervene in events and interact with the other characters, and he does so by 'getting into' character and costume and fully immersing himself in the role. In contrast, his assistant Ida, the man with the movie camera, is never seen or acknowledged by the other characters in these flashbacks, and remains a passive observer, recording everything that unfolds, even as he appears to be affected by the scenario around him. On one occasion, Ida notes with incredulity as the set morphs instantly around him: 'What the heck happened to Manchuria?' The effects of such metamorphoses are different from that of live action casting against a blue or green screen of cinematographic special effects. I argue that the 'real' world is even more closely conflated with the dreamworld in animation, given that these drawn characters (standing in for real people) are, in a sense, constituted of the same 'plasmatic' material as the background against which they are placed. The visual coherence of the diegetic world is enhanced even as the narrative sequencing is unsettled.

Cosmopolitan Cinema

Figure 2.8 *Millennium Actress*: Chiyoko on a bicycle

Thus, the real story of *Millennium Actress* could be read not, as Melek Ortabasi notes, Chiyoko's biography, but rather 'the history of one of Japan's proudest cultural products: live action cinema, particularly that of the "golden age" of the 1950s and 60s'.[74] To an extent, Chiyoko may be seen as representative of that lost era; her character not only experienced the height of her career during the 1950s and 1960s, but is also in the present a recluse. The character of Chiyoko is said to be inspired by a real-life actress, Setsuko Hara (1920–2015),[75] and indeed some of the styling of the characters Chiyoko plays are reminiscent of Hara's screen personae. The scene of Chiyoko as a young girl riding down a hill on a bicycle with her hair blowing behind her even references Hara (as Noriko) on her bicycle in Ozu's *Late Spring* (1949) (Figures 2.8 and 2.9). The film also draws on images from the films of the other Japanese director most well known to Western audiences, Akira Kurosawa. While Chang discusses cultural symbolism of the image of the old lady with the spinning wheel in *Millennium Actress* as 'a symbol of time', spinning 'a Buddhist prayer wheel',[76] it is difficult to ignore the reference to the spirit with the spinning wheel that opens Kurosawa's *Throne of Blood*, his 1957 adaptation of *Macbeth* (Figures 2.10 and 2.11). In another sequence, Ida, the cameraman, dodges a hail of flaming arrows in a similar way Washizu (Toshiro Mifune) reacts in terror at the arrows shot at him by his own men in *Throne of Blood* (Figures 2.12 and 2.13).

Cosmopolitan memory and self-reflexive cinema

Figure 2.9 *Late Spring*: Noriko on a bicycle

Figure 2.10 *Millennium Actress*: Old lady with a spinning wheel

In both instances, the profilmic arrangement of the mise-en-scène in *Millennium Actress* mirrors the scenes in Kurosawa's films.

There are also references to other film-related visual media, such as posters, and black-and-white newsreel images. In one sequence, Chiyoko's image is placed in a poster that recalls a 1953 melodrama, called *What Is Your*

Figure 2.11 *Throne of Blood*: Spirit with a spinning wheel

Figure 2.12 *Millennium Actress*: Ida is hailed by arrows

Cosmopolitan memory and self-reflexive cinema

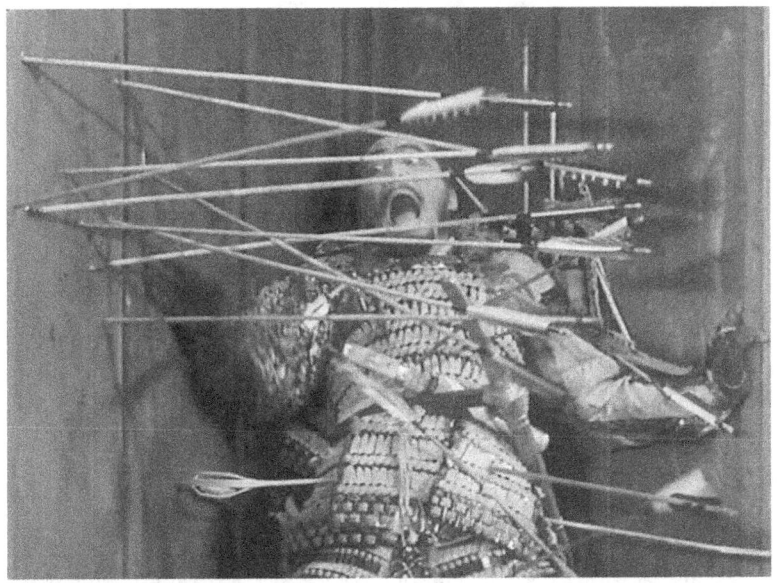

Figure 2.13 *Throne of Blood*: Washizu is hailed by arrows

Name? / Always in My Heart (Kimi no nawa), which was adapted from a popular radio drama at the time, and has since been remade for Japanese television in 1991–2. *Kimi no nawa* was Shochiku studio's most profitable postwar film in the mid-1950s and the female protagonist, dressed in her signature 'Machiko' shawl or wrap, became a popular culture icon. In *Millennium Actress*, Chiyoko appears in a similar wrap, and her image then morphs into a poster for a film (Figure 2.14). Ortabasi notes the 'dialogue between the poster and its surroundings', where 'several women in the foreground imitate the style, subtly indicating the huge popularity of Chiyoko's film and thus the pop-cultural importance of its source'.[77] In addition, the protest in the background references 'the social unrest of this period, such as the 1959–1960 Ampo demonstrations'.[78] The character of Chiyoko is thus not merely an elderly lady looking back on youthful times, but an actress who looks back upon very specific moments in Japanese cultural history. With the demolition of the old (fictional) Ginei film studio at the beginning of the film, *Millennium*

Figure 2.14 *Millennium Actress*: Chiyoko in a 'Machiko shawl'

Actress also acknowledges the end of a golden age of dream-making that is now popularly revived in re-makes, tributes, documentaries and other intertextual practices, including within the animated film itself.

The film suggests in parts that Chiyoko had continued to work tirelessly as an actress in order to travel to different parts of Japan to search for her lover; yet it also indicates that many of the films were shot on studio premises, suggesting that any journeys undertaken may have been purely in Chiyoko's mind. This is reinforced by the fact that as Chiyoko recounts her memories to Tachibana and Ida, the images of her memories become indistinguishable from the images of the films she had made – each one re-enacting a woman's search for the mystery lover and ending in inevitable frustration. Just before her death, Chiyoko admits to the two filmmakers that perhaps it was the chase that sustained her and not the man himself who remained a cipher to the very end. The chase in the film culminates cinematically in a climactic montage sequence depicting Chiyoko as a central figure travelling across Japan in time and space. The editing of the sequence has been described by Chang as constituting a 'number of unique transitions, especially the match-on-actions that jump between historical scenes [...] [and t]his seemingly uninterrupted continuity makes these dream-like scenes seem to run smoothly and reduce logical reasoning'.[79] This sequence is edited to the haunting, electronic rhythms of the musical piece, 'Run' (by Japanese electronic artist and composer, Susumu Hirasawa). In this sequence, Chiyoko literally 'runs', or more accurately gallops, rides and cycles, through time and history, as the scenes in the background morph from one historical time period to the next. As it does so, the scenes also morph from one aesthetic style to the next, paying tribute not just to Japanese cinematic history, as I have discussed, but also to even earlier forms of Japanese visual culture, such as the woodblock print, fabric design and scroll paintings. The director Satoshi Kon is said to have likened *Millennium Actress* to 'an animated form of *nishiki-e*',[80] the Japanese woodblock prints of vibrant colours originating in the 1760s. Following this reading, it could then be said that Chiyoko, through her films, travels through an even longer history of Japan than her own fictional lifespan, reaching back into medieval times and stretching into the space-age future. In this short one-minute sequence, encased within the full 87 minutes of *Millennium Actress*, more than a thousand years of Japanese history is encapsulated. And it is worth noting that as Chiyoko passes through this history, she also passes through this history as it has been *mediatised*.

While much of *Millennium Actress* negotiates with Japanese national and cultural histories as I have argued, this 'Run' sequence is often discussed as part of the film's wider series of intertextual allusions and quotations. At this level of analysis, the animated form is conceived of as a medium of adaptation, where cel animation is perceived to be an economical alternative to producing a live action film with high production costs. Chang notes that this has been suggested of Kon's films:

> Kon's works have also often caused authors to question whether these films may be more suitable as live action films [...] because of the realistic human character designs and the use of cinematography; the boundary between reality and the fantasies of the characters is usually blurred and interwoven with the progress of the story. Jumps often occur between scenes to emphasize the changes in the characters' states of mind, consciousness, or memories. The narrative discontinuity is similar to that with which fragments are constructed in our dreams.[81]

Why these themes may be seen to be better served by live action cinema points to implicit assumptions about the superiority of the live action film to the animated one, a bias Thomas Lamarre points out rather succinctly: 'for a variety of reasons, animation is often thought of as secondary, even inferior [to live action cinema] [...] there is the common wisdom that, if a film can be made in live action, then it should [...] [and] there is a bias that photography-based cinema inherently has greater reality effect than the drawings used for animation'.[82] Lamarre, speaking largely for Japanese *anime*, and for animation more generally, argues that far from being the cheap and childish cousin to live action cinema, *anime* and the cinema in fact constitute a 'constellation of relations'.[83] He cites Livia Monnet's analysis of *Ghost in the Shell* (1995) in which 'animation becomes *the* medium that remediates all others – a kind of hyper-metamedium'.[84] I would read Kon's *Millennium Actress* in a similar vein. Kon has articulated in an interview: 'I draw pictures. That's how I express my ideas and stories. When I make films, I cannot think of how to do it without drawings. Thus, it was out of [the] question for me to make *Millennium Actress* with real actors. I only thought about drawing a comic book or making an animated film'.[85] In one of his series of tutorial videos via his YouTube channel, *Every Frame a Painting*, professional film editor Tony Zhou summarises Kon's editing style and technique of matching scene transitions as one that builds 'a style out of match cuts' in order to link the world of 'dreams, memories, nightmares, movies and life'. Zhou notes that Kon 'edits in a way that a lot of live action editors could not' simply because his editing was 'too fast', often completing an action with considerably fewer frames: 'Kon felt that as an animator he could actually draw less information in the shot so that your eye could read it faster'.[86] This analysis resonates with Lamarre's assertion that one of the functions of animation is not to replicate live action cinema with drawings as such, but to 'decode' and then 'recode' how movement is captured in photographic film:

> Because there are real differences between the intervals that the hand will draw and those a shutter will take, the animator's work is not really an exact replication of the camera's procedures. It is a recoding of them. Such differences are not merely differences in precision: it is not simply that cinematography based on photography is more accurate or real than painting or drawing. Animation presents qualities of movement that differ profoundly from live-action cinema.[87]

This recoding, Lamarre further explains, 'is not the same thing as replicating, copying or reproducing. To say that animation recodes cinematic movement is not to say that animation is imitative, derivative or secondary in relation to cinema. On the contrary, recoding is intended to show the responsiveness and expressiveness of animation'.[88] In other words, animation can be said to be *cinema in another form*, rather than a form of cinema that simply employs drawn pictures.

Writing about the history of animation in Japan, Lamarre notes that a 'distinctive *anime* aesthetic' emerged in the 1970s,[89] when animators in Japan had to find a cost-effective way of rendering movement:

> The emergence of an *anime* aesthetic is typically traced back to the technical limitations placed on *anime* production during the global economic crisis of animation in the 1960s. Financial constraints were such that studios could not afford to produce 'full animation', in which animators draw as many as twelve frames per second, in which an image lasts only two frames. [...] Constrained to work with drawings that could be sustained for five or six frames, animators adopted different strategies for composing and conveying movement, other than drawing it frame to frame. The result was limited animation, which had profound aesthetic consequences.[90]

'Full animation', where the animator strives to draw each stage of movement across the frames, is the kind of smooth flowing animation we have come to associate with Disney, and big-budget *anime* films like *Spirited Away* produced by Studio Ghibli. 'Limited animation' is animation where instead of trying to draw movement, the animator strives instead to move the drawings, where 'The cel can be pulled across the background in various directions, or the background pulled under the cel'.[91] This results in a kind of '"induced movement", that is, an effect of relative movement'.[92] The 'Run' sequence in *Millennium Actress* employs this induced movement effect, which sets it apart from the full animated aesthetic of the rest of the film. Lamarre gives a description of the effects of limited animation: 'It is like that which arises when you feel that the platform not the train moves as your train leaves the station. Or, as two trains pass, one train seems to stand still [...] Induced movement brings into play a complex set of mobile relations between foreground, background and spectator'.[93]

The relation of foreground, middle ground and background and the relative speeds and directions at which they move across the frame in the 'Run' sequence is what contributes to the 'look' of limited animation. Chiyoko moves from left to right on a horse, a carriage and finally a rickshaw, sometimes occupying the foreground or the middle ground of the frame, and in general moves at a slower speed than the other planes which rush (or are pulled) past her from right to left. These relative speeds and oppositional directions generate the sense of movement and urgency in the sequence, as she appears to charge ahead into the future, urged on by the pulsating rhythms of Hirasawa's electronic score. I offer here a schematic description of the planes of movement here:

1. Chiyoko, in a kimono and traditional headdress, rides a horse side-saddle, which gallops from left to right and moves from foreground to middle ground in a battle scene of *static* figures from medieval Japan – soldiers, cannons, flags, all simulate but do not actually reproduce movement. Background and foreground move from right to left past Chiyoko as she gallops through them. Blast from cannon segues into next sequence (Figure 2.15).
2. Silkscreen image of rising / setting sun. Chiyoko, dressed in nineteenth-century Western dress, and seated on a horse-drawn carriage, continues to ride from left to right in middle ground. Foreground and background suggest a park with blossoming cherry trees. Mount Fuji appears in the background. Chiyoko moves into the foreground holding up a parasol while a train glides past her in middle ground from left to right at a faster speed. Background dissolves into an image of European architecture (Figure 2.16).
3. Chiyoko in the foreground wearing a kimono but sporting a modern girl's hairstyle, loosely tied back with a ribbon, and seated on a rickshaw. Ida with his camera glides into the middle ground and moves alongside though slightly ahead of Chiyoko. We later see he is seated on a moving car while Chiyoko is being pulled along by Tachibana on foot. Japanese soldiers march in the background and the flags of the Japanese Imperial army are prominent (Figure 2.17). The sequence ends when Tachibana stumbles and Chiyoko is hurled onto a bicycle, gliding downhill into the main narrative trajectory once again.

Cosmopolitan memory and self-reflexive cinema

Figure 2.15 *Millennium Actress*: Chiyoko rides through history

Figure 2.16 *Millennium Actress*: Chiyoko in European dress

This one-minute sequence is remarkably efficient both in capturing the sweep of history and the sense of its relentless pace as Japan hurtles into modernity. The use of the three *flat* planes – foreground, middle ground and background – does not in fact provide a sense of perspectival distance and spatial relations but instead reiterates what Lamarre calls the 'superflat' quality which has become characteristic of a certain 'anime-ic' style: 'In effect, the supposedly flat and depthless characters and figures in *anime* are

Figure 2.17 *Millennium Actress*: Chiyoko being filmed by Ida

superflat. In their very flatness, they are traversed by a potential for interaction, motion and transformation. They move on a specific field of forces'.[94] Limited animation, with its inherent jerkiness and awkwardness of movement, has thus evolved from a limitation into 'a distinctive form of expression' in itself, and in so doing 'does not only spin narratives of the future but also proposes futures of narrative'.[95] The iconoclastic animated sitcom, *South Park*, created by Trey Parker and Matt Stone employs the flatness and limitations of its construction paper cut-out animation as its central aesthetic.

While, on the one hand, it could be read that the 'Run' sequence in *Millennium Actress* acknowledges the film's debt to the cultural history of Japanese animation, as well as its live action films as I have argued, on the other hand, it is also possible to argue that the self-conscious insertion of the 'Run' sequence as the narrative climax of the film serves to suture animation, and *anime*, directly into the celebrated cultural history of Japanese cinema itself. Significantly, Ida, the cameraman, is inserted into the last part of the sequence, his camera pointing directly at us, filming not only Chiyoko but simultaneously the gaze of the 'camera' which is constituted by our viewing position, and which is also in effect filming the actions and events on screen. Ida's presence breaks the fourth wall and connects us to the film as the spectator is positioned on a fourth plane on this moving course of superflat planes. The self-reflexivity in *Millennium Actress* is thus not merely constituted by its performed awareness of filmic devices and various cultural screen memories, but also by the insertion of itself into the very process of filmic memory-making as well. The sequence may be read as an animated version of W. J. T. Mitchell's notion of 'metapictures': pictures that call attention to themselves as pictures, where 'the use of metapictures as instruments in the understanding of pictures seems inevitably to call into question the self-understanding of the observer'.[96] By these means, *Millennium Actress* is not simply paying tribute to history, it is in effect re-historicising history and re-memorialising memory itself. The cosmopolitan questions that *Millennium Actress* poses are not so much about whether animation can compete with live action film, or whether it is even cinema at all; instead, if animation is indeed part of the fabric of cinema as Kon's *Millennium Actress* seems to suggest, then it is time for us, as critics, historians, and fans, to revisit its place in various national and global cinemas[97] – besides Japan and the US, there are animation traditions in China, Estonia, Hungary, Iran, among others, and not least of all in Britain as well – especially as we begin to contemplate the digital era here and to come.

Concluding remarks

Self-reflexive cinema, as I have explored, offers a means of looking back on the past through the act of looking back upon its form. As a conscious mode of textual practice, self-reflexivity works via cultural memory and, perhaps even more importantly, cultural literacy. The success of recognising the text's ability to reflect upon itself depends upon the spectator's knowledge of a set of known tropes and gestures. Each of the films I have studied addresses particular moments in Chinese and Japanese national histories, as well as the medium's cultural histories. In each of these films, self-reflexivity operates on three levels: firstly, how it acknowledges its form; secondly, how it acknowledges its history; and thirdly, how that history is told through the history of the form. In analysing what self-reflexive modes of textual operation say about the relationship between cultural texts and historical memories, what cosmopolitanises these memories and forms is the invitation to engage with that history through the international *public performance* of that relationship through the medium of the cinema.

3

Film festivals and cosmopolitan affect

When considering questions of cosmopolitanism in film studies, the question of context is as important as the analysis of texts. Graeme Turner, in *Film as Social Practice*, now into its fourth edition, argues for 'the understanding of [a film's] production and consumption, its pleasures and its meanings, [as] enclosed within the study of the workings of culture itself'.[1] Turner's book, first published in 1988, introduced students of film studies to broader questions beyond formalist and aesthetic readings of the text. These questions explored the *conditions* – social, political, industrial – for film production and reception. This is an approach that is today taken for granted in the teaching and research of film studies. While reception and audience studies are now fully embedded within the field, the contexts and conditions for film distribution and exhibition remain still relatively under-explored. In this chapter, I offer a study of film festivals as a way of exploring some of the conditions of distribution and exhibition. There are many different types of festivals with different themes, programming priorities, management structures, funding regimes and so on, and it is not the place of this chapter to enter into such a typology except to suggest that the study of festivals more generally can offer us several routes into the study of film as social, cultural and political practice and process, particularly in terms of the kinds of encounters they bring into effect.

Festivals may be considered, variously, as sites of exhibition and circuits for distribution;[2] marketplaces for sales and city branding;[3] and increasingly also as producers of new work.[4] Along with film critics and reviewers, festival programmers can act as cultural gatekeepers and tastemakers, a group to whom Paul Willemen has tersely referred as 'PIPs – Plain-clothes Ideological Police'.[5] Yet festivals can also raise our awareness to certain causes, marginal groups, new aesthetics and alternative voices.[6] The expansion of LGBTQ film festivals is one example of this.[7] Willemen's own intervention via the Third Cinema conference during the Edinburgh Film Festival in 1986 is another example.[8] Festivals are also media events, or what Janet Harbord calls 'spaces of flow',[9] located in fixed places but transient in time: 'the festival, a market place, a designated space of transaction, brings together the determinants of film culture under the duress of space-time compression or the media event'.[10] The transitory nature of the film festival poses two main challenges for research. The first challenge is how one might research and write about an event that is over and already passed, and that leaves behind precious few material traces. Catalogues, reviews and reports can convey something of the occasion but very little of the atmosphere – what Cindy Wong describes as 'a week or two of glitz, buzz, myriad screenings, and jumbled events'.[11] These print materials, and today increasingly the material shared on social media, are nonetheless important and constitute part of the discourse of the festival as an event. Harbord identifies four main discourses underpinning film festivals: first, the discourse of filmmakers and producers; second, the discourse of 'media representation' (i.e., the press); third, the 'business discourse' that operates through the buying and selling of films; and fourth, 'the discourse of tourism and the service industry'.[12] Festival histories as memoir constitutes another form of discourse, even if they can sometimes seem to be dominated by memories of wild parties and extravagance.[13] Often written by festival 'insiders', usually a programmer or a critic, these biographical accounts both illuminate something of the inner workings of the festivals, whilst also reaffirming their exclusivity.

The second challenge is how one might research and write about an event that is ongoing, even if one is able to be present for part or all of the festival as it is happening. As the nascent field of film festival studies continues to establish itself with a growing body of work,[14] and because of the sheer size, scope and diversity of festivals, many different methodologies are being employed, and often mixed together, including ethnography[15] and network theory,[16] intersecting with cultural studies approaches that look at festivals as institutional structures of (state) power.[17] By and large, the research focuses on festivals as social-cultural-political phenomena. In this chapter, I explore these challenges within the critical frame of the notion of affect, through the exploration of a number of interlocking relationships that operate within the dynamics of a festival. These relationships may be understood as a political economy functioning through cultural and state institutions and market imperatives,[18] along with what can only be called the *affective encounter* that make up the experience of festivals.

Many people go to festivals for the *pleasures* they offer, though not necessarily for the same reasons. These pleasures are sometimes articulated as pleasures of discovery: to see something they have never seen before or have not had the chance to encounter, be it new aesthetics, genres, narrative content, authorial bodies of work, or national and cultural cinemas. A. O. Scott, writing for *The New York Times*, reflects on his initial encounter with Hirozaku Koreeda's *Still Walking* (2008), and credits the Toronto Film Festival for the positive experience:

> This is exactly the kind of film – quiet, modest, untroubled by ambitions of importance – that risks being lost in the news media shuffle. And yet it is so completely absorbing, so sure of its own scale and scope that while you're watching it the rest of the world fades into irrelevance. [...] This is one of the things film festivals are for, surely. Not escape from reality, exactly, but a reminder of just how much reality there is, and how many perspectives on it are possible.[19]

Cindy Wong notes that '[a]udiences are important to sustain the culture of cinephilia and to demand that festivals serve as guardians of quality cinema, especially as festivals have changed in the last few decades to accommodate the business of cinema'.[20] While festivals are certainly also marketplaces where the buying and selling of films take place, that industry professionals and audiences tend to speak of their experiences in affective terms tells us something about why they keep going back, business and commercial imperatives notwithstanding. An example of what Jeffrey Ruoff refers to as 'the travel genre of festival writing'[21] is Gerald Peary's recollection of having had to persuade various editors to send him on assignments to cover festivals, even if they could not necessarily cover his expenses.[22] For Peary, the business of festival reporting became the excuse to attend the festivals rather than the other way around. Wong's own recollection corroborates the experience: 'While professionals watch films at festivals with varied agendas, many festival audiences see these exhibitions as exciting glimpses of art cinema and other worlds. My media students in Hong Kong awaited the HKIFF [Hong Kong International Film Festival] catalog with real excitement, while those in New York look to the New York Film Festival, Tribeca, or MIX for the same thrills.'[23] Reflecting on the pleasures of her own experience while conducting her research on festivals, Wong further recalls: 'Whether reviewing student films at San Sebastián, taking my children to premiers in Hong Kong, or spending seemingly endless nights chasing down past prizewinners of Cannes, Locarno, Berlin, and Venice in libraries and on DVDs, I have learned, remembered and enjoyed the fact that festivals are about films.'[24]

What the environment – the 'buzz' – of the festival provides is not just a place where films are screened and watched by an audience – that could happen in any place with adequate resources, and much more easily in the digital age – but a mode, or modes, of engaging with the films that shape the experience of cinema as a cosmopolitan cultural experience. As I have already argued, there is an inherent tension between the particular and the universal within cosmopolitanism, which plays out in certain ways on filmic texts as I have discussed in previous chapters. In this chapter I explore this tension as it operates within the dynamics of a festival. Festivals *are* cosmopolitan spaces on many levels, not least because the cities hosting the festivals are frequently keen to market themselves as such, but what occurs within the space and duration of the festival may deliver an altogether alternative cosmopolitanism from what the marketeers intend.

By turning to affect in my discussion of cosmopolitan cinema, I do not make a case for reading affect in the aesthetic form of film,[25] nor for the emotional experiences of the spectator as they watch films.[26] Rather, I employ the notion of affect as exemplified by the series of vignettes compiled in Breakwell and Hammond's edited collection, *Seeing in the Dark* (1990). Now out of print and put together at a time before the 'turn to affect' had taken hold in humanities research, the collection brings together what is written in the blurb as 'a bizarre, funny collection of movie tales'.[27] These tales collected from friends, and later friends of friends, of the editors are not ethnographical studies, yet the sheer diversity of affective encounters they record of the cinema – ranging from memories of childhood terrors and delights to smells in the theatre – testifies to the fact that this quality of experience remains under-researched, or at least under-acknowledged in scholarly discourse on cinema. As Breakwell and Hammond write in their brief introduction to the compendium:

> Measuring applause does not reveal that the movie was memorable for the woman in the third row because the building on screen reminded her of where she went to school and all those childhood memories came flooding back intercut with the film while the auditorium gently shook as an underground train passed beneath and cigarette ash fluttered down from the balcony in the projector beam.[28]

In the introduction to their edited volume *The Affect Theory Reader* (2010), Seigworth and Gregg attempt to delineate what they see as the liminality of affect. They ascribe affect as a state of 'in-between-ness' that '*accumulates* across both relatedness and interruptions in relatedness, becoming a palimpsest of force-encounters traversing the ebbs and swells of intensities that pass between "bodies"'.[29] I explore affect as a way to conceptualise the dynamic forces that pull on all the cultural and economic actors, consumers and artefacts at work within a film festival.

Thinking of cosmopolitan encounters through the notion of affect may be productive if we imagine cosmopolitanism as a series of encounters with strangers (and strangeness), as I have been arguing throughout this volume. There is the encounter with strange worlds within the filmic text, and there is also the encounter with strangers within the theatre and with other participants. Through these various encounters festivals operate as a kind of imagined space of the cosmopolis as described by David Chaney:

> The cosmopolis is a place or political space that encompasses the variety of human culture. It promises the potential to meet and become acquainted with all the strands of cultural diversity. The cosmopolitan is therefore someone who can cope with

unpredictability. Cosmopolitans know what is expected in different cultural settings and can move between them with confidence and assurance.[30]

Participation in a film festival shares a similar set of assumptions, stemming mainly from the supposition that the participants know what they are doing: that they know what they want to see, when and where to see the films, and actively seek them out. This festival participant is presumed to think and act as a privileged, cosmopolitan, 'cultural citizen', for whose ease of mobility the cultural and geographical spaces of the festival are designed. However, as festivals take place in public spaces, they also offer room for the unpredictable to occur. Festival spaces can also accommodate accidental, serendipitous or alternative encounters – for example, among people who 'drop in' never having been to a festival film before. These may be people who turn up at festival films for reasons beyond the middle-class, middle-brow consumption of 'art cinema'; and they may be people who occupy the spaces of the festival with no intention of, nor inclination for, any of its prescribed activities. I argue that the *frisson* sparked by the contemporaneous existence of these different modes of engagement produces another kind cosmopolitan affect within the festival encounter, one that does not presuppose the harmonious universality of experience but rather accentuates their heterogeneity.

The following analysis is drawn from a series of personal encounters experienced while attending and working at the Singapore International Film Festival between 1997 and 2003. I worked during this period on different occasions as a volunteer and a paid freelancer, taking advantage of the job perk to watch as many films as I could fit into a day: four theatrical screenings a day remains my physical limit, not including screeners and partial viewings and previews. These encounters I cite may be deemed affective in that they are not recollected with empirical certitude but are reliant on impression, memory and personal notes. I do not reproduce verbatim dialogue or name names. I am not writing an ethnography and was not consciously researching one at the time. Instead my understanding is influenced by Mica Nava's approach, where she writes of her own multiple affiliations and attempts 'to integrate memories, the reworking of events, historical context and argument'.[31] The following constitutes my own efforts to invoke through personal engagement the affective nature of these encounters, which cannot be easily addressed when we speak of festivals in macrocosmic terms. Others may draw similar and different conclusions from their own festival and film-going memories.

Festivals are often described in energetic terms – such as 'buzz', 'flow', and general 'chaos' – to signal a certain suspension of 'normal life' within the city, even if the festival returns to the city at the same time each year. Kirstie Jamieson describes the self-styled 'festival city' of Edinburgh in terms that evoke its rough-and-tumble energy: 'Festival time signals jostling crowds, overspilling bars, and cacophones of multilingual conversations. [...] For 6 weeks, a thriving street life brings tourists, performers, and residents into proximity where difference in appearance, language, and behavior becomes the norm of city center public life'.[32] This suspension of 'normal life' invites particular modes of participation, even ritualised behaviour, depending on individual circumstances and inclination. The following is a schematic of my own personal semi-ritualised experience on first arrival at a film festival, where even after the advent on online booking in the early 2000s, there are certain pleasures to be sought from a kind of 'analogue' engagement with the paraphernalia of the event:

1. The first thing to do is to pick up the festival catalogue. Having the booklet in print makes it easier to have an overview of the entire programme as well as facilitates the flipping of pages from front to back. Online ticket purchasing may be convenient but browsing a catalogue of over 100 films online can be time-consuming and mentally exhausting.
2. The second thing to do is to find a café nearby, preferably a quiet one in view of the mental labour to be undertaken in the next hour or so.
3. The third task, best conducted with a caffeinated or fizzy beverage on the side and a good pen in hand, involves marking out all the films that look 'promising', although from the pithy descriptions, it can be difficult ascertaining which films are worth taking trouble to try and catch.
4. This 'trouble' worth taking, the fourth task, involves having to work out various logistics and priorities, such as any potential clashes in the schedule; the distance and time needed to travel between screening venues; and, crucially, the limits of the budget! (Procuring festival accreditation with an unlimited entry pass is ideal.)

Part of the pleasure of the festival experience is the sheer intensity and the adrenaline rush of trying to work out the priorities of the programme, organising meal breaks and negotiating distances between venues (often reached on foot or by public transport) between the screenings. If one were in an unfamiliar city, there is sometimes the added attraction of including a visit to a tourist landmark or two within the itinerary! At the 2006 Toronto International Film Festival, I moved between the different screening venues via the city's hop-on, hop-off tourist sightseeing bus. It was a great convenience and really enhanced my trip as not only was the bus ticket valid for three days, the bus route took in 21 tourist destinations, nearly all the festival locations, and, best of all, a stop near my hotel. Of course, it is entirely possible to engage film festival screenings at a more leisurely pace, by perhaps trying to catch one or two prize-winners and the odd auteur retrospective after work or during the weekends. However, the 'intense' version produces a particular form of cosmopolitan sociality that interests me in the context of this discussion on affect. The festival experience as I have outlined above is, for me (and anecdotally for other festival goers I know), a largely *solitary* one. It is an experience of compressed encounters completely unlike its more leisurely counterpart. The latter tends to take place within a broader social context, where one is likely to attend the film with a friend or family and maybe to take in a meal or a drink as well. In the solitary, intense version, the pressure of having to rush from venue to venue does not always make for good social interaction, unless one's companion shared similar priorities. In this context, if there is a plan to meet up with friends or colleagues socially at the festival, this usually takes place after the day's screenings are done. Alternatively, there may be a designated bar or café in a central location where people know to drop in for the chance of meeting acquaintances, industry contacts and perhaps even the odd film star or two. Serendipity is very much a part of the affective cosmopolitanism of a festival.

What form of cosmopolitan encounter does this frenzied solitary travel take? I explore three overlapping encounters. Firstly, there is the encounter with the films. Secondly, there is the encounter with the spaces of the festival: such as the venues, buildings, outdoor screenings, alternative site screenings and so on. And, thirdly, there is the encounter with a particular form of 'imagined community' that runs concurrent to the kind of imagined community first introduced by Benedict Anderson to describe nationalism and national imaginaries, as Dina Iordanova observes with particular reference to diasporic identities:

> In the 'live' space of the festival, organisers and audiences form a community, an actual one, that congregates face-to-face for the purpose of fostering an 'imagined community' that comes live in the act of watching a film and imagining distant human beings becoming part of one's own experiences. Thus, the festival's set-up extends an invitation to engage in what is essentially a political act of imagined belonging and to continue the nation building process that is pre-supposed by extending it to the diaspora and beyond.[33]

The kind of 'imagined community' I would also add to the mix is not a community drawn along national or ethnic or even cultural lines, where 'culture' is designated according to its ethnological delineation, but a community of participants drawn together by a kind of common cultural literacy and shared practice that enable one to navigate successfully the spaces of the festival and to draw pleasure from it.

Filmic encounters

The primary pleasure of a film festival is the encounter with new films. However, the criteria for choosing which new films to see depend largely on personal tastes and preferences. This is one of the reasons why auteur cinema thrives at festivals: authorial style can function as a known 'brand'.[34] My preference, in accordance with my research interests and cultural curiosity, leans towards East Asian cinema, but also national cinemas of 'small' nations such as those defined by Hjort and Petrie (2007),[35] whose films can struggle to be picked up for wider distribution. I also lean towards cinema that crosses linguistic and cultural boundaries, am partial to 'quirky' themes and films that whimsically play with form and genre. These are also less likely to be picked up by mainstream distributors. Other individuals may seek out films with different characteristics. However, as Bill Nichols notes, the main draw of a film festival remains the possibilities of 'an encounter with the unfamiliar, the experience of something strange, [and] the discovery of new voices and visions'.[36] The fascination of the encounter with the new and the strange, and the wonder and novelty of the experience, can be traced to the fascination of the first audiences who were drawn to the early 'cinema of attractions'.[37] If rarity and scarcity are added the mix, the resulting sense of urgency is what contributes to the 'compression' of festival encounters that I have described above. There is often a sense at a festival that one may not get a second chance to see the film again, especially if the film is particularly obscure, unusual or 'weird'.[38] And a large part of the pleasure extends beyond the experience of the film to the effort it takes to get to it. Seigworth and Gregg's particularly evocative description of affect speaks to the certain urgency produced by the transience of the festival encounter:

> Affect [...] is the name we give to those forces – visceral forces beneath, alongside, or generally *other than* conscious knowing, vital forces insisting beyond emotion – that can serve to drive us toward movement, toward thought and extension, that can likewise suspend us (as if in neutral) across a barely registering accretion of force-relations, or that can leave us overwhelmed by the world's apparent intractability.[39]

This desire for the discovery of the new in cinema, and its gratification, are frequently self-generating and self-fulfilling. As Nichols notes, 'this experience inflects and constructs the meanings we ascribe to one of the newest in a continuous succession of "new cinemas" while we at the same time constitute the very audience needed to recognize and appreciate such cinemas as distinct and valued entities'.[40] On the one hand, a 'festival circuit' is generally conceived of in terms of routes of distribution and exhibition; on another, there is a parallel circuit of audience desire and expectation, which fuels funding and production in another kind of loop, including a phenomena identified as 'film-induced tourism'[41] or 'film-motivated tourism'.[42]

Navigating these different loops and circuits is what makes festival research exciting at this juncture. One particularly vivid example from personal autobiography is my encounter with the 'small' Icelandic film, *Cold Fever* (1995) at the Singapore International Film Festival. Set in the harsh but hauntingly beautiful landscape of Iceland in winter, the film tells the whimsical story of a Japanese man on a road trip across Iceland to perform last rites at the site on which his parents had died. The film, in effect an international co-production between USA, Japan, Iceland, Denmark and Germany, mobilises genre conventions and geographical remoteness to produce a quirky mode of address, where film not only provides a window into a mythical, touristic 'Iceland', but also through an intelligent self-reflexive register comments on its own practice of self-representation. In experiencing Iceland through the eyes of a Japanese 'foreigner' the film self-consciously presents Iceland for the touristic gaze, yet it is not the gaze of the mass tourist which is sought, who may have no interest in travelling beyond its modern capital, Reykjavik, or its famous hot spring, the Blue Lagoon. Instead, the film invites the spectator on a journey into the heart of the country, albeit into equally touristic vistas of icy plains and rugged mountains. This is travel aimed at the adventurous for whom the rigours of the journey are a source of pleasure rather than resistance. In so doing, the film deftly sutures the spectator as a participant into a community of festival film enthusiasts presumed to be capable of decoding its intertextual references and genre revisions.[43] This venture into unknown yet familiar territory is part of the pleasure of discovery in festival cinema. It is also a solitary pleasure that ties us into a wider community of festival participants that in turn produces what we experience as the international film festival 'circuit'. Nichols describes the pleasures of his own discovery of Iranian cinema in the mid-1990s:

> This is a distinctive pleasure: it accompanies the discovery that the unknown is not entirely unknowable. As festival-goers we experience a precarious, ephemeral moment in which an imaginary coherence renders Iranian cinema no longer mysterious but still less than fully known. Like the tourist, we depart with the satisfaction of a *partial knowledge*, pleased that it is of our own making. Beyond it lie those complex forms of local knowledge that we have willingly exchanged for the opportunity to elect Iranian cinema to the ranks of the international art film circuit. Hovering, like a spectre, at the boundaries of the festival experience, are those deep structures and thick descriptions that might restore a sense of the particular and local to what we have now recruited to the realm of the global.[44]

It is this *feeling* of taking pleasure in partial comprehension that evokes a cosmopolitan affect, one which signals an equal desire to be at ease with difference while accepting the limits of restricted perspectives.

Films may also have afterlives outside of festivals, though not all do. Although *Cold Fever* made its international première at the Toronto International Film Festival in 1995, the DVD only became available in UK Region 2 in 2004. Since the film made such an impression on me when I first saw it, I took the opportunity to put it on an undergraduate course where I taught it as an example of a 'festival film'.[45] However, one key feature of the film which was only experienced during festival screenings is not replicated on DVD: that is, the film's shift in aspect ratio from 1.66:1 in the opening sequences in Tokyo to 2.35:1 when the narrative moves to the wide panorama of Iceland. This shift, experienced at the theatrical screening, is not seen on the DVD and my students have to be asked to imagine it.[46] Some students wrote in their essays about the missed opportunity to see the event 'live'; others later emailed with news of visits to Iceland during the summer break, their curiosity for the country having been piqued by the film. These modes of circulation, while not read as part of the film's original festival route and circuit, nonetheless constitute another kind of cosmopolitan encounter, which has traversed time (1995 to 2004 to the present) and space (from Iceland, to Toronto, to Singapore, to the UK, and back to Iceland again), via different platforms. These modes of circulation cannot be easily traced through box office numbers and theatrical bookings, but may go some way in trying to read the politics of film festivals beyond 'the power and distortion of the European gaze in film knowledge mediated through key festivals and the alternatives visible from other positions within the festival world'.[47]

Spatial encounters

Festival and city spaces have symbiotic relationships. Festivals utilise spaces within the city and also its infrastructure networks, and cities are keen to use festivals to promote themselves as a destination. As Wong notes: 'Film festivals also celebrate place: the city that hosts them, the nation and national/regional industries that often underpin them, and the globalization of relations of production and film markets. Festivals define the very cultural capital that cities and nations embrace as brand-name events for cities of the creative class'.[48] Julian Stringer argues for the re-consideration of the festival city as an 'exhibition site' constituting 'a new kind of counter public sphere',[49] and one that could in particular counter the predominance of 'national cinemas' as the organising principle around which to discuss the cultural politics of film production.[50] According to Stringer, 'the international film festival circuit' suggests 'the existence of a socially produced space unto itself, a unique cultural arena that acts as a contact zone for the working through of unevenly differentiated power relationships – not so much a parliament of national film industries as a series of diverse, sometimes competing, sometimes cooperating, public spheres'.[51] His position stems from the understanding that the crowdedness of the festival marketplace and the competition amongst cities produces a hierarchy that mirrors a 'geographically uneven development' reinforced by structures that reproduce global inequalities'.[52] In addressing cities, rather than national film industries, as 'the nodal points on this circuit', Stringer invites us to 'pay as much attention to the spatial logics of the historical and contemporary festival circuit as we do to the films it exhibits', especially since the 'circuit exists as an allegorization of space and its power relationships; it operates through the transfer of value between and within distinct geographic localities'.[53]

When festival goers encounter the city as a destination for business and leisure, the intensity of the festival experience can also create unexpectedly visceral relationships with the more intimate spaces of the festivals, and in this section, I focus on the spatial logics within a city, and particularly on the function and the locale of the exhibition venue. While film festivals may screen films in multiplexes, the status of the festival as an extraordinary event means that films are sometimes screened in other venues, such as old picture palaces, nondescript conference rooms and warehouses. They may also be screened in outdoor venues, in town squares or even on beaches. Each venue will have a story to tell regardless of the film programme, and like the films they host, some stories will be more interesting than others. In this section, I explore the example of the historic Majestic theatre located in Singapore's Chinatown district and its use as a screening venue during the Singapore International Film Festival in the 1980s until the theatre's closure in 1998, before it was turned into a shopping mall in 2003. I approach my experience of the Majestic in the spirit of Gaston Bachelard's *The Poetics of Space* (1958), where he describes the attraction, and a certain magnetism, of intimate spaces: 'Space that has been seized upon by the imagination cannot remain indifferent space subject to the measures and estimates of the surveyor. It has been lived in, not in its positivity, but with all the partiality of imagination'.[54] Although Bachelard writes largely of the spaces of a house, its interior spaces and its outside, its secret nooks and crannies and drawers and chests, it is possible to argue that at certain moments and in certain places, one might build up an intimate relationship with a structure like an old cinema theatre. Many films reify similar intimacies of place: see for example *Cinema Paradiso* (1988), *Hugo* (2011) and *The Purple Rose of Cairo* (1985). The film theatre, it could be said, becomes a cultural home of sorts.

When I worked for the Singapore International Film Festival from 1997 to 2003, I spent a lot of time as a volunteer at the Majestic theatre. My duties ranged from merchandise selling, to ticket tearing, to ushering and as a general runner for the festival's organisers. Sometimes these duties included reminding the veteran Chinese-speaking projectionist repeatedly that he was not to put the house lights on until the end credits had run their course – he often worried about the health-and-safety consequences of audiences tripping over themselves as they left the theatre in the dark. The festival's organisers insisted on this practice as a way of aligning itself with the European arthouse and of distinguishing itself from mainstream, 'popcorn' cinema. Keeping the house lights off pressed upon audiences the import of staying through the end credits and thus the festival's ethos of 'serious' cinema practice, never mind that the majority of the audience chose to stumble out of the darkened auditorium anyway. My other informal duties included fielding questions from members of the public, and on more than one occasion having to explain to (or, more usually, placate) ticket holders about cancelled or delayed screenings (for example when the Board of Film Censors ratings had not been issued on time), the lack of subtitles (when the wrong print had been delivered) and any other hiccup in the proceedings. During calmer periods, passers-by from nearby stalls and markets in Chinatown where the theatre was located would sometimes drift in to the lobby, and their questions ranged from 'Film festival? What's on?' to 'Film festival? What's that?'

On these occasions, I am reminded of how the Majestic can be read as a cultural anachronism. The building is located in Singapore's Chinatown, which in a nation whose population is made up of an ethnic

Chinese majority as Yeoh and Kong note is 'an anachronistic place name'.[55] Nevertheless, it is this very anachronism that has allowed the space to be inscribed by various notions of 'Chineseness', which are continually 'reconstituted and transformed to shape state practices and to serve new purposes within the independent State'.[56] Following the state's attempt to clean up its streets according to the ordered principles of modernist rationalisation in the 1960s (through demolitions and repurposing of public spaces), and later in the 1980s to 'conserve' at least cosmetically what was left of the old colonial architecture, by the 1990s Chinatown was constituted by a mixed bag of architectural styles, economies (formal and informal) and cultural imaginaries. Yet like modernist projects elsewhere, this process of rationalisation remains incomplete. Pockets of resistance continue to exist, and Chinatown continues to evolve as a 'multicoded space inscribed with a multiplicity of meanings'.[57] The fate of the Majestic could be said to embody many of the contradictory forces within the cultural geography of the Chinatown area in Singapore (Figure 3.1).

The Majestic theatre was built as a Cantonese opera house in 1928 in the heart of Singapore's Chinatown district by the Chinese business tycoon and philanthropist Eu Tong Sen. Designed and constructed by

Figure 3.1 The Majestic theatre in Singapore, *c.* 1950s. Bels Collection, courtesy of the National Archives of Singapore

British colonial architectural firm Swan and Maclaren, the theatre combined a mix of Western art deco and traditional Chinese architectural styles. In 1938, it was rented by Shaw Organisation, at the time one of the largest production studios and exhibitors in the region,[58] to screen films. During the Japanese occupation of British-ruled Singapore during World War II, the Majestic screened Japanese propaganda films.[59] In 1956, the building was bought by Cathay Organisation, Shaw's rival in film production and exhibition at the time, and continued to run as a cinema until 1998 when it was closed and converted into a shopping mall in 2003. The refurbished mall retained the building's exterior facade but hollowed out the interior to accommodate a myriad of faceless shops, removing all of its distinctive interior architectural period features. These included the tiered cinema seating and a disused 1930s bar on the first floor, its art deco features still discernible beneath the dust and cobwebs when it was in use by the Singapore International Film Festival in the late 1990s, a haunting echo of a more glamorous past when the theatre was frequented by the great and the good in Chinese entertainment in the pre- and immediate postwar period. The mall itself failed as a commercial venture and closed in 2007, following which the building was sold on to be turned into a betting centre and then a cash converters, prompting locals to lament its decline.[60]

In fact, by the mid-1990s, the closure of the Majestic was already imminent, and as festival volunteers we were already acutely aware of its anachronistic status within a rapidly expanding exhibition culture of multiplexes, IMAX screens and sophisticated sound systems, not only in the downtown areas of Singapore but in the suburban new towns as well.[61] The Majestic was crumbling at the edges, and the irony of its name was palpable. It was one of the few standalone theatres left in the hyper-modern nation still housing a single screen projection and tiered stall and circle seating. On non-festival days (about 50 weeks of the year), the lady in the ticket booth still sold tickets printed on soft paper which she marked with a grease pencil – the kind that needed no sharpener as the lead was lengthened by pulling on the attached string and tearing off the encasing paper; another anachronism when all the multiplexes had already moved to computerised ticketing. The one middle-aged usher employed at the theatre met us enthusiastically each year – he never saw crowds as large as ours on normal days. The ageing plumbing systems meant that the toilets sometimes leaked. And on occasion, we received reports of rats scampering across the feet of unsuspecting patrons during screenings. Kenneth Chan's reading of Tsai Ming-liang's *Goodbye, Dragon Inn* (2003), set in a soon-to-be-closed theatre in Taiwan, resonates with the fate of the Majestic towards the end of its life as a film theatre:

> The Fu Ho Theatre represents a pre-video, pre-multiplex cinema, one that often occupies a single building, has a huge screen for Cinemascope movies, and has a large audience sitting capacity. As an instance of these 'grand ole dames of yore', the theatre offers a singular cinematic experience, where everyone gathers to enjoy one movie, simply because there is only one giant screen. The singularity of the filmic experience, of course, implies that there is a greater imagined sense of cultural and social connectivity in terms of the movie-going experience, vis-à-vis the diversity and multiplicity of cinematic choices in an era of the DVD and the multiplex.[62]

Indeed, the large audience capacity and single screen was one of the main reasons why the Majestic was in use during the festival. It was one of the few single hall theatres left in Singapore in the age of the shopping mall multiplex and its globalised, standardised product.[63]

The 'singularity of the filmic experience' is one that is increasingly relegated to the past; as Philip Cheah, the director and programmer for the festival at the time noted, 'Audiences are fragmenting'. During the annual festival season, this singular experience was reclaimed for a brief two weeks, and despite its ageing structure, the Majestic frequently played to full houses during the festival, even hosting Q&A events with filmmakers and other festival guests. People came to the theatre because the screening was a 'one-off' event. If they did sometimes complain about the state of the building, these occurrences were infrequent: surprising and unusual in a city known for its fastidiousness and obsession with cleanliness, both physical and moral. The rats even became a running joke amongst the regulars. Experiencing the festival at the Majestic in the mid-1990s evoked an affective sense of a lost past not just of place but also of time; borrowing from Kenneth Chan's reading of *Goodbye, Dragon Inn* once again:

Film festivals and cosmopolitan affect

> Of course, the actuality of the cinematic experience in these theatres is not commensurate with the nostalgic sense that one has, especially when one compares it to the digital-quality sound, pristine picture quality, and comfortable plush seating of the contemporary multiplex halls. While it is true that nostalgia imbues a past experience with a kind of retroactive glow and aura, I want to suggest that it also activates through a memory trace a powerful cultural significance, or 'structures of feeling' […], in an otherwise mundane everyday occurrence. In *Goodbye, Dragon Inn*, the notion of place evokes these memory traces or fragments.[64]

Watching new festival films in an old cinema like the Majestic brought together the desire for discovery with the nostalgia for an older mode of viewing and thus a different time. This nostalgia must also be taken in the context of a nation that remains on a relentless track of urban renewal, in spite of more recent attempts at 'heritage conservation'. The city-state is continually building and rebuilding itself, reconfiguring spaces, demolishing landmarks, altering roadways, to the extent that 'place identity' for individuals and communities is put under severe strain.[65]

However, issues of modernisation and nostalgia in Singapore are never just a matter of looking back with rose-tinted glasses or a benign fondness for days gone by. In a territory where the provision of space and place is closely tied up with the authoritarian control of the state, the search (if not the fight) for space – encompassing physical, creative and psychic spaces – is always political.[66] Artists and intellectuals in particular frequently seek out these spaces, all the while negotiating with state processes and policies of control.[67] The transmutation of the Majestic theatre into yet another faceless mall in a city of faceless malls and a betting centre with no acknowledgement of its cultural past encapsulates in microcosm the trauma brought on by such cultural violence that accompanies the state's unending lurch towards modernity. Yet it is a trauma that is largely unvoiced in the public domain.[68] Privately, family, friends and colleagues regularly express frustration and helplessness at this constant change, experienced as a kind of psychic, if not physical, dislocation. It is a sense of dislocation that may be contextualised within Laurent Berlant's notion of how to think of the present (in this case, an ever-shifting, destabilising present) 'as part of an unfolding historic moment [exemplifying] the affective experience not of a break or a traumatic present, but of crisis lived within ordinariness'.[69]

The Singapore International Film Festival was one of the few spaces through which alternative voices could be heard, though it was not a fully open space. Singapore's authoritarian, and some would say 'draconian',[70] state censorship laws have undergone several revisions in the past two decades, and the old 'screen / screen-with-cuts / or ban-outright' practice has evolved into a classification system.[71] However, it should be noted that even an R21 (Restricted 21) rating does not exempt a film from cuts. The Singapore International Film Festival had made it a matter of practice not to screen a film with cuts, and had on a number of occasions preferred to have the films withdrawn from its programme instead.[72] This included withdrawing Oshima Nagisa's 1976 film, *In the Realm of the Senses*, now deemed a classic, from the 2000 edition of the festival, when the censors insisted on cuts to the film even at a time when the R(A) (Restricted Artistic) rating was already in force. However, the censors have also on other occasions made a number of exceptions for the festival and allowed it a one-off screening of a film that would be restricted from commercial exhibitors. One example is Zhang Yuan's *East Palace, West Palace* (1996), released in the US as *Behind the Forbidden City*. It was a film noted to be the first from mainland China with explicitly male homosexual themes, and which was itself banned in China and had to be smuggled out of the country to the Cannes film festival. The film played at the 1997 Singapore International Film Festival to a full house at the Majestic theatre. Another example is Singapore filmmaker, Royston Tan's film, *15* (2003), set amidst 'real' youth gangs in Singapore, one of the reasons for which it was censured. Nevertheless, *15* was given special permission to be screened uncut at the Singapore International Film Festival in 2003, the film's international première, after a delayed deliberation by the censors. Having gained international press attention and festival accolade overseas, the film was later allowed a general release in Singapore under the R(A) rating only after the filmmaker agreed to make 27 cuts to the film amounting to about five minutes of footage.[73] It would be fair to say, albeit speculatively, that had the film not be shown and received positively at the Singapore International Film Festival and later abroad, it might not have received a general release in Singapore at all.

In offering rare and hard-won – cosmopolitan – space to a film like *15*, which exposes the underbelly of a city-state keen to maintain its shiny, prosperous exterior (the other, market-savvy version of cosmopolitanism), and in a country where foreign imports tend to be valued over home-grown products, the extent of the festival's cultural and political interventions and contributions to a Singapore national cinema and film culture should not be underrated. It is perhaps not entirely coincidental that the 'revival' of a Singapore cinema, following a period of post-independence decline, emerged in tandem with the birth of the Singapore International Film Festival as an organisation in 1987.[74]

Cultural literacy and cosmopolitan affect

In providing this space for art and alternative cinema in Singapore, the festival also succeeded in expanding the film education and cultural literacies of a generation of Singaporeans from the late 1980s to 2000s, especially in the period before the advent of the worldwide web and the flood of cheap DVDs, and in a period when VHS was prohibitively expensive.[75] For many of us, the film festival offered a cosmopolitan glimpse, not into 'the world' as such, but in fact many different worlds. Among these worlds were the Canadian independent cinema (as an alternative voice from North America); Icelandic films as discussed above (from tropical Singapore, remote Iceland seemed pretty exotic); Southeast Asian cinema from Malaysia, Thailand, Indonesia and beyond (and the chance to engage with our Southeast Asian neighbours we hardly knew[76]); and crucially to witness the birthing (or, as some would say, the revival) of a post-independence Singapore 'national cinema'. The opportunity to encounter different, especially non-European, auteurs was irresistible, as was the chance to see work by established and emerging talent alike from around the world (Mohsen Makhmalbaf, Abbas Kiarostami, Kim Ki-duk, Ousmane Sembene, Naomi Kawase, Hal Hartley, just to name a handful) as well as nearer home (Eric Khoo, Royston Tan, Tan Pin Pin, Yasmin Ahmad, Garin Nugroho, Apichatpong Weerasethakul, among others). The list is as eclectic as it is long.

However, exciting as these developments were, as Kirstie Jamieson notes, the 'festival gaze' can be a practised one, belonging to 'a leisured modality experienced in the company of strangers. It belongs to those comfortable and skilled in looking and being looked at in an urban environment where emotional distance and acceptance of "strangeness" communicate educated good manners [...] and the practiced art of looking'.[77] Again writing of the Edinburgh festival, Jamieson argues that those unaccustomed to the gaze and who may be 'excluded from the cultural values and economy of Edinburgh's festival culture are either rendered a feature of the spectacle or rendered invisible by the geographical and social boundaries of festival spaces'.[78] Here Jamieson refers specifically to the city's homeless community who are turfed out of the spaces where they normally gather as the city's streets are 're-claimed during the festival season by the authorities and re-configured as performance and market stall spaces'.[79] In her chapter on film festivals and the public sphere, Cindy Wong argues that: 'Film festivals evoke a place and position that is very close to the traditional bourgeois public sphere, given the middle-class status and locales in which they foster informed debates and discussions'.[80] Even as festivals promote a liberal agenda of inclusivity, they also 'clearly construct their own myths of film knowledge, modernity, and diversity', to the extent that 'the constructed hierarchy of the current film festival circuit also means that the top festivals, with their ability to endow distinctions in their specific film world, can be seen as analogous to the idealized liberal bourgeoisie public sphere that limits the voices of women and the lower classes or less powerful regions'.[81] Festivals are as much about selection, exclusivity and canon formation as they are about innovation, experimentation and alternative perspectives.

In this section, I consider not so much those who are excluded from the festival gaze, but rather who possess *alternate* festival gazes. They look upon the festival with different priorities and intentions to those whose social and cultural capital feed the festival circuit with regularity. Unlike the homeless people of Edinburgh in Jamieson's analysis, who have no choice but to share the space of the city with the festival, I refer to some people (in Singapore) who actively and purposefully *purchase tickets* for a film or films at the festival, but to whom the festival is not necessarily marketed or addressed. These include those who maybe stumble upon a venue and decide to drop in, or were perhaps recommended by a friend; as well as those who purchased tickets with intent but whose experience takes place beyond what Jamieson calls the 'social boundaries' of the festival gaze.[82] These participants, I argue, are equally constituent of the *cosmopolitan affect* of the festival, not just those partaking of its cultural samplings. I explore three personal encounters during my experience at the Singapore International Film Festival, each one offering a particularly visceral experience of the festival, and in my view a particularly affective mode of alternative engagement to the festival as a cosmopolitan space. When we speak of festivals as spaces of flow and as celebrations of difference, how do we speak of encounters which, if not to serve as disruptions to the business of the festival, certainly occur as spontaneous irruptions of dissonance within its established discourse. What is even more interesting is that these modes of alternative engagement can elicit similar affective responses to the event as those who participate 'properly' in it – responses ranging from curiosity, outrage, bewilderment and delight. What follows are three encounters selected for their vividness, both within my memory, and for how well they give form to what I am trying to articulate.

'What a wonderful film!'

In the same period that I was volunteering and freelancing at the Singapore International Film Festival, I was also teaching on an adult education degree programme held on weekday evenings. Many students on the programme were 'returners' to further education having missed their chances on leaving school for various reasons to do with individual circumstances. Many students came to the course (on art and the humanities) as mature individuals with 'life experiences' and social routines shaped by the demands of family and work. Many were parents, carers, managers, business owners and employees, and most were hard pressed for time and resources. Sharing with them the value of the arts and film festivals was altogether different from simply asking full-time undergraduates not long out of their teens to attend a few exhibitions and screenings. I am not suggesting that one group are more receptive learners than the other, merely that each group came to the subject with different priorities and social capital. I shared with these adult learners all that I outlined above: about the alternatives to Hollywood cinema, the importance of alternate voices and perspectives, and the pleasures of discovering something new. One former student, a female homemaker in her late thirties or early forties with two young children, had a particularly visceral experience of the festival, whose intensity rocked me out of what I can only now acknowledge as my bourgeois liberal complacency at the time.

On hearing about the Singapore International Film Festival from me, she chose to attend the film by Iranian filmmaker, Mohsen Makhmalbaf, known as *The Silence* (1998). The story is set in Tajikistan and follows the daily journey of a 10-year-old blind boy to his job as a tuner in a musical instrument shop. Along the way, the boy is constantly distracted by the music he hears from street musicians and other people's radios, and frequently turns up late for work, putting his job and family's livelihood in jeopardy. The day after the screening, I received a long, enthusiastic email from the student about the lyricism of the film and what a cultural revelation it had been to her. 'Fantastic,' I thought, feeling smugly pleased with my contribution to her cultural education. A week later, I received another email from the same student; this time very evidently distressed. She had been to a second film at the festival and enjoyed it very much but her two excursions had caused trouble at home. Her family (husband and in-laws) had taken issue with her uncharacteristic independence and unusual act of *going out alone at night* to see a film, and not just any film but a film at a *festival*, an event and a concept they did not understand. The tone of her email swung from the extremes of frustration to guilt: frustration at being misunderstood, and guilt at acting out of character and thus potentially being perceived as a bad wife and mother. This distress further caused her to question the value of the humanities education she had embarked on and whether she should stay on to complete the part-time degree programme.

At the time, I was completely taken aback by the force of the encounter. This was twentieth-century Singapore, and for all its conservative politics, any social or cultural resistance to women venturing out at night, alone or in groups, was rare. Women were an active part of the workforce whose contribution to consumer spending was considerable.[83] In addition, the city-state prided itself on its safe streets for all, even at night.[84] In my naiveté, I had of course taken my own social – and cosmopolitan – mobility and independence entirely for granted, not to mention the politics of women's leisure in Singapore.[85]

Film festivals and cosmopolitan affect

'How can you show a film like this?!'

In 1997, the Singapore International Film Festival screened a French-language film called *The Life of Jesus* (1997) at the Majestic theatre, the debut film of French filmmaker, Bruno Dumont. It is an angry film set in the north of France and centred on a group of socially marginalised youth there. In spite of, or perhaps because of, its unsentimental depiction of sex and an instance of sexual assault, the film would go on to win a number of international festival awards. When the screening in Singapore ended and the crowds poured out, I noticed that several of my colleagues were attempting to placate a small group of patrons. There was a great deal of shouting. It turned out that several people had purchased tickets to what they thought was a film about the life of *Jesus of Nazareth*. They were demanding refunds, but also questioning the festival's integrity for proffering what they saw as an intentional deception to lure in the religious market. There are many questions that could be asked of the irate, such as: why had they not read the blurb before purchasing the tickets, or why had they chosen to sit through nearly all of the film before protesting? What was the experience in the theatre even like, trying to make sense of what was unfolding on screen and attempting to reconcile it with the expectations one had brought to it? But in the face, and force, of anger, no rational questions could be posed, nor answers to be found. Nonetheless, it is the very irrationality of the encounter, the very rawness of mistranslation, the failure to explain, and the failure to comprehend – it is the whole messy mix that constitutes the affective cosmopolitanism of the moment.

'That film, very good!'

When Singapore introduced a film classification system for the first time in 1991, the authorities had not calculated beyond policing the morals of the young for other unintended social consequences. When the first R – Restricted – rating was introduced, it opened the floodgates to a sudden slew of arthouse erotica as well as exploitation films, many of which were from Hong Kong's Category III genre, a classification introduced in Hong Kong in 1988 restricting viewership to over 18 years of age. Because the R classification incorporated a wide range of films including the erotic comedy *Sex and Zen* (1991) and its sequels, as well as the arthouse *Happy Together* (1997) by Wong Kar-wai, the rating was modified a few months later to R(A), or Restricted (Artistic), in that only films deemed to be of 'artistic' value would be allowed to be screened. The R(A) rating ensured that while, for example, Anglo-European and Hong Kong arthouse cinema may be let through, other more salacious fare would be kept out. Who defined and what determined a film's 'artistry' largely depended on cultural gatekeeping mechanisms like overseas film festival selections and international prize winners, as well as 'OB markers' (out of bounds markers), a term widely used in political discourse in Singapore denoting the boundaries of what is deemed acceptable by the authorities. These markers are, however, only vaguely delineated and subject to interpretation.

Arbitrary as the '(Artistic)' qualifier might have been, the R(A) rating, a classification that would remain until 2004,[86] radically altered the film culture of Singapore, and the programming interventions of the Singapore International Film Festival. As former programmer Cheah notes: 'The rating system is important for us at the festival because prior to 1991 lots of films were cut and we had a very tough time. The filmmakers were naturally very upset and the distributors were reluctant to show their films in Singapore'.[87] Although, as noted above, this ratings system did not mean that no cuts were made to films, it certainly exposed Singapore audiences to more adult-themed films, including a wide range of world cinemas, and enabled Singapore-made films to explore more mature themes as well, such as Eric Khoo's debut film, *Mee Pok Man* (1995), which gestures towards necrophilia.

The initial influx of softporn exploitation films in 1991, many of which were shown in Chinatown theatres, although shortlived, also created a largely undocumented, and unacknowledged, audience category – that of middle-aged, working-class and less-educated men who were anecdotally seen and believed to attend R(A) films for their sexual titillation, rather than their artistic merits. Although the R(A) rating covered other mature themes like violence, these patrons seemed to know which films offered the most frequent and explicit (usually heterosexual) sex scenes. Several of these 'R(A) men', as they became almost affectionately known amongst festival volunteers, would be recognised as regulars who came back year on year for multiple screenings at a time. One particular regular would even shake our hands at the end of the screening, thanking us approvingly with 'Good film! Good film!' One year, faced with the perennial challenge of fund-raising for the festival, a colleague jokingly welcomed the 'R(A) Man' singularly as 'Patron of the Arts'. The anonymity of this demographic did not however render them invisible, if unacknowledged. They tended to dress unfashionably, sometimes in cotton vests and flip flops, in the kind of attire Singapore residents would have associated with going to local markets, not with 'downtown' urban activities like going to a film festival. They often came to screenings with crinkly plastic food bags and sometimes shouted out loud during screenings, disrupting the unspoken etiquette of the shared space. Indeed, their whole body language set them apart from the rest of the middle-brow festival crowd. These individuals would also be unlikely to have access to internet pornography; the official ban on pornography aside, exclusion from internet access in an extensively networked city further marks their social exclusion.

So, who are these men? What are their backgrounds? Why are they mainly men? How are they drawn to the festival? What criteria govern their choices? Do they refer to the catalogue or any of the press reviews? What do they know of the films? How do they choose the 'right' ones? Do they discriminate between language films? Do they rely on the English subtitles? In Singapore, despite English being the official language of government and commerce, competency and literacy in the language are by no means uniform across the population, and the exclusive use of English subtitles in 'foreign films' in Singapore invariably restricts their access to certain groups.[88] If I had been trained as an anthropologist, I might have thought to conduct an ethnography at the time, but as Singapore's rapacious rebuilding programme would have it, with the recent closing of the Yangtze cinema,[89] another musty Chinatown theatre known for its softcore programming, the phenomenon of 'the R(A) man', if not quite relegated to the past, has certainly lost one of its last affective spaces.[90]

Concluding remarks

In considering the space of the festival as a cosmopolitan space, where cultures meet and collide, it is also worth considering those who are displaced from, ironically, the normativity of difference. However, as these individuals also *participate* in the festival through the act of purchasing tickets, they are not so much displaced by the institutional structures of the festival as compel us to rethink the norms of participation and the politics of inclusivity inscribed onto these festival spaces. As Mica Nava writes, 'The cosmopolitan habitus, it must be noted, does not consist only of feelings and practices of inclusivity; it is also the breeding ground of loss, humiliation and rebellion. These darker moods are also part of the historical picture'.[91] Applied uncritically, the idealism of cosmopolitanism may well exude Lauren Berlant's 'cruel optimism', which 'names a relation of attachment to compromised conditions of possibility whose realization is discovered either to be *im*possible, sheer fantasy, or *too* possible, and toxic'.[92] However, cosmopolitan spaces are far from harmonious – they can be chaotic and extemporaneous, and often it is the encounter with their very contradictions that produces their most visceral, and thus compelling, affect. As Seigworth and Gregg put it, 'Affect marks a body's belonging to a world of encounters or; a world's belonging to a body of encounters but also, in *non-belonging*, through all those far sadder (de)compositions of mutual in-compossibilities'.[93] The world of the film festival and the city that hosts it can be said to be one such body, a body constituted by a miscellany of strange(r) encounters.

4

Embodiment as (cosmopolitan) encounter

Throughout this book, I have argued that cosmopolitanism is not to be found necessarily in the content of the films, but rather read through the dynamics of film form and context. As a socio-cultural formation in and of the world, the experience of cinema occurs in places with dimensions of materiality and temporality, that is, in places like cinema halls, shopping malls, film festivals, crumbling old opera houses, and of course in our own homes and on our personal smartphones and other digital devices as well. Inhabiting and interacting with these spaces are bodies – of spectators, ushers, volunteers, popcorn sellers, passers-by. So far, I have discussed the affective encounter as a cultural and experiential one, as a quality of experience. However, as Seigworth and Gregg further note, the notion of affect bears a direct relation to the materiality of the *body* – a body that can, they argue, have the 'capacity to affect and to be affected'.[1] Even as we consider the liminality of the cinematic experience, it should not be forgotten that there is also the presence of a physical body responding in physiological ways – in anger, delight, frustration, curiosity, even incredulity (perhaps when a rat scampers across one's feet in the theatre) – not to mention also the bodies on the screen. In her work on phenomenology and the cinema, Vivian Sobchack theorises 'the meaningful relationship between cinema and our sensate bodies', and wonders what we 'as contemporary theorists, [are] to do with such tactile, kinetic, redolent, resonant, and sometimes even tasteful descriptions of the film experience?'. She calls for a reconsideration of 'cinema's sensual address', 'the carnal sensuality of the film experience and what – and how – it constitutes meaning'. Such bodily experiences make us 'cinesthetic subjects' (merging 'cinematic' with 'synaesthetic'),[2] in ways that can challenge the dominance of visuality in film culture.

In this chapter, I explore an aspect of such 'cinesthesia' by drawing on the affective nature of the cosmopolitan encounter within the context of film work exhibited in art galleries, rather than in conventional cinemas. The gallery film offers particular scope for what I see as affective encounters between bodies – the bodies of the films, of the performers, and of the roving spectators interacting on the body of the exhibition space as well. I read gallery films here not as what cinema might be in the 'post-moviegoing age'[3] but how in looking at the cinema in this form, outside of the theatre, enables us to rethink our (bodily) relationship to the cinema and the encounters it proffers. I explore the work of Singapore-born, Berlin-based performance artist, Ming Wong, who specialises in re-enacting and re-configuring iconic filmic scenes and images as a way of rethinking cinema's place in cultural history.

Gallery bodies and films

Writing on cinema only occasionally takes into account the medium's relationship to the other arts, such as the theatre and visual art, even as these art forms are increasingly mobilising screen media in their work. Although these screen media forms in theatre and visual art are not conventionally thought of as 'cinema' per se, it is worth noting that the medium itself has never remained static. Long before the digital age, cinema has continually negotiated with the proliferation of technological formulations, alternative distribution pathways and experimental exhibition platforms. The advent of VHS in the 1980s not only impacted on theatrical film exhibition but also the way films were first, and then repeatedly, experienced. Far from accelerating the imminent 'death' of cinema, the rise of home video offered some films at least 'an indefinitely extended shelf life'.[4] This development also changed the way the post-1980s generation first encountered the cinema, that is, on video cassette in their homes. Home video profoundly changed what Richard Allen calls 'the character of the experience of cinema'.[5] Allen recalls his own daughter's first encounters with the cinema as a child and how she had employed

> a range of engagement strategies, including but not limited to: rapt, attentive viewing; successive obsessive attachments to one particular film and/or one particular scene in that film; distracted viewing; sleeping; humming, singing or speaking along with the film's soundtrack; acting out scenes from the film; dressing up like characters in the film; attempting to dress up others in the same room as characters in the film; performing scenes from the film; playing computer games based upon the film; playing with plush toy simulacra of characters in the film; eating breakfast cereal simulacra of characters in the film; wearing pyjamas depicting characters from the film; drawing characters from the film; manipulating the remote control to zip through disturbing or boring scenes, songs or dialogue sequences; replaying the same scene, song or dialogue sequence multiple times; increasing the volume in conjunction with replaying the same scene; pausing display of the film; making narrative, causal and moral queries and commentary regarding the film to whomever happened to be in the same room.[6]

Allen's list is long but worth quoting in its entirety for its comprehensiveness, and for its likely familiarity to the friends, family and acquaintances of a generation who 'understands cinema as a textually disintegrated phenomenon experienced through multiple and unpredictably proliferating sites and modalities'.[7] The age of the DVD and online streaming platforms have further proliferated and fragmented those modalities. In this environment, Allen suggests that theatrical exhibition may be increasingly relegated to the past, to the realm of memory. He writes, 'As theatrical moviegoing becomes a thing more remembered than experienced, we will be reminded that one of the most striking features of the experience of cinema for a hundred years was its sociality'.[8] What or where is cinema in this multi-modal environment? What forms of cultural encounter emerge from these modalities, and how can the notion of a cosmopolitan cinema help us understand it?

Gallery films are not traditional objects of study within the discipline of film studies, except perhaps as experimental cinema.[9] Nonetheless, some of the most thought-provoking new ideas about film form and how we engage with it have emerged from such untraditional studies. These include Laura Marks' influential introduction of a 'haptic visuality, or a visuality that functions like the sense of touch'.[10] Following from phenomenology, Marks explores the haptic as the embodiment of a quality of experience in a form of cinema she calls 'intercultural'. The haptic for Marks is born out of 'a lack of faith in the visual archive's ability to represent cultural memory', and so it is the haptic that lends a tangible articulation to intercultural works that 'begin from the inability to speak, to represent objectively one's own culture, history, and memory; they are marked by silence, absence, and hesitation'.[11] Marsha Meskimmon makes the cosmopolitan case for contemporary art by arguing not for 'bland representational forms of interpretation' but for 'concepts of affect and figuration that posit art's agency'.[12] For Meskimmon, artworks can find political efficacy when they 'offer spaces to us that may be taken up imaginatively', and allow us to 'dwell at the threshold of response-ability and responsibility', a threshold that is also 'a figuration, a conceptual structure capable of connecting a range of critical interrogations of subjectivity, location and power'.[13]

The added difference of gallery films to mainstream theatrical screenings is not just the experimental nature of the films' content but also their modes of exhibition and reception. Gallery films are sometimes projected on the white walls of the contemporary gallery space, or set apart in a darkened room (usually with seating for no more than five people). On some occasions, gallery films may play on multiple screens simultaneously, sometimes projected onto the wall space, or at other times on stand-alone screens. In addition, gallery films are likely to have to compete for the viewer's attention (and time) with other exhibits in the shared space. This fragmentary mode of reception can compel us to perceive the films, not just as flickers of light on a silver screen, but also as 'sculptural objects that invite our movement around and about them'.[14] While the syntax of the language of cinema has enabled us to engage with off-screen spaces (through framing, editing, sound and so on), the off-screen and off-frame space in the gallery is often also affectively present as a space that encourages, and almost insists upon, the mobility of the spectator. In a gallery, one is not usually seated and only faced by a frontally flat screen, but must walk around, in front of, and sometimes even behind it. Often one is required to walk round other spectators too. Gallery films in small black box auditoria may indeed be utilising the frontally flat screen in the conventional sense. However, by virtue of being located in a larger (white) gallery space alongside other artforms and artefacts vying for attention, and being played in a loop, these films cannot guarantee the uniformity of spectatorial experience. Spectators come and go at different times of day, and arrive and leave at different points in the film. They also stay for different durations of time, and in most modern galleries nearly every spectator will have to emerge from the dark space and have their experience of the film 'disturbed by [the] exit into the light of the white cube'.[15]

These mobile, fragmentary, and indeed momentary, modes of reception alter the customary conception of the cinematic spectator both as an individualised subject (assumed to be lost in their own world within the darkened space of the theatre) and as a member of a collective, a group of spectators constituting an 'audience'. The immersion offered by a gallery film is of another sort. Writing of Maya Deren's *Meshes of the Afternoon* (1943), Fowler describes her own experience of immersion as one where 'it is possible to lose one's sense of causality, of meaning being made in succession and of the end being the finish'.[16] Gallery films, she adds, 'need to be read from within film theory, in terms of what they offer both in-frame – a play with framing, mise-en-scene, and editing – and out-of-frame – a connection to the space outside the frame that forces us to read in a more involved, embodied way'.[17] By being compelled to move around the gallery space, spectators are also required to contend with the presence of other bodies, other strangers, who occupy and use the same space. The rest of this chapter reads the artistic production of Ming Wong and his cultural experiments with embodiment within the frame of Sara Ahmed's notion of 'embodied others', where '[a] concern with strange encounters involves a concern with the dialogic production of different bodies and texts', of which there is always an ethical dimension'.[18]

Embodiment and encounter

Ming Wong's artistic career spans about a decade and a half, although his work came to public attention largely in 2009 when his installation, *Life of Imitation*, commissioned by the National Arts Council for the Singapore Pavilion, garnered a Special Jury Mention Award for 'Expanding Worlds' at the 53rd Venice Biennale. The work yokes together Douglas Sirk's *Imitation of Life* (1959) and Wong Kar-wai's *In the Mood for Love* (2000) by running simultaneous re-creations of each film alongside the other. Reinventing Sirk's 1950s melodrama, in which a mixed race young woman rejects her black mother and attempts to pass for white in American society, Ming Wong re-casts the characters from Sirk's film within his own *Life of Imitation* (Figure 4.1). In the latter, 'three male actors from three ethnic groups in Singapore (Chinese, Malay and Indian) take turns playing the black mother and her mixed-race daughter, with the identity of each actor changing after each shoot'.[19] Angie Baecker reflects on the vividness of the sequence:

> in this iteration, the scene is a video installation by Ming Wong, recasting Sarah Jane and Annie with male actors from Singapore's three main ethnic groups: Chinese, Malay, and Indian, making praxis of the country's ubiquitous CMIO (Chinese, Malay, Indian, and Others) categorization system. With each shot, the actors rotate roles, further destabilizing the racial binaries otherwise ascribed to them. The men are all too old to pass for Sarah Jane and too young to pass for Annie. Dressed in cheap wigs and ill-fitting cocktail dresses, the effect is both visually preposterous and mesmerizing, sustained in equal parts by the melodrama of the original and the complete dissonance of the new.[20]

Figure 4.1 *Life of Imitation.* Courtesy of Ming Wong

Likewise, re-enacting the scene in *In the Mood for Love* where Mrs Chan (played by Maggie Cheung) rehearses a confrontation with her philandering husband, stood in for by Mr Chow (played by Tony Leung Chiu-wai), Ming Wong's *In Love for the Mood* re-casts Caucasian actors to play both roles. Meta-film meets meta-film as 'Ming Wong's interpretation is a rehearsal of this rehearsal scene, and we watch the actress as she grapples with the intricacies of speaking Cantonese. Aided by the artist's off-screen prompts, the actress' progressive attempts at the script are shown separately across three screens, with her mistakes and apologies remaining in the final work.'[21] In these works, it is the incongruity and imperfect performances (rather than performances of imperfection?) that are the key conceit. Wong's curator and collaborator, Tang Fu Kuen, refers to this practice as 'disruptive role-playing'.[22] According to Tang, Wong '[miscasts] actors of different ethnic backgrounds, including himself. Imperfect mimicry allows for a critical recognition of difference and ambivalence. In Ming Wong's world of parroting, the sly and tragicomic performances of speech and gesture expose cultural mis-translations and connections at the same time'.[23] What these miscastings also expose are the performative praxes inherent in any identity formation, refracted through Wong's own position as a Singaporean working within and outside of its political and cultural spheres. In Wong's own words, 'I do what I do because of where I come from'.[24]

Although *Life of Imitation* did not see Wong cast himself in any of the roles, its performances of 'imperfect mimicry' draw on a mode he has explored time and time again throughout his career. His primary medium of practice is the video installation, which he employs in tandem with other media, such as posters, paintings and other installation objects. What these videos work with is not just the filmed content they depict but also the surrounding environment of the exhibition space and the films' relationship to the placement of other objects, offering as Fowler puts it, 'a connection to the space outside the frame'.[25] The cosmopolitanism of these works lies in the dynamic encounters of the filmed content and their contextual engagements.

Wong's video work largely centres on casting himself within the re-creations and re-enactments of iconic sequences from well-known films, ranging from Ingmar Bergman's *Persona* (1966) to Luchino Visconti's

Death In Venice (1971) to Roman Polanski's *Chinatown* (1974). However, these are neither re-makes nor re-productions, but rather a kind of 'ersatz cinema'.[26] Because Wong can never successfully pass for Liv Ullman or Jack Nicholson (or indeed Faye Dunaway, in spite of a blonde wig and dark glasses), or rather never really tries to, each performance foregrounds the very incongruity of the performer's presence in the text. The following analysis draws from Wong's *Chinatown* series, a re-performance of Polanski's disturbing neo-noir feature, which has travelled from Los Angeles to Toronto to Liverpool and Manchester, and adapting on each occasion to the specific locale.

In Polanski's film, 'Chinatown' is constructed as a murky, mysterious space, nestled in the dark underbelly of sunny Los Angeles. It is a space where any attempt to delve into its dubious morals, motivations and manoeuvres is repeatedly fobbed off with, or perhaps produced by, the cryptic utterance of 'it's Chinatown' by various characters: 'C'mon, Jake – it's Chinatown', or 'Forget it, Jake. It's Chinatown'. That the films uses 'Chinatown' as a cipher socially, culturally and metaphorically is not being disputed: William Galperin praises the formal complexities of the film that enable it to operate as a 'disruptive or deconstructed presence', whose 'emphasis consequently is not on China or the Chinese per se (both of which are subjected to the usual stereotyping), but on China-"town," on the alien order that has infiltrated our own, challenging our idealized conceptions'.[27] Yet, that 'the usual stereotyping' of the Chinese figures in the film is summarily dismissed in favour of the film's admired sophistication in manipulating the terms of representation is particularly *troubling* (though not necessarily 'troublesome' as cited below). Galperin proceeds to analyse the 'bad for glass' sequence in some detail. 'Bad for glass' is the pidgin phrase Evelyn Mulwray's (played by Faye Dunaway) nameless Chinese servant uses when he is talking about the *grass*. This instance of mis-translation is inscribed into the dominant (white, patriarchal) narrative of the film as a pivotal moment, crucial to the plot and its denouement:

> [Gittes, played by Jack Nicholson] is met at the door by Khan, a Chinese servant, ushered through a room where another Chinese domestic is cleaning and then onto a veranda where yet a third Chinese, the gardener, is working rather frantically. When we first see him – when he is first the subject of the

shot – the gardener is peering into a pool which at the moment is still and reflective. [...] As for the object the gardener sees but does not retrieve, it is essentially forgotten. Thus, it is not important that the object turns out to be crucial to the film's denouement or that its retrieval, necessarily deferred, is a metaphor as well for the ensuing action between Dunaway and Nicholson.[28]

'Glass' as pidgin for 'grass' has now been transferred (in the psychoanalytic sense) onto something that is actually made of glass: the object the gardener sees in the grass is a pair of broken bifocals. This transference is then further read as an exemplar of a kind Derridean *différance*: 'Content not just to represent representation (the "film" reflected in the pool), Polanski must deconstruct it by disrupting the mimetic plane that the central action imposes on "something" (a pair of broken bifocals as it turns out) for which the gardener reaches'.[29] In this reading, the shadowy Chinese figure has performed his function: he has advanced a crucial plot point and, job done, this Chinese gardener disappears, serving no more than a trace of 'a signpost to otherness, to the presence or "background" we would mystify into absence'.[30] If otherness is mystified in a film about Chinatown, it is because it has been so constructed, as post-1980s post-colonial thinking shaped by scholars such as Edward Said and Gayatri Spivak has uncovered, among others. What is interesting for me in this analysis is the *form* that this mystification has taken – as silence, as absence and crucially as (stereotypically) *Chinese*. Imagine black or Latino figures in place of these Chinese wraiths and the politics of representation are instantly reconfigured. Writing of the Black Arts movement in Britain of the 1980s, where for a time the term 'black' politically encompassed non-white identities, even 'Chinese', susan pui san lok notes how this form of political alignment can render Chinese identities even more invisible ('Asian' in the British context largely refers to 'South Asian'): 'If black can be Asian, but Asian is not always Asian, Chinese – among others – does a disappearing act. As the third largest minority in Britain, Chinese has often been positioned as the "unspoken and invisible other" of black as well as white aesthetic discourses'.[31] In other words, 'otherness' is not all othered in the same way.

If 'Chinatown' is thus a kind of formless space, then it is into the very formlessness of this space that Ming Wong makes his own – very formal – intervention. Initially commissioned for REDCAT (Roy and Edna Disney / CalArts Theater), the California Institute of the Arts' 'downtown center for contemporary arts' in Los Angeles, Wong's *Making Chinatown* (2012) casts the artist himself in all the principal roles played by Jack Nicholson, Faye Dunaway, John Huston and Belinda Palmer, and 'key scenes are reenacted in front of printed backdrops that are digitally rendered from film stills and kept intact within the video installation'.[32] Wong's performative intervention immediately throws up what Krishtalka notes as the 'troublesome' gender and racial politics of the film, which I have preferred to deem 'troubling'. Citing the post-coital sequence where Wong casts himself both as Jake Gittes and Evelyn Mulwray (and thus Nicholson and Dunaway respectively), Krishtalka notes its dissonance:

> There's something profoundly strange in hearing the pillow talk between two Asian men – the same Asian man, one in drag as a femme fatale, one in drag as a hyper-masculine sleazy gumshoe – talk about the orientalist dangers and mysteries of the mythically debauched Chinatown, or re-tell an awful joke about how a 'Chinaman' fucks.[33]

Wong's re-enactments are not aimed at raising the visibility of the incidental characters, like the Chinese servants, but rather in boldly inserting a Chinese / Asian body into the roles played by Caucasian actors, Wong activates a kind of 'reverse yellowfacing'. In blatantly failing (or refusing) to pass, Wong's gesture both mirrors the clumsiness of yellowface in Hollywood while forcing us to confront the radical politics of their subversion. Yellowface during Hollywood's studio era, Robert Ito notes, had never aspired towards cultural authenticity, citing, amongst other examples, Luise Rainer's 'heroin chic' appearance in *The Good Earth* (1937) and Shirley MacLaine's dolling up for *My Geisha* (1962). Ito grumbles that, 'The actors don't look Asian at all, but exactly what they are: white actors wearing a weird combination of eyepieces, rubber bands, and makeup'.[34] However, as Yiman Wang argues, it is precisely the validation of yellowface (however ill-construed) as a performance that contributes to its persistence: 'when a white actor acts in yellowface or blackface, he or she is taken as a skillful performer of someone apparently not him- or herself, hence the impossibility of conflating the actor with the role of the racial Other'.[35]

Wang identifies this form of masquerade as 'screen passing' which she distinguishes from 'conventional racial passing': 'Contrary to conventional racial passing, which hinges on erasing all traces of performance and disguise, screen passing in the form of yellowface or blackface masquerade highlights the white actor or actress behind the racially marked screen persona'.[36] Screen passing, she argues, involves acting, or even over-acting, certain racialised roles.[37] Within mainstream Anglo-American casting practice, Wang notes that the racial and ethnic identities of non-white actors are often taken as mimesis, indexing 'a homogenous Orient', rather than judged for their performative abilities or strategies.[38]

By refusing the indexicality of racial performance, ironically by overplaying the incongruity of his casting in white roles, Ming Wong plays a wry game of visual and cultural translation with the audience here, that also operates as a kind of 'haunting by history', a phrase used by B. Ruby Rich to describe the work when it was exhibited at the Toronto International Film Festival. Rich called it 'a sort of séance for Hollywood ghosts'.[39] The echo of this haunting, this cross-cultural historical encounter, is what stops Wong's performances, both straight-facedly sincere yet slyly self-reflexive, just at the edge of burlesque. As Krishtalka puts it, Wong's performances 'though stilted, are nevertheless genuine, straight-faced; no sly winks or mockery of any kind. It's just as much a dedicated homage as it is a deconstruction'.[40] History is chastised inasmuch as it is also, paradoxically, celebrated. Yet the thoughtfulness these encounters provoke are not so much cop-outs as signalling the inherent ambivalence we all have to face up to when re-reading texts in and out of their contexts.

Cosmopolitan geographies

As argued above, Wong's re-performances of iconic roles are not attempts at authentic recreations. In fact, many of them are awkward, dissonant and even decidedly *fake*. Nonetheless, it is a fakeness that seeks authentication, not from the acts of performance themselves, but from *where* they take place.[41] In an obverse view to the work being 'haunted by history' as discussed above, one could also read the encounter as that of the haunting precisely being authenticated by history. The work is not haunted by history because it travels, but rather history authenticates the haunted nature of the work precisely *because* it travels, and with each incarnation striking a similar yet different affect of the occasion and the place of encounter. Here, context is not only social, political, historical and theoretical, but also *geographical*.

So while 'Chinatown' in Polanski's film may function narratively as a cipher, its efficacy as a cipher is derived from the psycho-socio-cultural histories and geographies of Chinatowns in various cities across Europe and North America. Kay Anderson rightly notes that 'Chinatown' is not simply a descriptive nomenclature of an ethnic enclave, but 'a social construction with a cultural history and a tradition of imagery and institutional practice that has given it a cognitive and material reality in and for the West'.[42] In other words, 'Chinatown' is not created by Chinese inasmuch as it is created by the gaze of the dominant white community on the Chinese. In taking his filmed performances and installations from Los Angeles (the setting of Polanski's *Chinatown*) to Toronto, and later San Francisco, Liverpool and Manchester, the works speak to the political geographies of Chinatowns in these locations both on the levels of macro-, as well as micro-, histories.

In an interview Wong speaks of his continued fascination with Chinatown as a concept following his exhibition in Los Angeles: 'I could not forget Chinatown, and in the subsequent months after "Making Chinatown", I delved into research into the history of the Chinatowns in Los Angeles and San Francisco'.[43] San Francisco's Chinatown was formed in tandem with the influx of large numbers of Chinese immigrants in the 1850s following the 1849 gold rush, while in the case of Liverpool,[44] many Chinese were employed as seamen on the Blue Funnel Shipping Line, and later set up laundries and takeaways in the city. The social discrimination and institutional racism that contributed to the formation of these ethnic enclaves, while similar in terms of a broader grand narrative, also differed with the specificities of local histories. In San Francisco, Chinese immigrants were subject to the Chinese Exclusion Act (1882–1943) in US law which restricted the naturalisation of Chinese workers and prevented them from bringing over their families from China. Severe restrictions on female immigration and punitive anti-miscegenation laws preventing interracial marriage resulted in Chinatowns turning into bachelor societies.

This research led to the discovery of Liverpool's Chinatown history. In 2012, Wong staged his follow-up work, *After Chinatown*, for the Liverpool Biennial (Figure 4.2), as a response to the stories of forced separations of

Embodiment as (cosmopolitan) encounter

Figure 4.2 *After Chinatown*. Courtesy of Ming Wong

Chinese seamen from their families, as well as to the comic orientalism and casual racism of 'yellow peril' representations of Chineseness in pulp fiction and cinema like Sax Rohmer's Dr Fu Manchu and many classic noir films, such as Orson Welles' *The Lady From Shanghai* (1947). In Liverpool, thousands of Chinese seamen, some married to English women, and many of whom served on British ships during World War II, were forcibly 'repatriated' between 1946 and 1947. Many disappeared without warning and the civil war in China at the time made communication all but impossible. The trauma inflicted upon the families left behind in Liverpool, many of whom believed for decades that they had been abandoned by their fathers and husbands, only surfaced in the public consciousness in 2002.[45] The unveiling of this forgotten history has since led to a search by the surviving families for their lost histories, and small gestures have been made to commemorate this history in the form of a plaque and public art. Wong's work in Liverpool, via his re-formulation of Polanski's *Chinatown*, speaks directly to the silences and forgotten memories of Liverpool's Chinese histories.

However, the exhibition of *After Chinatown* at the Liverpool Biennial did not simply transport the original *Making Chinatown* from San Francisco to a geographical location. Alongside Wong's re-performances of Polanski's *Chinatown*, there are new videos depicting Wong walking through the streets of Los Angeles, San Francisco and Hong Kong dressed in a trenchcoat, fedora, a blonde wig and sunglasses, as well as a pair of novelty plastic eye glasses with 'slit eye' inserts. As if to prove these racist novelty toys were not something he made up, attached to the gallery wall opposite the screen was a packet containing these glasses labelled, 'Chop Suey Specs: Fool Your Friends with this Oriental Disguise!'[46] A number of different stereotypes and cultural tropes are called into play all at once, including that of the nameless (Chinese) *femme fatale* character played by Brigitte Lin Ching-hsia in Hong Kong auteur Wong Kar-wai's *Chungking Express*. Dressed in a blonde wig, trenchcoat and dark glasses, Lin's character in *Chungking Express* is herself a nod towards the noir genre. Inscribed on the body of this wandering figure, this *flâneur / flâneuse* played by Wong is a kind of racial queering of the Chinese body as it is re-inserted into familiar historical and filmic locales, and a kind of obverse 'yellow yellowface' performance as conceptualised by Yiman Wang in her analysis of Anna May Wong's performative strategy as a Chinese actress working in a racially discriminatory Hollywood of the 1920s and 1930s. Wang analyses the camp excesses of the actress' roles in the perennial 'lotus flower' or 'dragon lady' stereotypes as a conscious or instinctive strategy which 'denaturalized the category of the Asian by mimicking and highlighting the process of producing stereotypical Asian images'.[47] In other words, Anna May Wong, already stereotyped as an oriental female figure in Hollywood, overplayed the stereotype in order to reclaim the racial politics in her favour. Wang reads the self-reflexivity in Anna May Wong's performances as self-conscious acts of self-irony: 'Understood as camp, [Anna May] Wong's yellow yellowface impersonation of the Chinese prostitute, and multiple other racialized roles, was fundamentally opposed to the mimetic assumption of Wong's "authentic" Chineseness'.[48] Wang acknowledges that this self-conscious self-performance had largely gone unread during Anna May Wong's tenure as an actress,[49] and it was a mode of performance that was, in its time, 'short-circuited due to the lack of an appropriate audience'.[50]

Read abstractly and a-historically, Ming Wong's often exaggerated performance of cultural mistranslations could be construed as merely comic, a kind of extravagant gesture towards performance as playfulness, towards comic incongruity as a subversion of identity politics. However, read in the context of yellow yellowfacing (the issues of which remain prescient) and in the context of Norman Denzin's idea of 'performance ethnography',[51] Wong's work begins to take on an affective resonance that speaks simultaneously to personal, national and cultural histories. An 'autoethnographer-performer', according to Denzin, is one who 'insert[s] their experiences into the performances that they study'.[52] Yet autoethnographic performances are not re-enactments of individual lives as such, but situate themselves as 'text-as-event [within] a complex system of discourse where traditional and avant-garde meanings – of the real, the hyperreal, mimesis and transgression, audiences, performances, performance video and performance art pedagogy – all circulate and inform one another'.[53] Russell Storer describes Wong's 'shape-shifting' efforts in the context of his personal history, in the context of Wong having grown up in multicultural Singapore in which difference has been consciously and conspicuously 'systematised': 'There is a continual need for re-evaluation, renegotiation and reinterpretation. Wong's video works propose new contexts for thinking about where we are in the world and how we relate to our surroundings; and remind us that every time we speak to another, we are creating something new, even if we are not quite sure what it means'.[54] Navigating these intersecting paths is the figure of Wong's *flâneur*.

The *flâneur* as a literary conceit has been imbued since the eighteenth century with a high degree of self-awareness and theatricality, a 'gentleman walker' who oscillates between dandy and critical observer. Writing of *flâneurie* in Hong Kong film, Tsung-yi Huang sums up Walter Benjamin's depiction of the *flâneur*: 'While deriving voyeuristic pleasure from observing the crowd, he also experiences a sense of loss in the crowd. Seeing the crowd as inferior to him the *flâneur* can never completely identify himself as one of them. On the other hand, since the *flâneur* cannot resist the fascinating spectacle the crowd presents, he is never a total outsider'.[55] Ming Wong's *flâneur* makes a number of symbolic journeys: the journeys of the first immigrants to these enclaves, the journeys of the characters in films, as well as the journeys of the films themselves across time and place. Wong speaks of the production of his film: 'It was shot over the summer on location in Los Angeles, San Francisco and Hong Kong, so in a way I was retracing the journeys made by the early Chinese immigrants'.[56]

An implicit journey could also be said to be made through Singapore's Chinatown, a Chinese enclave created by British colonialism amidst a country where over 70 per cent of the population are ethnic Chinese (see Chapter 3). Singapore's Chinatown may be an anachronism but it thrives precisely because it functions both as a place of ethnic identification and dislocation at the same time, the cultural dissonances of which could not be lost on the artist who himself hails from the republic.

Significantly for Wong this perpetual search for identity is consistently played out in contexts *other* to Singapore, and other to himself. The return of *Life of Imitation* to be 'restaged' at the Singapore Art Museum (SAM) in 2010 'with a new design and additional works'[57] thus had a flavour of a homecoming, in which the presence of the artist's work in a particular space allowed once again multiple historical trajectories to cross and re-cross on the site of, and the encounter with, the exhibition. As with his other works, traces of authenticity and inauthenticity to rub up against, blend into and bounce off each other. I offer here a snapshot of some of these trajectories.

In the first instance, there is the physical structure of the Singapore Art Museum itself. Located on the site of the historic St Joseph's Institution, a former boys' school founded as a missionary establishment by the La Salle Brothers in 1852, the appropriation of the colonial structure serves as a reminder of Singapore's consistent national and cultural narratives of perpetual renewal.[58] Within this structure, the new design of the exhibition consisted of re-purposing three galleries within the museum into three small cinemas, 'recreating the atmosphere of peephole cinemas'.[59] The foyer, meanwhile, 'was transformed into a cinema hall filled with old seats and billboards painted in the 1950s style by the last surviving billboard painter, Neo Choon [sic] Teck' (Figure 4.3).[60] Secondly, the presence of Neo Chon Teck's hand-painted billboards within the installation evokes the sense of a lost past and inevitable change that is a constant present in Singapore's self narrative. In harking back to an earlier time in cinema history before multiplexes and digital printing, the billboards reference the time of early modernity when movie-going seemed more like a collective social activity and movie- and poster-making still evoked, in the spirit of Benjamin, an aura of *craftsmanship*. Thirdly, this sense of personal intimacy with the work is echoed further by the reference to the peephole

Embodiment as (cosmopolitan) encounter

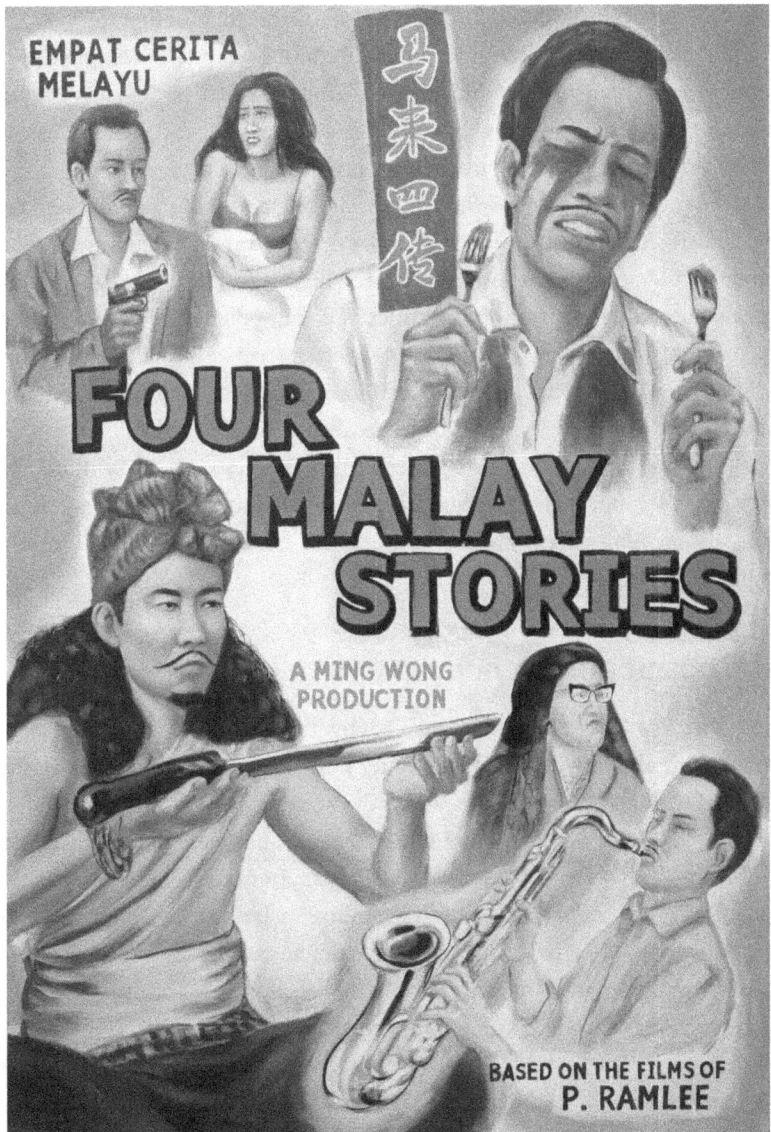

Figure 4.3 Billboard of *Four Malay Stories*. Courtesy of Ming Wong

cinema, and all its intimations of voyeurism and salaciousness. Fourthly, within the re-purposed space of the museum that was once a school, was included a gallery with perhaps the least obtrusive exhibit of the series,

Filem-Filem-Filem (2008–10), a showcase of instant photographs of old standalone cinema buildings in Singapore and Malaysia. These 'architectures of entertainment', Wong's curator Tang Fu Kuen writes, serve as an 'ode to the last remaining cinema buildings [...] once beautiful but now forgotten "dream palaces" built by the early film entrepreneurs'.[61]

Geography, I contend, is central to thinking about cosmopolitan practice in art and film – *where* cosmopolitan encounters occur impacts on how they occur, in what form and with whom. For Jeff Popke, geography speaks directly to debates on the ethics of cosmopolitanism because it can be brought to bear on what he calls different 'registers': of 'urban space, migration and hospitality, and postcolonial studies'.[62] Cosmopolitan art and cinema yokes together history, memory, and geography, in ways that can feel quite visceral. As Sara Ahmed puts it, 'bodies materialise in a complex set of temporal and spatial relations to other bodies, including bodies that are recognised as familiar, familial and friendly, and those that are considered strange'.[63]

The cosmopolitan body

The cosmopolitan encounter enabled by the cinema could be said to require a body on which that encounter may take place. It could be on the body of the text (as we have explored through processes of translation) or the medium (as we have explored by looking at animated films); or it could be on the body of the character, especially that of the female body (as we have explored through the analyses of films such as *Lust, Caution* and *24 City*); or it could be on the bodies of participants, spectators and workers (as we have explored through the festival encounter); and the bodies of performers (as we have explored for much of this chapter).

Vivian Sobchack writes of the importance of a reconsideration of the 'somatic effects' of cinema and a return to a phenomenological understanding of the cinema. She argues that cinema is 'somatically intelligible' and posits 'the film viewer's lived body as a carnal "third term" that chiasmatically mediates vision and language, experience and image'.[64] Cinema, according to Sobchack, is a bodily, physiological, sensuous and *carnal* encounter, an experience too complex and nuanced to be simply denigrated to pornographic and horror films. We are what she calls 'cinesthetic subjects' (blending notions of cinema and synaesthesia), who both touch and are 'touched by the screen, able to commute seeing to touching and back again *without a thought* and through sensual and cross-modal activity able to experience the movie as both here and there rather than clearly locating the site of that cinematic experience as "on-screen" or "off-screen".'[65] In other words, the cinesthetic subject, by taking into account the totality of the bodily experience, is freed from the hegemony of vision[66] that has so long dominated the study of film.

But this body, I argue, cannot just be *any* body. Bodies – whether of migrants, workers or performers – come with their own histories, contexts and frailties. The most effective cosmopolitan performances are ones that *know themselves*, in the sense of knowing the limits of translation. In contrast to film adaptations and remakes, Wong's re-enactments repeatedly reiterate their failure to pass for authentic. They are, it could be said, mere *imitations*: to be acknowledged as imitation is to acknowledge the failure to *pass*, but also to concede the effort to do so. Liora Moriel writes that 'passing in film affords us an examination of ways in which the knowledge that passing is possible affects those who are invested in the fixedness of the frontiers of their own identity of origin – the tension between the desire for fixed frontiers and the fear that frontiers are fluid, porous and blurred'.[67] Passing is therefore not the same as representing. Wong's efforts at re-performance are not representations of identity but conscious presentations of their fracture.

I turn in my final analysis to the inclusion of Wong's earlier work *Four Malay Stories* (2005) within the larger *Life of Imitation* exhibition in Venice and in Singapore. It consists of a four-channel video installation which sees Wong repeatedly inhabiting, performing and re-enacting several scenes from films by P. Ramlee, once again playing both the male and female roles. Ramlee was an iconic filmmaker whose career spanned the end of the colonial period in British Malaya to the early years of independence both for the Federation of Malaysia and the Republic of Singapore, and in paying homage to him, Wong is acknowledging a longer cinematic history of Singapore before independence and a cultural history of the territory beyond the life of the modern city-state.

The four P. Ramlee films referenced in Wong's installation are *Semerah Padi* (1956); *Ibu Mertua Ku / My Mother-in-Law* (1962); *Labu dan Labi*

(1962); and *Doktor Rushdi* (1970). The first three films were produced by Malay Film Productions, and the fourth by Merdeka Film Productions, and the citing of these two production houses makes direct reference to these national and cultural histories. Malay Film Productions was the Malay-language production unit of Shaw Brothers studios, a film production empire that dominated Chinese-language filmmaking between the 1950s and 1960s, extending from colonial Hong Kong to Singapore in Southeast Asia. Between 1947 and 1967, what is now known as the 'golden age' of Malay cinema, Shaw's Malay Film Productions made over 150 films, and at least 60 of these films were helmed by P. Ramlee. Malay Film Productions was located in what was colonial Singapore (and thus part of British Malaya), and its success put Singapore at the centre of the Malay film world at the time. In 1957, the Federation of Malaya achieved independence from British colonial rule and was reconstituted as the Federation of Malaysia in 1963, comprising Peninsular Malaysia, Singapore, Sabah (then North Borneo) and Sarawak. In 1965, Singapore was expelled from the federation and became a republic. These two key events are central to modern Singapore's national formation and self-conception, where they are simply referred to locally as 'merger' and 'separation'.

Following Singapore's independence from Malaysia in 1965, the Shaw Brothers closed their Malay production unit in Singapore in 1967 and moved Malay-language film production to their facility in Kuala Lumpur, the capital of Malaysia, and took P. Ramlee with them. In Kuala Lumpur, Merdeka Films never achieved the success of its predecessor in Singapore and Malay-language cinema was never to recover the heights of its golden age again. The reasons for this decline are manifold, including the advent of black-and-white television and colour films from Indonesia, Hong Kong and Hollywood. In the 1960s, the Ramlee films were still in black-and-white. However, while other film markets recovered from similar challenges of television and colour films by innovating, the political and social unrest in the region at this time made innovation and investment difficult. In Singapore, the period between merger and separation is historically noted to have been afflicted by 'race riots' between the Malay and the Chinese populations. In addition, Indonesia, one of Shaw's largest markets for Malay-language films, clashed with Malaysia during a period of violent conflict between 1963 and 1966, known as *Konfrontasi*, where Indonesia's

Sukarno government objected to the inclusion of Sarawak and North Borneo (Sabah) within the new Malaysian federation. Today, Indonesia controls about 70 per cent of Borneo island (historically the Dutch East Indies, now known as Kalimantan). It is these two key political events in the history of the region that would exert a profound impact on Malay-language film production in Singapore in particular, but also on the industry as a whole.

This history, albeit exceedingly condensed, is important here because the fourth Ramlee film, *Doktor Rushdi*, in Wong's tetralogy, *Four Malay Stories*, was made by Merdeka Film Productions, the studio in Kuala Lumpur to which Shaw had relocated their Malay film production unit. Together with the separation of national histories between Malaysia and Singapore, there followed the separation of national film histories. After 1965, 'Malay films' were no longer associated with Singapore's cultural and film histories, and P. Ramlee was brought into the fold of Malaysian national film history,[68] even though most of his best-loved films were made in Singapore.[69] Narratives of Singapore's film history tend to focus on contemporary Singapore cinema's 'revival' in the 1990s, when a number of English and Chinese language films came to be produced after the long hiatus.[70] Baecker notes that when Ming Wong inserts himself into 'sixteen different [male and female] Malay characters from films by popular postwar Malay entertainer P. Ramlee', local audiences are being invited 'to suspend their disbelief and accept an ethnic Chinese in a host of Malay roles';[71] I would add that beyond the suspension of disbelief, local audiences are being challenged to suspend their *social conditioning* reinforced by public policy and education to accept racial classifications based on oversimplified, essentialist criteria. The racial queering of the roles can only be funny to an audience conditioned into accepting that Chinese people cannot be expected to speak or understand Malay, much less be interested in Malay films. This is reinforced today in Singapore when programmes on the state-run dedicated Malay television channel are not subtitled in English (the lingua franca), while the programmes on the Chinese channel are. Like the Caucasian actress in *In Love for the Mood* who had to learn her Cantonese lines by heart, Wong had to learn the Malay dialogue for *Four Malay Stories* by rote; he says, 'I had to repeat each line in Malay over and over again, which I captured on camera, until I got it almost perfect, before moving on the next line or shot. I can't speak Malay fluently, but I can suprise [sic] my Malay friends by quoting from the movies they hold so dearly to their hearts'.[72] The performances are 'almost perfect', but not quite, and each repetition constitutes a valiant grasp at a cultural authenticity that is nonetheless elusive. In film history, the body that fails to pass is often the subject of melodrama – Sirk's *Imitation of Life* is a case in point. Here, the politics of passing intersects with the politics of representation when the failure to pass exposes the utter failure of representation as a heuristic force.

As Storer notes, while 'Wong acknowledges the historical fact that his hometown was the cultural centre of the Malay world during the 1950s. […] As a Chinese Singaporean, however, Wong's claim on these stories is a little less secure'.[73] To an extent, it could be argued that this form of performance, as enactment, embodiment and ultimately misappropriation, is itself an emblem of a cosmopolitan project – at once (re-) constructed yet authentic in its desire for authentication, expressing universal aspirations of self-understanding and local preoccupations through visceral bodily encounters; a life authenticated by, it could be said, its multiple imitations.

Postscript

Critical cosmopolitanism and comparative cinema

The challenge of cosmopolitanism, as I have put forward throughout this book, is not so much to theorise difference as it is to posit the problem of universality. I posit that the celebration of the ability to cross borders must be attended by the acknowledgement of the *conditions* of difference and their resultant transformations across each translative border. This includes or incorporates any resistances and obstructions to the process. Gerard Delanty's delineation of a 'critical cosmopolitanism' offers a useful way of avoiding the trap of universalism when thinking about cosmopolitanism – especially when we would not all want to be 'cosmopolitan' in the same way. For Delanty, a critical cosmopolitanism is one that is not only 'post-universal' but also capable of 'self-problematization and [...] reflexive and critical self-understanding'.[1] He places this understanding of cosmopolitanism in dialogue with the 'tendency within modernity towards self-problematization', what he calls the 'dimensions of critical cosmopolitanism',[2] which ultimately involves some form of 'internal transformation of social and cultural phenomena through self-problematization and pluralization [...] through the interplay of self, other and world'.[3] Unlike multiculturalism, where the goal lay in 'the management of cultural diversity within established structures',[4] the cosmopolitan process according to Delanty is also a 'learning process' involving 'an internal cognitive transformation', which invariably impacts upon external social, political and cultural conceptions of the world.[5] In (my) idiomatic terms, a critical cosmopolitanism may be framed as: *learning to live with paradox*.

However, embedded within the cosmopolitanism that prides itself on being open to encounters is an ethical dimension that cannot be left out of the conversation. It is entirely possible to live with paradox (by promising one thing and doing another, for example), but without the ethical struggle, living with paradox amounts to deception, whether of self or others. The operative word within Delanty's conception and mine is the emphasis on *learning* – learning to live with the paradoxes of cosmopolitanism is to grapple with the process of making ethical choices in the encounter with difference, to test the limits of one's knowledge, familiarity and tolerance, and to be prepared to confront them. Marsha Meskimmon, writing of contemporary art and the cosmopolitan imagination, asks: 'what are the ethical and political implications of be(long)ing at home everywhere, of a "cosmopolitan imagination" that is premised upon an embodied, embedded, generous and affective form of subjectivity in conversation with others in and through difference?'[6]

This imaginary dimension to cosmopolitanism finds germane expression in the cinema with its capacity for 'plastic realism'.[7] Delanty writes that 'the cosmopolitan imagination occurs when and wherever new relations between self, other and world develop in moments of openness'.[8] Meskimmon further asserts that the 'cosmopolitan imagination' is something 'fully sensory'[9] –Nava's 'visceral cosmopolitanism' may be brought to bear here – through which '[u]nderstanding ourselves as wholly embedded within the world, we can imagine people and things beyond our immediate experiences and develop our ability to respond to very different spaces, meanings and others'.[10] Although Meskimmon writes of the role of contemporary art in fostering the cosmopolitan imagination, her argument can be readily extended to the cinema, at least to the cinema I have been exploring thus far, which provides us with the cultural space to engage with liminality and limited knowledge. Meskimmon further calls for a critical mode of engagement that she terms 'affirmative criticality', a mode of praxis designed not 'solely to analyse and interpret things as they are or have been (present, past); [but] to engage actively with the constitution of the future and proposing the future is, by necessity, speculative and contingent'.[11] This is the aspirational dimension of cosmopolitanism, which by virtue of its futurism can only at this moment engage the imagination.

Nevertheless Lauren Berlant's 'cruel optimism' warns against the paradoxical condition of the desire for *something* (for example, 'the good life'), which in effect contributes to the opposite of what it is one desires, and questions the ethics of institutional structures and practices that sustain and support such an impasse:

> Cruel optimism is, then, like all phrases, a *deictic*, a phrase that points to a proximate location: as an analytic lever it is an incitement to inhabit and to track the affective attachment to what we call 'the good life,' which is for so many a bad life that wears out the subjects who nonetheless, and at the same time, find their conditions of possibility within it. My assumption is that the conditions of ordinary life in the contemporary world even of relative wealth, as in the United States, are conditions of the attrition or the wearing out of the subject, and that the irony that the labor of reproducing life in the contemporary world is also the activity of being worn out by it has specific implications for thinking about the ordinariness of suffering, the violence of normativity and the 'technologies of patience' or lag that enable a concept of the later to suspend questions of the cruelty of the now.[12]

A way to reconcile Meskimmon's affirmative criticality and Berlant's cruel optimism is to accept that both contradictory positions exist in tension within cosmopolitanism. Cosmopolitanism as I have argued emerges from a process of questioning and a condition of relationality, rather than constituting an end-goal of utopian understanding. If cosmopolitanism is to have value in cultural debates, being able to articulate its capacity for self-critique and ethical reflection is important, and thus attractive to cultural critics seeking a more nuanced alternative to multiculturalism and diversity in cultural discourse.

For instance, Robert Spencer argues for a cosmopolitan criticism as an approach to post-colonial literature, which takes into account the present forces of globalisation and 'more expansive forms of citizenship and community', insofar as they 'incite a desire for cosmopolitanism at the same time as they arouse indignation at the way in which the structures and attitudes of the present frustrate cosmopolitanism's realisation'.[13] Similarly Meskimmon affirms the 'inter-subjective political agency' of art and texts,[14] as well as the active engagement of the reader, who 'complete the thought, undertake a passage, [and] become part of a transitive economy'.[15] Neither author is advocating the kind of cultural sampling that popularly characterises cosmopolitanism in the cultural marketplace; each stresses instead a form of critical engagement that is prepared to challenge structures of knowledge and epistemic frameworks. Meskimmon refers to the process as a 'figure of passage', invoking the notion of travel, movement and encounter that have come to signal a kind of cosmopolitan disposition:

> I want to suggest that the figure of passage can participate in the project to reconceive world citizenship beyond either a multicultural fantasy of 'cosmopolitans', whose open-mindedness simply transcends material differences between themselves and others, or the bleak prognosis of the world as an inevitably iniquitous sphere, populated by monadic individuals designed to consume or destroy others. The trope of passage suggests a critical exploration of world citizenship that is both material and yet mutable, operating at the level of the subject (figuring an intersectional subject of circulation) and at the level of practice (figuring global belonging).[16]

Spencer's understanding of cosmopolitanism as 'a system of trans-national relationships embodied in structures and institutions',[17] not merely in textual representations, grounds this movement of passage in the social, economic and political worlds, and prevents it from dissolving into ephemera, into the nebulousness of belonging everywhere and nowhere.

How can cinema contribute to this conversation? As an industrialised cultural form, cinema bears both the capacity for imagination and the force of institutions, as well as their critique. It both travels and offers the experience of travel. It requires and desires translation and sometimes fails in the quest for understanding. Cosmopolitanism may sometimes gesture towards globalism, but global cinema is not necessarily cosmopolitan. Sean Cubitt equates what he calls the 'cosmopolitan film' with global, commercial cinema: 'some films that have tried to win a global audience, and which, in the process, have had to invent as a special effect an address to the audience that might constitute it as global'.[18] Cubitt, who cites Ang Lee's

Postscript: Critical cosmopolitanism and comparative cinema

Crouching Tiger, Hidden Dragon (2000) as an example of a cosmopolitan film, argues that in the cultural and economic regime of global commercial cinema, the global audience becomes 'dimensionless',[19] subsumed by the power of consumption that these films exact:

> The cosmopolitan cinematic object is no longer the world, or a world, but the audience. It attains autonomy from human interests by assimilating rather than rejecting them. It opens itself to all interests, to the universality of interests, not least by picking from every tradition what can be picked, addressing itself to that entirely abstract object, the universal audience: not people, but the addresses of cinema in their universality.[20]

While Cubitt takes on the universalism in cosmopolitanism, he does not really explore the ethical dilemmas cosmopolitanism prompts, ethical dilemmas that are raised precisely by when local specificities come into tension with the 'universal'. In spite of its global success, the apparent universality of a film like *Crouching Tiger, Hidden Dragon*, as I have argued elsewhere, was not initially taken for granted, but the result of a number of strategic cultural and economic interventions which do not in themselves automatically ease over the challenges of cultural translation.[21] The cosmopolitan challenge for such broad-reaching cinemas, especially those dealing with historical material, is precisely that negotiation between 'local' histories and memories – where the 'local' could be constituted either geographically or culturally – and the address of those not party to such 'local' knowledge and literacies.

I have explored a range of examples where local knowledge and limited literacies have been brought into contention with institutional structures of production, distribution and exhibition. I have explored multilingual and self-reflexive cinema through both their desire to articulate and to translate history, culture and identity, as well as their inability to do so. I have also explored the pull of cultural memory, the affective spaces of the film festival, and the embodiment of these. What threads through each chapter is not just the awareness that there is no such thing as full passage when it comes to cultural access and literacy, but also what the lack of access and understanding can tell us about cinema's place in the history and geography of a territory.

To address the critical cosmopolitanism of cinema, one would have to address its comparative dimension, not just between films, genres or whole national cinemas, but between the *address* of films and a wider (social, historical, political, economic) perspective from which to make sense of it. In his conception of a 'comparative film studies', Paul Willemen argues for a mode of engagement with the medium in a way that takes into account 'the common experience but divergent histories of the development of a capitalist mode of production and the impact of its reformatting dynamics on social, including cultural, relations'.[22] He writes: 'What *is* unstable is then not the compromise between local material and foreign form, but between local material and the transformative power and impact of industrialization itself, which is never simply "foreign"'.[23] What is being compared then is not 'cultures' as such – in the sense that a 'Chinese' film may approach a subject differently from a 'Japanese' one, which in turn is different from an 'American' one – but 'to sort out which of those local industrialized forms related to the encounter with capitalism *by* and *within* the local formation'.[24] These competing forces, Willemen argues, may be traced via the text's mode of address, in order to 'show how the representational aspects of a text may be conditioned by their non-representational aspects, and how regimes of address orchestrate (energize and regulate) the dynamics at work in the textual fabrics'.[25]

The comparative framework is thus a relational one that also, crucially, takes into account its own comparative position in relation to the work, and especially by being aware of the boundaries of one's own disciplinary discourse. Meaghan Morris rues the difficulty of overcoming 'disciplinary borders [...] as conceptual barriers': 'Too often, we simply do not know enough to discuss cinema historically in a transnational register, even on a regional scale – as distinct from talking with cultural compatriots "about" transnational cinema'.[26] As I have argued in my analyses, the cosmopolitan nature of cinema can emphasise rather than diminish the feeling that we can never 'know enough', as Morris puts it. Perhaps another way of perceiving the situation is to construct the state of 'not knowing enough' as a position of productive inquiry, where the critic is not just partially blind, partially deaf, and perhaps even partially inarticulate, but also conscious of and secure with being so. To this degree, it may be possible to argue that the comparative perspective *is* a cosmopolitan position, one for which multiple positionalities not merely uncover the gaps in prevailing structures of knowledge, but also offer possibilities for how those structures themselves might be, eventually, transformed.

Notes

Foreword

1. Timothy Brennan, *At Home in the World: Cosmopolitanism Now* (Cambridge, MA: Harvard University Press, 1997).
2. Paul Gilroy, *After Empire: Melancholia or Convivial Culture?* (London: Routledge, 2004).
3. I am writing this foreword in the context of a recent referendum decision in the UK to leave the European Union (EU). The so-called Brexit campaign relied heavily on an anti-immigration platform, on xenophobic language and on a nostalgic fantasy of reclaiming Britain for the British. The catastrophic failure of Western European countries to respond appropriately to the refugee crisis, in part stemming from the war in Syria, forms one of many geo-political landscapes informing the current situation. There are thus multiple reasons to return to cosmopolitan aspirations in the current context.
4. For example: see Marsha Meskimmon, *Contemporary Art and the Cosmopolitan Imagination* (Abingdon, Oxon: Routledge, 2011); Bertolt Schoene, *The Cosmopolitan Novel* (Edinburgh: Edinburgh University Press, 2009); and Robert Spencer, *Cosmopolitan Criticism and Postcolonial Literature* (Basingstoke: Palgrave Macmillan, 2011).
5. See, for example, Dimitris Eleftheriotis, *Cinematic Journeys: Film and Movement* (Edinburgh: Edinburgh University Press, 2010), and Stephan K. Schindler and Lutz Koepnick (eds), *The Cosmopolitan Screen: German Cinema and the Global Imaginary, 1945 to the Present* (Ann Arbor, MI: University of Michigan Press, 2007).
6. Jacques Derrida, *On Cosmopolitanism and Forgiveness* [1997] (London: Routledge, 2001).
7. Zygmunt Bauman, *Modernity and Ambivalence* (Cambridge: Polity Press, 1991).
8. See Chapter 1, p. 24.
9. Giuliana Bruno, *Street Walking on a Ruined Map: Cultural Theory and the City Films of Elvira Notari* (Princeton, NJ: Princeton University Press, 1993).
10. There is now an extensive literature on trauma and memory. See for example: Cathy Caruth (ed.), *Trauma: Explorations in Memory* (Baltimore, MD: John Hopkins University Press, 1990); E. Ann Kaplan and Ban Wang (eds), *Trauma and Cinema: Cross-Cultural Explorations* (Hong Kong: Hong

Kong University Press, 2004); Susannah Radstone and Bill Schwarz (eds), *Memory: Histories, Theories, Debates* (New York: Fordham University Press, 2010).
11. Kaplan and Wang (eds), *Trauma and Cinema*.
12. Vivian Sobchack, 'What my fingers knew, the cinesthetic subject, or vision in the flesh', *Senses of Cinema* 5 (2000). Available at sensesofcinema.com/2000/conference-special-effects-special-affects/fingers/ (accessed 31 October 2014); Laura U. Marks, *The Skin of the Film: Intercultural Cinema, Embodiment, and the Senses* (Durham, NC: Duke University Press, 2000).
13. Mica Nava, *Visceral Cosmopolitanism: Gender, Culture and the Normalisation of Difference* (Oxford: Berg, 2007).
14. See Mary Ann Doane, *Femmes Fatales: Feminism, Film Theory, Psychoanalysis* (London: Routledge, 1991).
15. See Homi Bhabha, *The Location of Culture* (London: Routledge, 1994).

Introduction: Cosmopolitanism and the cinema

1. David Miller, 'Cosmopolitanism', in Garrett Wallace Brown and David Held (eds), *The Cosmopolitanism Reader* (Cambridge: Polity Press, 2010), p. 391.
2. Pheng Cheah, 'The cosmopolitical – today', in Pheng Cheah and Bruce Robbins (eds), *Cosmopolitics: Thinking and Feeling Beyond the Nation* (Minneapolis, MN: University of Minnesota Press, 1998), p. 36.
3. Robert Spencer, *Cosmopolitan Criticism and Postcolonial Literature* (Basingstoke: Palgrave Macmillan, 2011), p. 4.
4. Ibid., p. 13.
5. Ibid., p. 12.
6. Arjun Appadurai, 'Cosmopolitanism from below: some ethical lessons from the slums of Mumbai'. *JWTC: Johannesburg Workshop in Theory and Criticism* 4 (2011). Available at jwtc.org.za/volume_4/arjun_appadurai.htm (accessed 18 June 2014).
7. Gyan Prakash, 'Whose cosmopolitanism? Multiple, globally enmeshed and subaltern', in Nina Glick Schiller and Andrew Irving (eds), *Whose Cosmopolitanism?: Critical Perspectives, Relationalities and Discontents* (New York: Berghahn, 2015), p. 27.
8. Ibid., p. 28.
9. Nina Glick Schiller and Andrew Irving, 'Introduction: what's in a word? What's in a question?', in Nina Glick Schiller and Andrew Irving (eds), *Whose Cosmopolitanism?: Critical Perspectives, Relationalities and Discontents* (New York: Berghahn, 2015), p. 3.
10. Jackie Stacey, 'Hollywood memories', in Annette Kuhn and Jackie Stacey (eds), *Screen Histories: A Screen Reader* (Oxford: Clarendon Press, 1999), p. 39.

11. Poshek Fu, *Between Shanghai and Hong Kong: The Politics of Chinese Cinemas* (Stanford, CA: Stanford University Press, 2003), p. xi.
12. Laura Mulvey, *Death 24x a Second: Stillness and the Moving Image* (London: Reaktion Books, 2006), p. 34.
13. Galin Tihanov, 'Narratives of exile: cosmopolitanism beyond the liberal imagination', in Nina Glick Schiller and Andrew Irving (eds), *Whose Cosmopolitanism?: Critical Perspectives, Relationalities and Discontents* (New York: Berghahn, 2015), p. 141.
14. Ibid., pp. 141–2.
15. Ibid., pp. 152, 154.
16. Ibid., p. 155.
17. Ibid., p. 155.
18. Ibid., p. 141.
19. Dimitris Eleftheriotis, *Cinematic Journeys: Film and Movement* (Edinburgh: Edinburgh University Press, 2010), p. 76.
20. See Rosalind Galt and Karl Schoonover (eds), *Global Art Cinema: New Theories and Histories* (Oxford: Oxford University Press, 2010).
21. Zygmunt Bauman, *Modernity and Ambivalence* (Cambridge: Polity Press, 1991), p. 55.
22. Eleftheriotis, *Cinematic Journeys*, p. 179.
23. See Stephanie Dennison and Song Hwee Lim (eds), *Remapping World Cinema: Identity, Culture and Politics in Film* (London: Wallflower, 2006); and Lúcia Nagib, Chris Perriam and Rajinder Dudrah (eds), *Theorizing World Cinema* (London: I.B.Tauris, 2012).
24. Naoki Sakai, 'Translation', *Theory, Culture & Society*, 23.2–3 (2006), p. 73.
25. Agnieszka Szarkowska, 'The power of film translation', *Translation Journal* 9.2 (2005). Available at translationjournal.net/journal/32film.htm (accessed 29 April 2013).
26. Michael Phillips, 'Turns out Godard's worldview includes a llama', *Chicago Tribune* (10 June 2011). Available at articles.chicagotribune.com/2011-06-10/entertainment/ct-mov-0610-film-socialisme-20110610_1_godard-llama-film-socialisme (accessed 17 May 2013).
27. Walter Benjamin, 'The translator's task' (*'Die Aufgabe des Übersetzers'*), trans. Steven Rendall, *TTR* 10.2 (1997), p. 154.
28. Ibid., p. 152.
29. Ibid., p. 157.
30. 'Titanica' special issue of the journal, *Interdisciplinary Literary Studies* 5.1 (2003).
31. Tim Bergfelder and Sarah Street (eds), *The Titanic in Myth and Memory: Representations in Visual and Literary Culture* (London: I.B.Tauris, 2004).

32. Pamela McClintock, 'Box office report: Titanic 3D jumps $200 mil in only 12 days', *The Hollywood Reporter* (16 April 2012). Available at www.hollywoodreporter.com/news/titanic-box-office-james-cameron-312497 (accessed 18 June 2014).
33. Paul Willemen, 'Indexicality, fantasy and the digital', *Inter-Asia Cultural Studies* 14.1 (2013), pp. 110–35.
34. See Edna Lim, 'Displacing Titanic: history, spectacle and Hollywood', *Interdisciplinary Literary Studies* 5.1 (2003), pp. 45–69.
35. Nikos Papastergiadis, *Cosmopolitanism and Culture* (Cambridge: Polity Press, 2012), p. 11.
36. Ibid., pp. 11–12.
37. Ibid., p. 12.
38. Nelson Goodman, *Ways of Worldmaking* (Hassocks: Harvester Press, 1978), p. 7.
39. Pheng Cheah, 'What is a world? On world literature as world-making activity', *Daedalus* 137.3 (2008), p. 27.
40. Ibid., p. 28.
41. Ibid., p. 30.
42. Ibid., p. 35.
43. Ibid., p. 35.
44. Miriam Bratu Hansen, 'The mass production of the senses: classical cinema as vernacular modernism', *Modernism/Modernity* 6.2 (1999), p. 63. Critique of David Bordwell, Janet Staiger and Kristin Thompson, *The Classical Hollywood Cinema: Film Style & Mode of Production to 1960* (New York: Columbia University Press, 1985).
45. Edward W. Said, *The World, the Text and the Critic* [1983] (London: Vintage, 1991), p. 34.
46. Ricciotto Canudo, 'The birth of the sixth art (1911)', in Paul Willemen and Jim Pines (eds), *The Essential Framework: Classic Film and TV Essays* (London: EpiGraph, 1998), pp. 14–22. The citation references Canudo's 1911 essay 'The birth of the sixth art' where he lays out his arguments for the cinema. He later revised his list to include dance, making cinema the seventh art.
47. Murray Pomerance, 'Introduction', in Murray Pomerance (ed.), *Cinema and Modernity* (New Brunswick, NJ: Rutgers University Press, 2006), pp. 11–12.
48. Ibid., p. 12.
49. Ibid., pp. 12–13.
50. See www.uis.unesco.org/Culture/Pages/movie-statistics.aspx (accessed 30 June 2013).
51. Aida A. Hozic, *Hollyworld: Space, Power, and Fantasy in the American Economy* (New York: Cornell University Press, 2001).

52. Ramon Lobato, *Shadow Economies of Cinema: Mapping Informal Film Distribution* (London: British Film Institute, 2012).
53. Said, *The World, the Text and the Critic*, p. 53.
54. Nadine Chan Su-Lin, 'Cosmopolitan cinema: towards a new trajectory in cosmopolitan theory', unpublished dissertation submitted for the degree of Master of Arts, Department of English Language and Literature, National University of Singapore (2009).
55. Rey Chow, *Not Like a Native Speaker: On Languaging as a Postcolonial Experience* (New York: Columbia University Press, 2014), p. 37.
56. Mica Nava, *Visceral Cosmopolitanism: Gender, Culture and the Normalisation of Difference* (Oxford: Berg, 2007), p. 3.
57. Mica Nava, 'Cosmopolitan modernity: everyday imaginaries and the register of difference', *Theory, Culture & Society* 19.1–2 (2002), p. 90.

1 The cosmopolitan challenge of multilingual cinema

1. See Bhikhu Parekh, *Rethinking Multiculturalism: Cultural Diversity and Political Theory* (Cambridge, MA: Harvard University Press, 2002).
2. Jackie Stacey, 'The violence of idealizations and the ambivalence of self', in Nina Glick Schiller and Andrew Irving (eds), *Whose Cosmopolitanism?: Critical Perspectives, Relationalities and Discontents* (New York: Berghahn, 2015), p. 35.
3. Ibid., p. 35.
4. David Chandler, 'The cosmopolitan paradox: response to Robbins', *Radical Philosophy* 118 (2003), p. 25.
5. Bruce Robbins, 'Comparative cosmopolitanism', *Social Text* 31–2 (1992), p. 183. Emphasis mine.
6. Larry Rohter, 'Can you say "do it again" in Norwegian?', *The New York Times* (12 April 2013). Available at www.nytimes.com/2013/04/14/movies/two-versions-of-kon-tiki-in-two-different-lanugages.html (accessed 30 June 2014).
7. See Donald Crafton, *The Talkies: American Cinema's Transition to Sound, 1926–31* (Berkeley, CA: University of California Press, 1999).
8. Ella Sho[c]hat and Robert Stam, 'The cinema after Babel: language, difference, power', *Screen* 26.3–4 (1985), p. 46.
9. See also Marijke de Valck, *Film Festivals: From European Geopolitics to Global Cinephilia* (Amsterdam: Amsterdam University Press, 2007), p. 24.
10. Joseph L. Andersen and Donald Richie, *The Japanese Film: Art and Industry*, expanded edition (Princeton, NJ: Princeton University Press, 1982), pp. 21–34; Yingjin Zhang, *Chinese National Cinema* (New York: Routledge, 2004), pp. 14–17.

11. Laikwan Pang, 'Walking into and out of the spectacle: China's earliest film scene', *Screen* 47.1 (2006), p. 77.
12. Ibid., p. 77.
13. Ibid., p. 77.
14. Ibid., p. 77.
15. Andersen and Richie, *The Japanese Film*, pp. 439–44.
16. Hideaki Fujiki, 'Benshi as stars: the irony of the popularity and respectability of voice performers in Japanese cinema', *Cinema Journal* 45.2 (2006), p. 71.
17. Ibid., p. 71.
18. Hamid Naficy describes a similar practice of simultaneous interpretation, where '[s]ince these intermediaries had to translate the intertitles, the subtitles, or the foreign language dialog in real time, they often resorted to colorful Persian phrases and expressions, thereby indigenizing and enriching the film experience', in Hamid Naficy, 'Theorizing "third-world" film spectatorship', *Wide Angle* 18.4 (1996), p. 12.
19. Andersen and Richie, *The Japanese Film*, pp. 339–441.
20. Ibid., p. 441.
21. Fujiki, 'Benshi as stars', p. 74.
22. Ibid., p. 74.
23. Ibid., p. 76.
24. Ibid., pp. 79–80.
25. Junko Ogihara, 'The exhibition of films for Japanese Americans in Los Angeles during the silent film era', *Film History* 4.2 (1990), p. 3.
26. Ibid., p. 85.
27. Ibid., p. 86.
28. Pierre Bourdieu, *Language and Symbolic Power* (1982), edited and introduced by John B. Thompson, trans. Gino Raymond and Matthew Adamson (Cambridge: Polity Press, 1991), p. 45.
29. Luise von Flotow, 'When Hollywood speaks "international French": the sociopolitics of dubbing for Francophone Québec', *Québec Studies* 50 (2010), p. 27.
30. Ibid., p. 27.
31. Felicia Chan, 'When is a foreign-language film not a foreign-language film? When it has too much English in it; the case of a Singapore film and the Oscars', *Inter-Asia Cultural Studies* 9.1 (2008), pp. 95–105.
32. See Emanuel Levy, *All About Oscar: The History and Politics of the Academy Awards* (New York: Continuum, 2003).
33. Kwai-cheung Lo, *Chinese Face/Off: The Transnational Popular Culture of Hong Kong* (Urbana and Chicago, IL: University of Illinois Press, 2005), p. 3.
34. Stephen Teo, *Hong Kong Cinema: The Extra Dimensions* (London: British Film Institute, 1997), p. 207.
35. See Teo, *Hong Kong Cinema*; and Zhang, *Chinese National Cinema*.

36. See, for example, Gary Bettinson, *The Sensuous Cinema of Wong Kar-wai: Film Poetics and the Aesthetics of Disturbance* (Hong Kong: Hong Kong University Press, 2014); Peter Brunette, *Wong Kar-wai* (Urbana, Champaign, IL: University of Illinois Press, 2005); and Stephen Teo, *Wong Kar-wai: Auteur of Time* (London: British Film Institute, 2005).
37. 'He Zhiwu' in *pinyin* Mandarin, but rendered as 'He Qiwu' in the English subtitles in the international distribution of the film and the DVD. I have opted to use latter since it is likely to be the more familiar to English readers. Other critics sometimes use the other spelling.
38. Gordon Mathews, *Ghetto at the Center of the World: Chungking Mansions, Hong Kong* (Chicago, IL: University of Chicago Press, 2011).
39. Lo, *Chinese Face/Off*, p. 4.
40. Ibid., p. 26. There has been a move to study Hokkien / Fukien / Fujian / Amoy-language cinema, a cheaply produced vernacular cinema made in Hong Kong in the 1950s for direct export to other parts of the Chinese diaspora, including the Philippines, Taiwan and Singapore. See Jeremy E. Taylor, *Rethinking Transnational Chinese Cinemas: The Amoy-Dialect Film Industry in Cold War Asia* (London: Routledge, 2011).
41. Sheldon Lu, 'Dialect and modernity in 21st century Sinophone cinema', *Jump Cut: A Review of Contemporary Media* 49 (2007). Available at www.ejumpcut.org/archive/jc49.2007/Lu/text.html (accessed 13 June 2013).
42. Rey Chow, *Not Like a Native Speaker: On Languaging as a Postcolonial Experience* (New York: Columbia University Press, 2014), pp. 45–6.
43. Ibid., p. 45.
44. Ibid., p. 37.
45. Ackbar Abbas, *Hong Kong: Culture and the Politics of Disappearance* (Hong Kong: Hong Kong University Press, 1997), p. 28.
46. Teo, *Hong Kong Cinema*, pp. 11–60.
47. Zhang, *Chinese National Cinema*, pp. 150–1.
48. Ibid., p. 150.
49. Teo, *Hong Kong Cinema*, p. 14.
50. Zhang, *Chinese National Cinema*, p. 150.
51. Teo, *Hong Kong Cinema*, p. 14.
52. Ibid., p. 14.
53. Ibid., pp. 14–15.
54. Zhang, *Chinese National Cinema*, pp. 162–3.
55. Ibid., p. 151.
56. Ibid., p. 163.
57. Ibid., p. 166.
58. Ibid., p. 166.
59. Ibid., p. 174.
60. Ibid., p. 177.

61. Stephen Teo, *Wong Kar-wai*, p. 193.
62. Zhang, *Chinese National Cinema*, p. 185.
63. See Felicia Chan, 'Crouching Tiger, Hidden Dragon: Cultural migrancy and translatability', in Chris Berry (ed.), *Chinese Films in Focus II* (London: British Film Institute, 2009), pp. 73–81
64. Teo, *Hong Kong Cinema*; Cheuk-to Li, 'Hong Kong: zest and anguish', in Aruna Vasudev, Latika Padgaonkar and Rashmi Doraiswamy (eds), *Being and Becoming: The Cinemas of Asia* (Delhi: Macmillan, 2002), pp. 92–123.
65. Even today, the song is learnt in schools in the region as a folk song, without pupils necessarily having to learn about its cultural origins. I recall learning it in its original language in primary school in Singapore in the early 1980s, as part of the multiracial ideology of the state, without really understanding a word of it, alongside 'Danny Boy' and 'Sur le Pont d'Avignon / On the Bridge of Avignon' as if we were simply tapping into a vast universal cultural reservoir. Until I began researching this, I was not even aware that 'Bengawan Solo' was not an old Malay folk tune from Singapore, so embedded is it now in the country's cultural history and memory. It is thus resonant that in *In the Mood for Love* the song signals Chow's relocation to Singapore, enacting the ties between the two territories at the time of Singapore's own fledgling quests for identity following independence from Britain in 1959, the merger with Malaysia in 1963 and subsequent separation in 1965.
66. Lai Chee Kien, 'Imagining Nanyang: the framing of Southeast Asia in Wong Kar-wai's movies', in Lilian Chee and Edna Lim (eds), *Asian Cinema and Space: Interdisciplinary Perspectives* (London: Routledge, 2015), p. 109.
67. Ibid., p. 113.
68. Ibid., p. 121.
69. Lo, *Chinese Face/Off*, p. 53.
70. Ibid., p. 56.
71. Julian Stringer, '"Your tender smiles give me strength": paradigms of masculinity in John Woo's *A Better Tomorrow* and *The Killer*', *Screen* 38.1 (1997), p. 37; and quoted in Lo, *Chinese Face/Off*, p. 54.
72. Meaghan Morris, 'Transnational imagination in action cinema: Hong Kong and the making of a global popular culture', *Inter-Asia Cultural Studies* 5.2 (2004), p. 182.
73. Lo, *Chinese Face/Off*, p. 48.
74. Ibid., pp. 48, 49.
75. Ibid., p. 73.
76. Chua Beng Huat, 'Conceptualizing an East Asian popular culture', *Inter-Asia Cultural Studies* 5.2 (2004), p. 214.
77. Ibid., p. 214.
78. Lo, *Chinese Face/Off*, p. 51.

79. Abé Mark Nornes, *Cinema Babel: Translating Global Cinema* (Minneapolis, MN: University of Minnesota Press, 2007), p. 155.
80. There have been some exceptions in recent years, such as the use of some 'dialect' Hokkien and Cantonese in some Singapore films, such as Eric Khoo's *12 Storeys* (1997), but these are individual decisions that do not (yet) amount to a coherent policy or practice.
81. See Anthea Fraser Gupta, 'Singapore Colloquial English? Or deviant Standard English?', in Jan Tent and France Mugler (eds), *SICOL: Proceedings of the Second International Conference on Oceanic Languages Vol. 1* (Canberra: Pacific Linguistics, 1998), pp. 43–57.
82. Jacques Derrida, *Monolingualism of the Other; or, the Prosthesis of Origin* (Stanford, CA: Stanford University Press, 1998), p. 5.
83. Ibid., p. 31.
84. Ibid., pp. 30–1.
85. Chow, *Not Like a Native Speaker*, p. 20.
86. Lo, *Chinese Face/Off*, pp. 49, 50.
87. Ibid., p. 50.
88. The 'art-house ghetto' is a phrase Ang Lee used when talking about trying to distribute *Crouching Tiger, Hidden Dragon* beyond the specialist cinema circuit. See Bruce Kirkland, 'Ang Lee's a dragon in hiding', *canoe.com* (3 December 2000). Available at jam.canoe.com/Movies/Artists/L/Lee_Ang/2000/12/03/pf-759755.html (accessed 12 June 2013).
89. B. Ruby Rich, 'To read or not to read: subtitles, trailers, and monolingualism', in Atom Egoyan and Ian Balfour (eds), *Subtitles: On the Foreignness of Film* (Cambridge, MA: The MIT Press, 2004), p. 158.
90. Henri Béhar, 'Cultural ventriloquism', in Atom Egoyan and Ian Balfour (eds), *Subtitles: On the Foreignness of Film* (Cambridge, MA: The MIT Press, 2004), p. 85.
91. Lawrence Venuti, 'Introduction', in Lawrence Venuti (ed.), *Rethinking Translation: Discourse, Subjectivity, Ideology* (London: Routledge, 1992), p. 10.
92. Nornes, *Cinema Babel*, p. 155.
93. Venuti, 'Introduction', p. 10.
94. 'Specialist film' is a term used within the distribution and exhibition industries to loosely categorise films with a niche audience, especially non-English-language films.
95. Mark Betz, 'The name above the (sub)title: internationalism, coproduction, and polyglot European art cinema', *Camera Obscura* 46, 16.1 (2001), pp. 4–5.
96. Ibid., p. 9.
97. Margaret Talbot, 'The auteur of anime', *The New Yorker* (17 January 2005). Available at www.newyorker.com/magazine/2005/01/17/the-auteur-of-anime (accessed 5 May 2014).

98. Anne Cooper-Chen, 'Cartoon planet: the cross-cultural acceptance of Japanese animation', *Asian Journal of Communication* 22.1 (2012), pp. 44–57.
99. Betz, 'The name above the (sub)title', p. 4.
100. A phrase borrowed from Judith Still and Michael Worton, 'Introduction', in Judith Still and Michael Worton (eds), *Intertextuality: Theories and Practices* (Manchester: Manchester University Press, 1990), p. 30.
101. Naoki Sakai, 'Translation', *Theory, Culture & Society*, 23.2–3 (2006), p. 83.
102. See Sylvia Li-chun Lin, *Representing Atrocity in Taiwan: The 2/28 Incident and White Terror in Fiction and Film* (New York: Columbia University Press, 2007).
103. Ibid., p. 128.
104. Ibid., p. 128.
105. Leo Chanjen Chen, 'Cinema, dream, existence: the films of Hou Hsiao-Hsien', *New Left Review* 39 (May / June 2006), p. 89.
106. Ibid., p. 87.
107. Ibid., p. 90.
108. I am unable to date the broadcast of this interview, but it is excerpted on YouTube: 'Hsiao-hsien Hou talking about Tony Leung', available at www.youtube.com/watch?v=oecpR-dCfes (accessed 9 May 2014).
109. See 'Hou Hsiao-Hsien talks about Tony Leung [City of Sadness]', available at www.youtube.com/watch?v=BH4e8NVY3aE (accessed 9 May 2014).
110. See for example James Mudge, 'The melancholic charm of Tony Leung Chiu Wai', *yesasia.com* (16 January 2007). Available at www.yesasia.com/us/yumcha/the-melancholic-charm-of-tony-leung-chiu-wai/0-0-0-arid.106-en/featured-article.html (accessed 9 May 2014); Rodrigo Prieto, 'The "killer pizza light"', in *Lust, Caution: The Story, the Screenplay and the Making of the Film*, by Eileen Chang, James Schamus and Wang Hui Ling (New York: Pantheon, 2007), pp. 253–4; and Steve Rose, 'It never gets any easier', interview with Tony Leung, The *Guardian* (23 February 2004). Available at www.theguardian.com/film/2004/feb/23/1 (accessed 9 May 2014).
111. Chen, 'Cinema, dream, existence', p. 76.
112. Ibid., p. 93.
113. See Virginia Crisp, '"BLOODY PIRATES!!! *shakes fist*": reimagining East Asian film distribution and reception through online filesharing networks', *Journal of Japanese & Korean Cinema* 3.1 (2012), pp. 65–72.
114. Valentina Vitali, 'Hou Hsiao-Hsien reviewed', *Inter-Asia Cultural Studies* 9.2 (2008), p. 281.
115. Ibid., p. 287.
116. Ibid., p. 282.
117. Ibid., p. 286.

118. Ian Balfour and Atom Egoyan, 'Introduction', in Atom Egoyan and Ian Balfour (eds), *Subtitles: On the Foreignness of Film* (Cambridge, MA: The MIT Press, 2004), p. 21.
119. See for example Jorge Díaz-Cintas, 'Dubbing or subtitling: the eternal dilemma', *Perspectives: Studies in Translatology*, 7.1 (1999), pp. 31–40; Miguel Mera, 'Read my lips: re-evaluating subtitling and dubbing in Europe', *Links & Letters* 6 (1999), pp. 73–85; and Gilbert C. F. Fong and Kenneth K. L. Au (eds), *Dubbing and Subtitling in a World Context* (Hong Kong: The Chinese University Press, 2009).
120. Sho[c]hat and Stam, 'The cinema after Babel', p. 58.
121. Carol O'Sullivan, *Translating Popular Film* (Basingstoke: Palgrave Macmillan, 2011).
122. John Mowitt, *Re-takes: Postcoloniality and Foreign Film Languages* (Minneapolis, MN: University of Minnesota Press, 2005), p. 45.
123. Chow, *Not Like a Native Speaker*, p. 73.
124. Ibid., pp. 75–6.
125. Martin Kayman, 'The state of English as a global language: communicating culture', *Textual Practice* 18.1 (2004), pp. 1–22.
126. Rada Iveković, 'The watershed of modernity: translation and the epistemological revolution', *Inter-Asia Cultural Studies* 11.1 (2010), p. 47.
127. Ibid., p. 50.
128. Ibid., p. 59.

2 Cosmopolitan memory and self-reflexive cinema

1. Sigmund Freud, 'Screen memories', in *The Uncanny* (London: Penguin, 2003), p. 19.
2. Susannah Radstone, 'Cinema and memory', in Susannah Radstone and Bill Schwarz (eds), *Memory: Histories, Theories, Debates* (New York: Fordham University Press, 2010), p. 326.
3. Ibid., p. 326.
4. Ibid., p. 326.
5. Ibid., p. 326.
6. Ibid., p. 328.
7. Ibid., p. 336.
8. Ibid., p. 336.
9. E. Ann Kaplan, 'Melodrama, cinema and trauma', *Screen* 42.2 (2001), p. 202.
10. Ibid., p. 204.
11. Ibid., p. 204.
12. Daniel Levy and Natan Sznaider, *Human Rights and Memory* (University Park, PA: Pennsylvania State University Press, 2010), p. 5.

13. Ibid., p. 6.
14. See also Andreas Huyssen and Natan Sznaider, 'Memory unbound: the Holocaust and the formation of cosmopolitan memory', *European Journal of Social Theory* 5.1 (2002), pp. 87–106; Pawas Bisht, 'The politics of cosmopolitan memory', *Media, Culture & Society* 35.1 (2013), pp. 13–20; and Jessica Rapson, 'Mobilising Lidice: cosmopolitan memory between theory and practice', *Culture, Theory and Critique* 53.2 (2012), pp. 129–45.
15. See Patricia R. S. Batto, 'The world of Jia Zhangke', *China Perspectives* 60 (2005). Available at chinaperspectives.revues.org/2843 (accessed 6 June 2011).
16. Zhang Xudong, 'Poetics of vanishing: the cinema of Jia Zhangke', *New Left Review* 63 (2010), pp. 1–18.
17. Valerie Jaffee, 'Bringing the world to the nation: Jia Zhangke and the legitimation of Chinese underground film', *Senses of Cinema* 32 (2004). Available at http://sensesofcinema.com/2004/feature-articles/chinese_underground_film/ (accessed 9 July 2014).
18. Ibid.
19. Ibid.
20. Ibid.
21. Chris Berry, 'Getting real: Chinese documentary, Chinese postsocialism', in Zhang Zhen (ed.), *The Urban Generation: Chinese Cinema and Society at the Turn of the Twenty-first Century* (Durham, NC: Duke University Press, 2007), p. 122.
22. Thomas Austin, 'Indexicality and inter/textuality: *24 City*'s aesthetics and the politics of memory', *Screen* 55.2 (2014), p. 257.
23. Ibid., p. 258.
24. G. Allen Johnson, 'Review: 24 City', *San Francisco Chronicle* (31 July 2009). Available at www.sfgate.com/movies/article/Review-24-City-3223498.php (accessed 9 July 2014).
25. Manohla Dargis, 'An upscale leap forward that leaves many behind', *The New York Times* (4 June 2009).
26. Austin, 'Indexicality and inter/textuality', p. 259.
27. Laura Mulvey, *Death 24x a Second: Stillness and the Moving Image* (London: Reaktion Books, 2006), p. 66.
28. Austin, 'Indexicality and inter/textuality', p. 261.
29. Mulvey, *Death 24x a Second*, p. 67.
30. Jiwei Xiao, 'The quest for memory: documentary and fiction in Jia Zhangke's films', *Senses of Cinema* 59 (2011). Available at http://sensesofcinema.com/2011/feature-articles/the-quest-for-memory-documentary-and-fiction-in-jia-zhangke%e2%80%99s-films/ (accessed 18 August 2016).
31. Austin, 'Indexicality and inter/textuality', p. 257.
32. Ibid., p. 258.
33. Quoted in Xiao, 'The quest for memory'.

34. Xiao, 'The quest for memory'.
35. Austin, 'Indexicality and inter/textuality', p. 262.
36. Mulvey, *Death 24x a Second*, p. 33.
37. Xiao, 'The quest for memory'.
38. Ibid.
39. Mulvey, *Death 24x a Second*, pp. 52–3.
40. Rapson, 'Mobilising Lidice'.
41. Ibid., p. 133.
42. Hsien-hao Sebastian Liao, 'Becoming modernized or simply "modern"?: Sex, Chineseness, and diasporic consciousness in *Lust, Caution*', *Concentric: Literary and Cultural Studies* 36.2 (2010), p. 181.
43. I adopt the spellings of the names as they appear in the English subtitles of the film, which uses the Wade-Giles romanisation of Chinese names, although I am aware that other writings on the film sometimes choose to adopt the *pinyin* rendition of the names: so Wang Chia-chih (Wade-Giles) rather than Wang Jiazhi (*pinyin*). I do so largely to maintain my focus on the film as it has travelled transnationally, including with English subtitles, rather than on the 'character' or 'personality' of Wang within the diegesis, as well as to maintain the cultural politics of the Wade-Giles and *pinyin* systems of romanisation of the Mandarin Chinese language. See, for example, Melissa L. Curtin, 'Languages on display: indexical signs, identities and the linguistic landscape of Taipei', in Elana Shohamy and Durk Gorter (eds), *Linguistic Landscape: Expanding the Scenery* (New York: Routledge, 2009), pp. 221–69.
44. Leo Ou-fan Lee, 'Ang Lee's *Lust, Caution* and its reception', *boundary 2* 35 (2008), p. 234.
45. James Schamus, 'Introduction', in *Lust, Caution: The Story, the Screenplay, and the Making of the Film* (New York: Pantheon, 2007), p. xi.
46. Susan Daruvala surveys a number of critical positions making these connections in her chapter on 'Self as performance, lust as betrayal in the theatre of war', in Peng Hsiao-yen and Whitney Crothers Dilley (eds), *From Eileen Chang to Ang Lee: Lust/Caution* (Abingdon, Oxon: Routledge, 2014), pp. 101–21.
47. Peng Hsiao-yen and Whitney Crothers Dilley, 'Introduction', in Peng Hsiao-yen and Whitney Crothers Dilley (eds), *From Eileen Chang to Ang Lee: Lust/Caution* (Abingdon, Oxon: Routledge, 2014), p. 7.
48. J. L. Austin, *How to Do Things with Words* (Oxford: Clarendon Press, 1962), p. 6.
49. Ibid., p. 5.
50. Ibid., p. 8.
51. Andrew Parker and Eve Kosofsky Sedgwick, 'Introduction: performativity and performance', in Andrew Parker and Eve Kosofsky Sedgwick (eds), *Performativity and Performance* (New York: Routledge, 1995), pp. 10–11.
52. Liao, 'Becoming modernized or simply "modern"?', pp. 185, 192.
53. Ibid., p. 193.

54. Poshek Fu, *Between Shanghai and Hong Kong: The Politics of Chinese Cinemas* (Stanford, CA: Stanford University Press, 2003), pp. 44–6.
55. Ibid., p. 13.
56. Leo Ou-fan Lee, 'The urban milieu of Shanghai Cinema, 1930–40: some explorations of film audience, film culture, and narrative conventions', in Yingjin Zhang (ed.), *Cinema and Urban Culture in Shanghai, 1922–1943* (Stanford, CA: Stanford University Press, 1999), p. 82.
57. Matthew Chew, 'Contemporary re-emergence of the qipao: political nationalism, cultural production and popular consumption of a traditional Chinese dress', *The China Quarterly* 189 (2007), p. 144.
58. Ibid., pp. 150–3.
59. Ibid., p. 161.
60. Stephen Teo, *Hong Kong Cinema: The Extra Dimensions* (London: British Film Institute, 1997), pp. 3–27.
61. Fu, *Between Shanghai and Hong Kong*, p. 57.
62. Ibid., p. 57.
63. Ibid., pp. 58–9.
64. Yingjin Zhang, *Chinese National Cinema* (New York: Routledge, 2004), pp. 161–3.
65. Sean Cubitt, 'Ecocritique and the materialities of animation', in Suzanne Buchan (ed.), *Pervasive Animation* (London: Routledge, 2003), p. 96.
66. See Paul Willemen, 'On realism in the cinema', *Screen* 13.1 (1972), pp. 37–44.
67. Cubitt, 'Ecocritique and the materialities of animation', p. 100.
68. Ibid., p. 100.
69. Annalee Newitz considers the possibility that this spike in popularity of Japanese popular cultural products in the US, chiefly *manga* and *anime*, from the 1990s is 'both the result of and a cause for American anxieties about the potency of its national culture in the world'. Annalee Newitz, 'Magical girls and atomic bomb sperm: Japanese animation in America', *Film Quarterly* 49.1 (1995), p. 3.
70. Sergei Eisenstein, *Eisenstein on Disney*, ed. Jay Leyda, trans. Alan Upchurch (London: Methuen, 1988), p. 4.
71. Ibid., p. 7.
72. Ibid., p. 21.
73. Thomas Lamarre, 'From animation to *anime*: drawing movements and moving drawings', *Japan Forum* 14.2 (2002), p. 330.
74. Melek Ortabasi, 'Indexing the past: visual language and translatability in Kon Satoshi's *Millennium Actress*', *Perspectives: Studies in Translatology* 14.4 (2007), p. 278.
75. Hara is generally considered to be the face of that golden age of Japanese cinema, and known internationally especially for starring in Yasujiro Ozu's 'Noriko trilogy' (*Late Spring*, 1949; *Early Summer*, 1951; *Tokyo Story*, 1953).

Hara's sudden retirement into seclusion in the mid-1960s has prompted comparisons with Europe's Greta Garbo. See Peter Bradshaw, 'The heart-wrenching performance of Setsuko Hara, Ozu's quiet muse', *The Guardian* Film Blog, 16 June 2010. Available at www.theguardian.com/film/filmblog/2010/jun/16/setsuko-hara-birthday-tokyo-story (accessed 22 July 2014).

76. Yen-Jung Chang, 'Satoshi Kon's *Millennium Actress*: a feminine journey with dream-like qualities', *Animation* 8.1 (2013), p. 90.
77. Ortabasi, 'Indexing the past', p. 285.
78. Ibid., p. 286. 'Ampo' refers to the Japanese abbreviation of its name for the Treaty of Mutual Cooperation and Security between the United States and Japan, instituted in 1952.
79. Chang, 'Satoshi Kon's *Millennium Actress*', p. 95.
80. Chale Nafus, '*Millennium Actress* program notes', Austin Film Society screening (5 December 2006). Available at www.austinfilm.org/page.aspx?pid=2997 (accessed 23 July 2014).
81. Chang, 'Satoshi Kon's *Millennium Actress*', pp. 85–6.
82. Lamarre, 'From animation to *anime*', p. 332.
83. Thomas Lamarre, 'Introduction: between cinema and *anime*', *Japan Forum* 14.2 (2002), p. 187.
84. Ibid., p.187.
85. Quoted in Nafus, '*Millennium Actress* program notes'.
86. See detailed video analysis by Tony Zhou in 'Satoshi Kon – editing space and time' on his YouTube channel, 'Every Frame a Painting'. Available at www.youtube.com/watch?v=oz49vQwSoTE (accessed 15 September 2015).
87. Lamarre, 'From animation to *anime*', p. 331.
88. Ibid., pp. 331–2.
89. Ibid., p. 334.
90. Ibid., p. 335.
91. Ibid., p. 330.
92. Ibid., p. 330.
93. Ibid., p. 330.
94. Ibid., p. 338.
95. Ibid., p. 339.
96. W. J. T. Mitchell, *Picture Theory* (Chicago, IL: University of Chicago Press, 1994), p. 57.
97. For all its metafilmic ingenuity, *Millennium Actress* did not in fact travel well (see Ortabasi, 'Indexing the past', p. 278). As with *Whisper of the Heart* which I discussed in the previous chapter, *Millennium Actress* is not the child-centred or mechatronic animated film that Anglophone markets have come to expect from *anime*, though the film did achieve a modest US release by DreamWorks / GoFish as a subtitled foreign film on six screens, mainly in New York and Los Angeles, and critical acclaim at film festivals. In the UK,

it did not secure a theatrical release and went straight to DVD: contrast the performance of Hayao Miyazaki's *Spirited Away* (2001), which was released theatrically in the same year and won the Best Animated Film at the Oscars that year. Dubbed into English and marketed by Walt Disney Productions, *Spirited Away* earned USD10 million at the US box office and even more worldwide.

3 Film festivals and cosmopolitan affect

1. Graeme Turner, *Film as Social Practice IV* (Oxon: Routledge, 2006), p. 2.
2. Dina Iordanova, 'The film festival circuit', in Dina Iordanova with Ragan Rhyne (eds), *Film Festival Yearbook 1: The Festival Circuit*. (St Andrews: St Andrews Film Studies, 2009), pp. 23–39.
3. Julian Stringer, 'Global cities and the international film festival economy', in Mark Shiel and Tony Fitzmaurice (eds), *Cinema and the City: Film and Urban Societies in a Global Context* (Oxford: Blackwell, 2001), pp. 134–44.
4. Miriam Ross, 'The film festival as producer: Latin American films and Rotterdam's Hubert Bals Fund', *Screen* 52.2 (2011), pp. 261–7.
5. Paul Willemen, 'Pesaro', *Framework* 15/16/17 (1981), p. 96.
6. Liz Czach writes about 'critical capital' and the politics of tastemaking in festival programming. See Liz Czach, 'Film festivals, programming and the building of a national cinema', *The Moving Image* 4.1 (2004), pp. 76–88.
7. See Dina Iordanova and Leshu Torchin (eds), *Film Festival Yearbook 4: Film Festivals and Activism* (St Andrews: St Andrews Film Studies, 2012).
8. See Valentina Vitali and Ashish Rajadhyaksha, 'Introduction to the dossier: Paul Willemen (1944–2012)', *Inter-Asia Cultural Studies* 14.1 (2013), pp. 85–93.
9. Janet Harbord, *Film Cultures* (London: Sage, 2002), p. 59.
10. Ibid., p. 60.
11. Cindy Hing-Yuk Wong, *Film Festivals: Culture, People, and Power on the Global Screen* (Rutgers, NJ: Rutgers University Press, 2011), p. 5.
12. Harbord, *Film Cultures*, p. 60.
13. Some titles include: Peter Bart, *Cannes: Fifty Years of Sun, Sex and Celluloid* (New York: Miramax, 1997); Kieron Corless and Chris Darke, *Cannes: Inside the World's Premier Film Festival* (London: Faber and Faber, 2007); Brian D. Johnson, *Brave Films, Wild Nights: 25 Years of Festival Fever* (Toronto: Random House Canada, 2000); and Kenneth Turan, *Sundance to Sarajevo: Film Festivals and the World They Made* (Berkeley, CA: University of California Press, 2002).
14. A number of initiatives include the *Film Festival Yearbook* series, led by Dina Iordanova, and published by St Andrews Film Studies, and the Film Festival Research Network (FFRN), founded by Marijke de Valck and Skadi Loist, who

also compile a bibliography on www.filmfestivalresearch.org. See also Marijke de Valck and Skadi Loist, 'Film festival studies: an overview of a burgeoning field', in Dina Iordanova with Ragan Rhyne (eds), *Film Festival Yearbook 1: The Festival Circuit* (St. Andrews: St. Andrews Film Studies, 2009), pp. 179–215.
15. Wong, *Film Festivals*.
16. Marijke de Valck, *Film Festivals: From European Geopolitics to Global Cinephilia* (Amsterdam: Amsterdam University Press, 2007).
17. Thomas Elsaesser, *European Cinema: Face to Face with Hollywood* (Amsterdam: Amsterdam University Press, 2005), pp. 82–107.
18. See Mark Peranson, 'First you get the power, then you get the money: two models of film festivals', in Richard Porton (ed.), *Dekalog 3: on Film Festivals* (London: Wallflower, 2009), pp. 23–37; and Wong, *Film Festivals*.
19. A. O. Scott, 'In Toronto it's all about crowd pleasers and films that get lost in the shuffle', The *New York Times* (7 September 2008). Available at www.nytimes.com/2008/09/08/movies/08toro.html (accessed 29 July 2014).
20. Wong, *Film Festivals*, p. 10.
21. Jeffrey Ruoff, 'Introduction: programming film festivals', in Jeffrey Ruoff (ed.), *Coming Soon to a Festival Near You: Programming Film Festivals* (St Andrews: St Andrews Film Studies, 2012), p. 11.
22. Gerald Peary, 'Memories of a film festival addict', in Jeffrey Ruoff (ed.), *Coming Soon to a Festival Near You: Programming Film Festivals* (St Andrews: St Andrews Film Studies, 2012), pp. 41–58.
23. Wong, *Film Festivals*, p. 10.
24. Ibid., pp. 20–1.
25. See Simon O'Sullivan, 'The aesthetics of affect', *Angelaki* 6.3 (2001), pp. 125–35.
26. See Catherine Grant, 'On "affect" and "emotion" in film and media studies', *Film Studies for Free* blog (4 November 2011). Available at: http://filmstudiesforfree.blogspot.co.uk/2011/11/on-affect-and-emotion-in-film-and-media.html (accessed 31 July 2014).
27. Ian Breakwell and Paul Hammond (eds), *Seeing in the Dark: A Compendium of Cinemagoing* (London: Serpent's Tail, 1990).
28. Ibid., p. 8.
29. Gregory J. Seigworth and Melissa Gregg, 'An inventory of shimmers', in Gregory J. Seigworth and Melissa Gregg (eds), *The Affect Theory Reader* (Durham, NC: Duke University Press, 2010), pp. 1–2.
30. David Chaney, 'Cosmopolitan art and cultural citizenship', *Theory, Culture & Society* 19.1–2 (2002), p. 158.
31. Mica Nava, *Visceral Cosmopolitanism: Gender, Culture and the Normalisation of Difference* (Oxford: Berg, 2007), p. 134.
32. Kirstie Jamieson, 'Edinburgh: the festival gaze and its boundaries,' *Space & Culture* 7.1 (2004), p. 64.

33. Dina Iordanova, 'Mediating diaspora: film festivals and "imagined communities"', in Dina Iordanova with Ruby Cheung (eds), *Film Festival Yearbook 2: Film Festivals and Imagined Communities* (St Andrews: St Andrews Film Studies, 2010), p. 13.
34. Timothy Corrigan compares the 'commerce of auteurism' to the process of star branding. See Timothy Corrigan, 'The commerce of auteurism: a voice without authority', *New German Critique* 49 (1990), pp. 43–57.
35. Mette Hjort and Duncan Petrie (eds), *The Cinema of Small Nations* (Bloomington, IN: Indiana University Press, 2007).
36. Bill Nichols, 'Discovering form, inferring meaning: new cinemas and the film festival circuit', *Film Quarterly* 47.3 (1994), p. 17.
37. Tom Gunning, 'The cinema of attractions: early film, its spectator and the avant-garde', *Wide Angle* 8.3–4 (1986), p. 65.
38. Following an unbroken run from 1987 to 2011, the Singapore International Film Festival folded for a number of reasons, including problems with funding and management. It relaunched with a new identity in 2014. John Lui, writing for Singapore's national broadsheet, *The Straits Times*, called for the new festival to stay 'edgy' and 'weird'. 'Weirdness', he writes, 'inspires, creates zeal, sells tickets'. See John Lui, 'Keep the film festival weird – the way for the rebooted Singapore International Film Festival to go is to stay edgy and creative', *The Straits Times, Life!* Section (11 December 2013).
39. Seigworth and Gregg, 'An inventory of shimmers', p. 1.
40. Nichols, 'Discovering form, inferring meaning', p. 16.
41. Sue Beeton, *Film-Induced Tourism* (Clevedon: Channel View Publications, 2005).
42. Angelina I. Karpovich, 'Theoretical approaches to film-motivated tourism', *Tourism and Hospitality Planning & Development*, 7.1 (2010), pp. 7–20.
43. Felicia Chan, 'Genre as cultural whimsy: taking to the road in *The Bird People in China* and *Cold Fever*', in Felicia Chan, Angelina Karpovich and Xin Zhang (eds), *Genre in Asian Film and Television: New Approaches* (Basingstoke: Palgrave Macmillan, 2011), pp. 210–21.
44. Nichols, 'Discovering form, inferring meaning', p. 27, emphasis mine.
45. In effect, the 'festival film' is not a genre, although Peter Wollen suggests in his 'An alphabet of cinema' that 'Films in this genre were specially made according to their own rules and traditions in order to win prizes at festivals. They were immediately recognizable as festival films by juries, critics and audiences alike. They had become integrated into the institution of cinema', in Peter Wollen, *Paris Hollywood: Writings on Film* (London: Verso, 2002), p. 9.
46. The availability of VHS and later DVD as an inexpensive resource has contributed to the exponential expansion of the discipline, though it should be

47. Wong, *Film Festivals*, p. 4.
48. Ibid., p. 2.
49. Stringer, 'Global cities', p. 136.
50. See also Felicia Chan, 'The international film festival and the making of a national cinema', *Screen* 52.2 (2011), pp. 253–60.
51. Stringer, 'Global cities', p. 139.
52. Ibid., pp. 137–8.
53. Ibid., p. 139.
54. Gaston Bachelard, *The Poetics of Space* (Boston, MA: Beacon Press, 1994), p. xxxvi.
55. Brenda S. A Yeoh and Lily Kong, 'Reading landscape meanings: state constructions and lived experiences in Singapore's Chinatown', *Habitat International* 18.4 (1994), p. 19. Among Chinese speakers in Singapore, the area is not referred to as *Tangren jie* (street of Tang people) as it normally is in the Chinatowns of Europe or North America. Instead, the area is known in Mandarin Chinese as *Niu Che Shui*, in Hokkien *Gu Chia Cui*, or literally 'bullock cart water', and in Malay as *Kreta Ayer* (water cart), referring to its origins as an area where water was drawn from a well on a nearby hill and taken into town on bullock carts. Note that the place names in the local vernacular make no reference to ethnicity. It was the British colonial government that designated the area an ethnic enclave, 'Chinatown', which the modern post-independence nation state has appropriated for its own policies of cultural and racial management.
56. Ibid., p. 19.
57. Ibid., p. 33.
58. Poshek Fu, *Between Shanghai and Hong Kong: The Politics of Chinese Cinemas* (Stanford, CA: Stanford University Press, 2003).
59. One wonders if the acclaimed Japanese director, Yasujiro Ozu, ever attended any of the screenings when he was sent to Singapore by the Japanese government in 1943. Donald Richie's biography of Ozu notes that Ozu had managed to avoid making any propaganda films for the Japanese Imperial Army: 'When Singapore returned to British rule, Ozu busied himself burning negatives and prints. Having done his best to make no films at all, he did not want to be judged a war criminal by the Allied Tribunal'. It is said that Ozu spent his time in Singapore watching Hollywood films – such as those by John Ford, King Vidor, Alfred Hitchcock, William Wyler, Orson Welles and others. See Donald Richie, *Ozu* (Berkeley, CA: University of California Press, 1974), p. 231. BBC Radio 3's *Night Waves*' *Landmarks* series discussed Ozu's *Tokyo Story* (1953) on 18 December 2013, and covered among other topics Ozu's wartime experience

in Singapore between 1943 and 1946, where one panellist noted that Ozu had watched 'over 100 Hollywood films'.
60. Tay Suan Chiang, 'Theatre Majestic no more – The Majestic's unfriendly design and unattractive surrounds make it tough to find new uses that fit its cultural heritage', *The Straits Times, Life!* Section (19 November 2011).
61. See Neil Ravenscroft, Steven Chua and Lynda Keng Neo Wee, 'Going to the movies: cinema development in Singapore', *Leisure Studies* 20 (2001), pp. 215–32.
62. Kenneth Chan, '*Goodbye, Dragon Inn*: Tsai Ming-liang's political aesthetics of nostalgia, place, and lingering', *Journal of Chinese Cinemas* 1.2 (2007), p. 91.
63. The other was the iconic Capitol Theatre, built in 1903 and located in the metropolitan centre of the city-state, which also closed to the public in 1998. The Capitol was in slightly better shape than the Majestic and was also used by the Singapore International Film Festival in the same period. It has recently been redeveloped into a luxury hotel, retail arcade, residential units and a repurposed theatre.
64. Chan, '*Goodbye, Dragon Inn*', p. 91.
65. Belinda Yuen, 'Searching for place identity in Singapore', *Habitat International* 29 (2005), pp. 197–214.
66. See Eunice Seng, 'Politics of greening: spatial constructions of the public in Singapore', in William S. W. Lim and Jiat-Hwee Chang (eds), *Non-West Modernist Past: On Architecture and Modernities* (Singapore: World Scientific Publishing, 2012), pp. 143–60.
67. In 1995, the Substation, an independent arts centre founded in Singapore in 1990, organised a conference called *Space, Spaces and Spacing*. See Lee Weng Choy (ed.), *Space, Spaces and Spacing* (Singapore: The Substation, 1996). In 2009, profiles of and interviews with 20 industry practitioners, comprising writers, filmmakers, producers, composers, editors and cinematographers, were compiled into a commemorative volume called *My Creative Room*, partly to draw attention to creative talent in Singapore and also to raise funds for the Singapore International Film Festival, which was in financial straits at the time. See Chew Boon Leong, Kong Kam Yoke and Danny Yeo (eds), *My Creative Room* (Singapore: My Creative Room, 2009); also mycreativeroom.wordpress.com.
68. There are some exceptions such as Clarissa Oon's column in *The Straits Times* on the 'erosion of personal space' in Singapore, due to 'globalisation and breakneck economic growth [which] have overhauled Singapore's cityscape', in Clarissa Oon, 'The past is just a memory – heritage issues and conservation causes loomed large in 2011 as Singaporeans reeled from the erosion of personal space', *The Straits Times, Life!* Section (31 December 2011); and veteran journalist Cherian George's essay, 'Lost at home: a

nation's state of geographical confusion', in Cherian George, *Singapore, the Air-Conditioned Nation: Essays on the Politics of Comfort and Control, 1990–2000* (Singapore: Landmark Books, 2000), pp. 189–94. These articles and the numerous online blogs, however, tend to simply describe what is already a *fait accompli* and mourn their loss. There is rarely a call to action, partly because there is very little political space for it, and also because any action would likely be too late.

69. Lauren Berlant, 'Thinking about feeling historical', *Emotion, Space and Society* 1 (2008), p. 5. More recently in 2015, the 50th year of the founding of the Republic, an online 'memory portal' (www.singaporememory.sg/) has allowed residents to share photos and memories of places lost to modern Singapore and the portal is incrementally turning into an affective archive of sorts.

70. Eugene Tan Quancai, 'One rule to rule them all: a study of Singapore censorship', *SGNewwave* (10 March 2010). Available at sgnewwave.com/main/2010/03/one-rule-to-rule-them-all-a-study-of-singapore-censorship/comment-page-1/ (accessed 14 August 2014).

71. The classification system may be found on the Media Development Authority of Singapore's website: www.mda.gov.sg/RegulationsAndLicensing/ContentStandardsAndClassification/FilmsAndVideos/Pages/default.aspx (accessed 14 August 2014).

72. Richard Phillips, 'Film festival director talks to WSWS about censorship in Singapore', *World Socialist Web Site* (24 April 2000). Available at www.wsws.org/en/articles/2000/04/sff3-a24.html (accessed 14 August 2014).

73. Sherwin Loh, '15 actor back in school', *The Straits Times, Life!* Section (14 October 2003).

74. See Raphaël Millet, *Singapore Cinema* (Singapore: Editions Didier Millet, 2006); and Jan Uhde and Yvonne Ng Uhde, *Latent Images: Film in Singapore* (Singapore: Oxford University Press, 2000).

75. The prohibitive cost of VHS tapes in Singapore was compounded by its hot and humid climate where, if not stored properly, mould would grow on the tapes, destroying their contents.

76. See Felicia Chan and Dave Chua, 'Programming Southeast Asia at the Singapore International Film Festival', in Dina Iordanova, Ruby Cheung and Alex Fischer (eds), *Film Festival Yearbook 3: Film Festivals and East Asia* (St Andrews: St Andrews University Press, 2011), pp. 125–41.

77. Jamieson, 'Edinburgh', p. 71.

78. Ibid., p. 71.

79. Ibid., p. 71.

80. Wong, *Film Festivals*, p. 160.

81. Ibid., p. 161.

82. Jamieson, 'Edinburgh', p. 71.

83. See Chua Beng Huat, *Life is Not Complete Without Shopping: Consumption Culture in Singapore* (Singapore: Singapore University Press, 2003).
84. See Belinda Yuen, 'Safety and dwelling in Singapore', *Cities* 21.1 (2004), pp. 19–28.
85. In *Women's Leisure, What Leisure?* (1990), Green, Hebron and Woodward conducted a study on women in Sheffield between 1984 and 1987, exploring in particular 'leisure as a site of potential conflict, which highlights the contradictory nature of the "freedom" and "pleasure" labels traditionally attached to it' (p. ix). See Eileen Green, Sandra Hebron and Diana Woodward, *Women's Leisure, What Leisure?* (Basingstoke: Macmillan, 1990).
86. Since its first introduction in 1991, the film classification system in Singapore has undergone a number of revisions, introducing various age-restricted categories over the next two decades: PG13 (in 2011), NC16 (in 2003), M18 (in 2004) and R21 (in 2004).
87. Quoted in Richard Phillips, 'Film festival director'.
88. The intersections of language, racial identification and class in Singapore are complex and multi-layered and it would take much more than a chapter to unpack all of its implications. See Nirmala Srirekam PuruShotam, *Negotiating, Language, Constructing Race* (Berlin: de Gruyter, 1997); and Tan Ern Ser, *Does Class Matter? Social Stratification and Orientations in Singapore* (Singapore: World Scientific Publishing, 2004). Nonetheless, the use and efficacy of subtitles ought to be factored into any study of cultural translation in film, and at film festivals in particular. Festivals in multilingual locations sometimes offer several sets of subtitles in addition to the one etched onto the film (usually English for international distribution but sometimes in German or French). At Locarno, these appear under the main projection via an additional device akin to a 'ticker tape'. At the Pusan festival, which I attended in 2006, Korean subtitles were projected vertically on the side of the screen via PowerPoint slides, and manned by festival volunteers. (The city of Pusan changed the romanised spelling of its name to Busan in 2000 but the festival only followed suit in 2011.)
89. Yip Wai Yee, 'Goodbye to softcore cinema Yangtze', *The Straits Times* (1 March 2016). Available at www.straitstimes.com/lifestyle/entertainment/goodbye-to-softcore-cinema-yangtze (accessed 1 March 2016).
90. See, also, RemSG, 'A last look at Pearls Centre and its Yangtze Theatre', *Remember Singapore* (20 September 2015). Available at remembersingapore.org/2015/09/20/pearls-centre-yangtze-cinema-closure/ (accessed 1 March 2016); and Low Beng Kheng. 'Yangtze Cinema: guerilla [*sic*] curating to the masses', *Singapore Memory Project* (February 2012). Available at www.singaporememory.sg/contents/SMA-39cb3836-858b-4ee6-a9df-26c19c6ccb2b (accessed 1 March 2016).
91. Nava, *Visceral Cosmopolitanism*, p. 14.

92. Lauren Berlant, 'Cruel optimism', in Gregory J. Seigworth and Melissa Gregg (eds), *The Affect Theory Reader* (Durham, NC: Duke University Press, 2010), p. 94.
93. Seigworth and Gregg, 'An inventory of shimmers', p. 2.

4 Embodiment as (cosmopolitan) encounter

1. Gregory J. Seigworth and Melissa Gregg, 'An inventory of shimmers', in Gregory J. Seigworth and Melissa Gregg (eds), *The Affect Theory Reader* (Durham, NC: Duke University Press, 2010), p. 2.
2. Vivian Sobchack, 'What my fingers knew, the cinesthetic subject, or vision in the flesh', *Senses of Cinema* 5 (2000). Available at sensesofcinema.com/2000/conference-special-effects-special-affects/fingers/ (accessed 31 October 2014).
3. Richard C. Allen, 'Re-imagining the history of the experience of cinema in a post-moviegoing age', in Richard Maltby, Daniel Biltereyst and Philippe Meers (eds), *Explorations in New Cinema History: Approaches and Case Studies* (Chichester: Wiley-Blackwell, 2011), pp. 41–57.
4. Ibid., p. 42.
5. Ibid., pp. 42–3.
6. Ibid., p. 43.
7. Ibid., p. 44.
8. Ibid., p. 44.
9. See Catherine Fowler, 'Room for experiment: gallery films and vertical time from Maya Deren to Eija Liisa Ahtila', *Screen* 45.4 (2004), pp. 324–43.
10. Laura U. Marks, *The Skin of the Film: Intercultural Cinema, Embodiment, and the Senses* (Durham, NC: Duke University Press, 2000), p. 22.
11. Ibid., p. 22.
12. Marsha Meskimmon, *Contemporary Art and the Cosmopolitan Imagination* (Abingdon, Oxon: Routledge, 2011), p. 6.
13. Ibid., p. 44.
14. Catherine Fowler, 'Into the light: re-considering off-frame and off-screen space in gallery films', *New Review of Film and Television Studies* 6.3 (2008), p. 253.
15. Ibid., p. 259.
16. Fowler, 'Room for experiment', p. 343.
17. Ibid., p. 343.
18. Sara Ahmed, *Strange Encounters: Embodied Others in Post-Coloniality* (London: Routledge, 2000), p. 40.
19. Carla Bianpoen, 'Ming Wong's "Imitation of Life"', *The Jakarta Post* (20 May 2010).

20. Angie Baecker, 'Melodrama and metissage: the art of Ming Wong', *LEAP* 10 (1 September 2011). Available at www.leapleapleap.com/2011/09/melodrama-and-metissage-the-art-of-ming-wong/ (accessed 21 January 2012).
21. Jon Lowther, 'Ming Wong re-casts classics to reveal our roles in modern society', *The Japan Times* (8 July 2011).
22. Tang Fu Kuen, 'Notes from the curator', *Ming Wong: Life of Imitation*, exhibition catalogue (Singapore Art Museum, 2010), p. 51.
23. Ibid., p. 51.
24. Quoted in Bianpoen, 'Ming Wong's "Imitation of Life"'.
25. Fowler, 'Room for experiment', p. 343.
26. Sholem Krishtalka, 'Ersatz cinema', *Toronto Standard* (17 September 2012). Available at www.torontostandard.com/culture/ersatz-cinema/ (accessed 10 June 2014).
27. William Galperin, '"Bad for the glass": representation and filmic deconstruction in *Chinatown* and *Chan is Missing*', MLN 102.5 (1987), p. 1157.
28. Ibid., p. 1158.
29. Ibid., p. 1158.
30. Ibid., p. 1158.
31. susan pui san lok, 'A to Y (entries for an inventory of dented "I"s)', in David A. Bailey, Ian Baucom and Sonia Boyce (eds), *Shades of Black: Assembling Black Arts in 1980s Britain* (Durham, NC: Duke University Press, 2005), p. 61.
32. REDCAT, 'Ming Wong: making Chinatown', REDCAT website (February–April 2012). Available at www.redcat.org/exhibition/ming-wong-making-chinatown (accessed 10 June 2014).
33. Krishtalka, 'Ersatz cinema'.
34. Robert Ito, '"A certain slant": a brief history of Hollywood yellowface', *Bright Lights Film Journal* (2 May 2014). Available at brightlightsfilm.com/certain-slant-brief-history-hollywood-yellowface/#.V2qDWY7ccz4 (accessed 10 June 2014).
35. Yiman Wang, 'The art of screen passing: Anna May Wong's yellow yellowface performance in the art deco era', *Camera Obscura* 60, 20.3 (2005), p. 168.
36. Ibid., p. 168.
37. Ibid., pp. 160–1.
38. Ibid., p. 161.
39. B. Ruby Rich, 'Toronto 2012: haunted by history', *Fandor* (13 September 2012). Available at www.fandor.com/blog/toronto-2012-haunted-by-history (accessed 11 June 2015).
40. Krishtalka, 'Ersatz cinema'.
41. Credit to a friend and colleague, Dr Robin Loon, who researches intercultural theatre at the National University of Singapore, for sharing this idea with me one afternoon over coffee in the courtyard of Liverpool's Bluecoat. The 'authentication of fakeness' is his phrase.

42. Kay J. Anderson, 'The idea of Chinatown: the power of place and institutional practice in the making of a racial category', *Annals of the Association of American Geographers* 77.4 (1987), p. 581.
43. Rhizome + FACT, 'Five videos: Ming Wong's "Forget it, Jake ... it's Chinatown"', *Rhizome* (18 September 2012). Available at rhizome.org/editorial/2012/sep/18/five-videos-ming-wongs-forget-it-jake-its-chinatow/ (accessed 11 June 2015).
44. Huiping Ling and Allan Austin (eds), *Asian American History and Culture: An Encyclopedia* (Abingdon, Oxon: Routledge, 2015), p. 147.
45. See Ian Herbert, 'Son's hunt for father exposes betrayal of war heroes', *The Independent* (1 February 2002). Available at www.independent.co.uk/news/uk/this-britain/sons-hunt-for-father-exposes-betrayal-of-war-heroes-9156231.html (accessed 11 June 2015).
46. See blog.angryasianman.com/2007/01/chop-suey-specs-again.html (accessed 11 June 2015).
47. Wang, 'The art of screen passing', p. 171.
48. Ibid., p. 177.
49. Ibid., p. 177.
50. Ibid., p. 179.
51. Norman K. Denzin, *Performance Ethnography: Critical Pedagogy and the Politics of Culture* (London: Sage Publications, 2003), p. 14.
52. Ibid., p. 12.
53. Ibid., p. 36.
54. Russell Storer, 'Repeat after me', *Ming Wong: Life of Imitation*, exhibition catalogue (Singapore: Singapore Art Museum, 2010), p. 62. For an early seminal text that self-consciously read against the grain the state's rhetoric on multiracialism and multiculturalism in Singapore, see Geoffrey Benjamin, 'The cultural logic of Singapore's "multiracialism"', in Riaz Hassan (ed.), *Singapore: Society in Transition* (Kuala Lumpur: Oxford University Press, 1976), pp. 115–33.
55. Tsung-Yi Huang, 'Hong Kong blue: *flâneurie* with the camera's eye in a phantasmagoric global city', *Journal of Narrative Theory* 30.3 (2000), p. 386.
56. Rhizome + FACT, 'Five videos'.
57. Bianpoen, 'Ming Wong's "Imitation of Life"'.
58. William Siew Wai Lim, *Architecture, Art, Identity in Singapore: Is There Life After Tabula Rasa?* (Singapore: Asian Urban Lab, 2004).
59. Bianpoen, 'Ming Wong's "Imitation of Life"'.
60. Ibid.
61. Tang, 'Notes from the curator', p. 55.
62. Jeff Popke, 'Geography and ethics: spaces of cosmopolitan responsibility', *Progress in Human Geography* 31.4 (2007), p. 510.
63. Ahmed, *Strange Encounters*, p. 40.
64. Sobchack, 'What my fingers knew'.

65. Ibid.
66. David Michael Levin (ed.), *Modernity and the Hegemony of Vision* (Berkeley, CA: University of California Press, 1993).
67. Liora Moriel, 'Passing and the performance of gender, race, and class acts: a theoretical framework', *Women & Performance: A Journal of Feminist Theory* 15.1 (2005), p. 184.
68. See Mahyuddin Ahmad and Yuen Beng Lee, 'Negotiating class, ethnicity and modernity: the "Malaynisation" of P. Ramlee and his films', *Asian Journal of Communication* 25.4 (2015), pp. 408–21.
69. Interestingly, as late as 2014, UNESCO recognises 'a cache of Malay movies made in Singapore from the 1950s to the 1970s ... as an important part of the region's heritage'. This is a cache of 91 films made by the Cathay-Keris Studio, a rival of Shaw's. See John Lui, 'Cache of Singapore Malay films recognised by Unesco as part of region's heritage', *The Straits Times* (11 December 2014). Available at www.straitstimes.com/lifestyle/entertainment/cache-of-singapore-malay-films-recognised-by-unesco-as-part-of-regions (accessed 15 June 2015).
70. Raphaël Millet, *Singapore Cinema* (Singapore: Editions Didier Millet, 2006).
71. Baecker, 'Melodrama and metissage'.
72. Selina Ting, 'Interview: Ming Wong', *Initiart Magazine* (Summer 2009). Available at www.initiartmagazine.com/interview.php?IVarchive=12 (accessed 21 January 2012).
73. Storer, 'Repeat after me', p. 58.

Postscript: Critical cosmopolitanism and comparative cinema

1. Gerard Delanty, 'The cosmopolitan imagination: critical cosmopolitanism and social theory', *The British Journal of Sociology* 57.1 (2006), p. 35.
2. Ibid., p. 40.
3. Ibid., p. 41.
4. Gerard Delanty, *Community* (London: Routledge, 2010), p. 72.
5. Delanty, 'The cosmopolitan imagination', p. 41.
6. Marsha Meskimmon, *Contemporary Art and the Cosmopolitan Imagination* (Abingdon, Oxon: Routledge, 2011), p. 6.
7. André Bazin, 'The ontology of the photographic image', trans. Hugh Gray, *Film Quarterly* 13.4 (1960), p. 6.
8. Delanty, 'The cosmopolitan imagination', p. 27.
9. Meskimmon, *Contemporary Art and the Cosmopolitan Imagination*, p. 8.
10. Ibid., p. 8.
11. Ibid., p. 91.

12. Lauren Berlant, 'Cruel optimism', in Gregory J. Seigworth and Melissa Gregg (eds), *The Affect Theory Reader* (Durham, NC: Duke University Press, 2010), p. 97.
13. Robert Spencer, *Cosmopolitan Criticism and Postcolonial Literature* (Basingstoke: Palgrave Macmillan, 2011), pp. 12–13.
14. Meskimmon, *Contemporary Art and the Cosmopolitan Imagination*, p. 68.
15. Ibid, p. 63.
16. Ibid., p. 69.
17. Spencer, *Cosmopolitan Criticism and Postcolonial Literature*, p. 6.
18. Sean Cubitt, *The Cinema Effect* (Cambridge, MA: MIT Press, 2004), p. 331.
19. Ibid., p. 339.
20. Ibid., p. 356.
21. Felicia Chan, '*Crouching Tiger, Hidden Dragon*: cultural migrancy and translatability', in Chris Berry (ed.), *Chinese Films in Focus II* (London: British Film Institute, 2009), pp. 73–81. See also Wu Huating and Joseph Man Chan, 'Globalizing Chinese martial arts cinema: the global–local alliance and the production of *Crouching Tiger, Hidden Dragon*', *Media, Culture & Society* 29.2 (2007), pp. 195–217.
22. Paul Willemen, 'For a comparative film studies', *Inter-Asia Cultural Studies* 6.1 (2005), p. 98.
23. Ibid., p. 103.
24. Ibid., p. 103.
25. Ibid., p. 107.
26. Meaghan Morris, 'Transnational imagination in action cinema: Hong Kong and the making of a global popular culture', *Inter-Asia Cultural Studies* 5.2 (2004), p. 183.

Bibliography

Abbas, Ackbar, *Hong Kong: Culture and the Politics of Disappearance* (Hong Kong: Hong Kong University Press, 1997).
Ahmad, Mahyuddin and Yuen Beng Lee, 'Negotiating class, ethnicity and modernity: the "Malaynisation" of P. Ramlee and his films', *Asian Journal of Communication* 25.4 (2015), pp. 408–21.
Ahmed, Sara, *Strange Encounters: Embodied Others in Post-Coloniality* (London: Routledge, 2000).
Allen, Richard C., 'Re-imagining the history of the experience of cinema in a post-moviegoing age', in Richard Maltby, Daniel Biltereyst and Philippe Meers (eds), *Explorations in New Cinema History: Approaches and Case Studies* (Chichester: Wiley-Blackwell, 2011), pp. 41–57.
Andersen, Joseph L. and Donald Richie, *The Japanese Film: Art and Industry*, expanded edition (Princeton, NJ: Princeton University Press, 1982).
Anderson, Kay J., 'The idea of Chinatown: the power of place and institutional practice in the making of a racial category', *Annals of the Association of American Geographers* 77.4 (1987), pp. 580–98.
Appadurai, Arjun, 'Cosmopolitanism from below: some ethical lessons from the slums of Mumbai', *JWTC: Johannesburg Workshop in Theory and Criticism* 4 (2011). Available at jwtc.org.za/volume_4/arjun_appadurai.htm (accessed 18 June 2014).
Austin, J. L., *How to Do Things with Words* (Oxford: Clarendon Press, 1962).
Austin, Thomas, 'Indexicality and inter/textuality: *24 City*'s aesthetics and the politics of memory', *Screen* 55.2 (2014), pp. 256–66.
Bachelard, Gaston, *The Poetics of Space* (Boston, MA: Beacon Press, 1994).
Baecker, Angie, 'Melodrama and metissage: the art of Ming Wong', *LEAP* 10 (1 September 2011). Available at www.leapleapleap.com/2011/09/melodrama-and-metissage-the-art-of-ming-wong/ (accessed 21 January 2012).
Balfour, Ian and Atom Egoyan, 'Introduction', in Atom Egoyan and Ian Balfour (eds), *Subtitles: On the Foreignness of Film* (Cambridge, MA: The MIT Press, 2004), pp. 21–30.
Bart, Peter, *Cannes: Fifty Years of Sun, Sex and Celluloid* (New York: Miramax, 1997).
Batto, Patricia R. S., 'The world of Jia Zhangke', *China Perspectives* 60 (2005). Available at chinaperspectives.revues.org/2843 (accessed 6 June 2011).
Bauman, Zygmunt, *Modernity and Ambivalence* (Cambridge: Polity Press, 1991).

Bibliography

Bazin, André, 'The ontology of the photographic image', trans. Hugh Gray, *Film Quarterly* 13.4 (1960), pp. 4-9.

Beeton, Sue, *Film-Induced Tourism* (Clevedon: Channel View Publications, 2005).

Béhar, Henri, 'Cultural ventriloquism', in Atom Egoyan and Ian Balfour (eds), *Subtitles: On the Foreignness of Film* (Cambridge, MA: The MIT Press, 2004), pp. 79-88.

Benjamin, Geoffrey, 'The cultural logic of Singapore's "multiracialism"', in Riaz Hassan (ed.), *Singapore: Society in Transition* (Kuala Lumpur: Oxford University Press, 1976), pp. 115-33.

Benjamin, Walter, 'The translator's task' (*'Die Aufgabe des Übersetzers'*), trans. Steven Rendall, *TTR* 10.2 (1997), pp. 151-65.

Bergfelder, Tim and Sarah Street (eds), *The Titanic in Myth and Memory: Representations in Visual and Literary Culture* (London: I.B.Tauris, 2004).

Berlant, Lauren, 'Thinking about feeling historical', *Emotion, Space and Society* 1 (2008), pp. 4-9.

——, 'Cruel optimism', in Gregory J. Seigworth and Melissa Gregg (eds), *The Affect Theory Reader* (Durham, NC: Duke University Press, 2010), pp. 93-117.

Berry, Chris, 'Getting real: Chinese documentary, Chinese postsocialism', in Zhang Zhen (ed.), *The Urban Generation: Chinese Cinema and Society at the Turn of the Twenty-first Century* (Durham, NC: Duke University Press, 2007), pp. 115-34.

Bettinson, Gary, *The Sensuous Cinema of Wong Kar-wai: Film Poetics and the Aesthetics of Disturbance* (Hong Kong: Hong Kong University Press, 2014).

Betz, Mark, 'The name above the (sub)title: internationalism, coproduction, and polyglot European art cinema', *Camera Obscura* 46, 16.1 (2001), pp. 1-45.

Bhabha, Homi, *The Location of Culture* (London: Routledge, 1994).

Bianpoen, Carla, 'Ming Wong's "Imitation of Life"', *The Jakarta Post* (20 May 2010).

Bisht, Pawas, 'The politics of cosmopolitan memory', *Media, Culture & Society* 35.1 (2013), pp. 13-20.

Bordwell, David, Janet Staiger and Kristin Thompson, *The Classical Hollywood Cinema: Film Style & Mode of Production to 1960* (New York: Columbia University Press, 1985).

Bourdieu, Pierre, *Language and Symbolic Power* (1982), edited and introduced by John B. Thompson, trans. Gino Raymond and Matthew Adamson (Cambridge: Polity Press, 1991).

Bradshaw, Peter, 'The heart-wrenching performance of Setsuko Hara, Ozu's quiet muse', The *Guardian* Film Blog 16 June 2010. Available at www.theguardian.com/film/filmblog/2010/jun/16/setsuko-hara-birthday-tokyo-story (accessed 22 July 2014).

Bibliography

Breakwell, Ian and Paul Hammond (eds), *Seeing in the Dark: A Compendium of Cinemagoing* (London: Serpent's Tail, 1990).
Brennan, Timothy, *At Home in the World: Cosmopolitanism Now* (Cambridge, MA: Harvard University Press, 1997).
Brunette, Peter, *Wong Kar-wai* (Urbana, Champaign, IL: University of Illinois Press, 2005).
Bruno, Giuliana, *Street Walking on a Ruined Map: Cultural Theory and the City Films of Elvira Notari* (Princeton, NJ: Princeton University Press, 1993).
Canudo, Ricciotto, 'The birth of the sixth art (1911)', in Paul Willemen and Jim Pines (eds), *The Essential Framework: Classic Film and TV Essays* (London: EpiGraph, 1998), pp. 14–22.
Caruth, Cathy (ed.), *Trauma: Explorations in Memory* (Baltimore, MD: John Hopkins University Press, 1990).
Chan, Felicia, 'When is a foreign-language film not a foreign-language film? When it has too much English in it; the case of a Singapore film and the Oscars', *Inter-Asia Cultural Studies* 9.1 (2008), pp. 95–105.
——, '*Crouching Tiger, Hidden Dragon*: cultural migrancy and translatability', in Chris Berry (ed.), *Chinese Films in Focus II* (London: British Film Institute, 2009), pp. 73–81.
——, 'Genre as cultural whimsy: taking to the road in *The Bird People in China* and *Cold Fever*', in Felicia Chan, Angelina Karpovich and Xin Zhang, *Genre in Asian Film and Television: New Approaches* (Basingstoke: Palgrave Macmillan, 2011), pp. 210–21.
——, 'The international film festival and the making of a national cinema', *Screen* 52.2 (2011), pp. 253–60.
Chan, Felicia and Dave Chua, 'Programming Southeast Asia at the Singapore International Film Festival', in Dina Iordanova, Ruby Cheung and Alex Fischer (eds), *Film Festival Yearbook 3: Film Festivals and East Asia* (St Andrews: St Andrews University Press, 2011), pp. 125–41.
Chan, Kenneth, '*Goodbye, Dragon Inn*: Tsai Ming-liang's political aesthetics of nostalgia, place, and lingering', *Journal of Chinese Cinemas* 1.2 (2007), pp. 89–103.
Chan Su-Lin, Nadine, 'Cosmopolitan cinema: towards a new trajectory in cosmopolitan theory', unpublished dissertation submitted for the degree of Master of Arts, Department of English Language and Literature, National University of Singapore (2009).
Chandler, David, 'The cosmopolitan paradox: response to Robbins', *Radical Philosophy* 118 (2003), pp. 25–30.
Chaney, David, 'Cosmopolitan art and cultural citizenship', *Theory, Culture & Society* 19.1–2 (2002), pp. 157–74.
Chang, Yen-Jung, 'Satoshi Kon's *Millennium Actress*: a feminine journey with dream-like qualities', *Animation* 8.1 (2013), pp. 85–97.

Bibliography

Cheah, Pheng, 'The cosmopolitical – today', in Pheng Cheah and Bruce Robbins (eds), *Cosmopolitics: Thinking and Feeling Beyond the Nation* (Minneapolis, MN: University of Minnesota Press, 1998), pp. 20–41.

——, 'What is a world? On world literature as world-making activity', *Daedalus* 137.3 (2008), pp. 26–38.

Chen, Leo Chanjen, 'Cinema, dream, existence: the films of Hou Hsiao-Hsien', *New Left Review* 39 (May / June 2006), pp. 73–106.

Chew Boon Leong, Kong Kam Yoke and Danny Yeo (eds), *My Creative Room* (Singapore: My Creative Room, 2009).

Chew, Matthew, 'Contemporary re-emergence of the qipao: political nationalism, cultural production and popular consumption of a traditional Chinese dress', *The China Quarterly* 189 (2007), pp. 144–61.

Chow, Rey, *Not Like a Native Speaker: On Languaging as a Postcolonial Experience* (New York: Columbia University Press, 2014).

Chua Beng Huat, *Life is Not Complete Without Shopping: Consumption Culture in Singapore* (Singapore: Singapore University Press, 2003).

——, 'Conceptualizing an East Asian popular culture', *Inter-Asia Cultural Studies* 5.2 (2004), pp. 200–21.

Cooper-Chen, Anne, 'Cartoon planet: the cross-cultural acceptance of Japanese animation', *Asian Journal of Communication* 22.1 (2012), pp. 44–57.

Corrigan, Timothy, 'The commerce of auteurism: a voice without authority', *New German Critique* 49 (1990), pp. 43–57.

Corless, Kieron and Chris Darke, *Cannes: Inside the World's Premier Film Festival* (London: Faber and Faber, 2007).

Crafton, Donald, *The Talkies: American Cinema's Transition to Sound, 1926–31* (Berkeley, CA: University of California Press, 1999).

Crisp, Virginia, '"BLOODY PIRATES!!! *shakes fist*": reimagining East Asian film distribution and reception through online filesharing networks', *Journal of Japanese & Korean Cinema* 3.1 (2012), pp. 65–72.

Cubitt, Sean, 'Ecocritique and the materialities of animation', in Suzanne Buchan (ed.), *Pervasive Animation* (London: Routledge, 2003), pp. 94–114.

——, *The Cinema Effect* (Cambridge, MA: MIT Press, 2004).

Curtin, Melissa L. 'Languages on display: indexical signs, identities and the linguistic landscape of Taipei', in Elana Shohamy and Durk Gorter (eds), *Linguistic Landscape: Expanding the Scenery* (New York: Routledge, 2009), pp. 221–69.

Czach, Liz, 'Film festivals, programming and the building of a national cinema', *The Moving Image* 4.1 (2004), pp. 76–88.

Dargis, Manohla, 'An upscale leap forward that leaves many behind', *The New York Times* (4 June 2009). Available at www.nytimes.com/2009/06/05/movies/05twen.html (accessed 9 July 2014).

Bibliography

Daruvala, Susan, 'Self as performance, lust as betrayal in the theatre of war', in Peng Hsiao-yen and Whitney Crothers Dilley (eds), *From Eileen Chang to Ang Lee: Lust/Caution* (Abingdon, Oxon: Routledge, 2014), pp. 101–21.

de Valck, Marijke, *Film Festivals: From European Geopolitics to Global Cinephilia* (Amsterdam: Amsterdam University Press, 2007).

de Valck, Marijke, and Skadi Loist, 'Film festival studies: an overview of a burgeoning field', in Dina Iordanova with Ragan Rhyne (eds), *Film Festival Yearbook 1: The Festival Circuit* (St. Andrews: St. Andrews Film Studies, 2009), pp. 179–215.

Delanty, Gerard, 'The cosmopolitan imagination: critical cosmopolitanism and social theory', *The British Journal of Sociology* 57.1 (2006), pp. 25–47.

——, *Community* (London: Routledge, 2010).

Dennison, Stephanie and Song Hwee Lim (eds), *Remapping World Cinema: Identity, Culture and Politics in Film* (London: Wallflower, 2006).

Denzin, Norman K., *Performance Ethnography: Critical Pedagogy and the Politics of Culture* (London: Sage Publications, 2003).

Derrida, Jacques, *On Cosmopolitanism and Forgiveness* [1997] (London: Routledge, 2001).

——, *Monolingualism of the Other; or, the Prosthesis of Origin* (Stanford, CA: Stanford University Press, 1998).

Díaz-Cintas, Jorge, 'Dubbing or subtitling: the eternal dilemma', *Perspectives: Studies in Translatology*, 7.1 (1999), pp. 31–40.

Doane, Mary Ann, *Femmes Fatales: Feminism, Film Theory, Psychoanalysis* (London: Routledge, 1991).

Eisenstein, Sergei, *Eisenstein on Disney*, ed. Jay Leyda, trans. Alan Upchurch (London: Methuen, 1988).

Eleftheriotis, Dimitris, *Cinematic Journeys: Film and Movement* (Edinburgh: Edinburgh University Press, 2010).

Elsaesser, Thomas, *European Cinema: Face to Face with Hollywood* (Amsterdam: Amsterdam University Press, 2005), pp. 82–107.

Fong, Gilbert C. F. and Kenneth K. L. Au (eds), *Dubbing and Subtitling in a World Context* (Hong Kong: The Chinese University Press, 2009).

Fowler, Catherine, 'Room for experiment: gallery films and vertical time from Maya Deren to Eija Liisa Ahtila', *Screen* 45.4 (2004), pp. 324–43.

——, 'Into the light: re-considering off-frame and off-screen space in gallery films', *New Review of Film and Television Studies* 6.3 (2008), pp. 253–67.

Freud, Sigmund, 'Screen memories', in *The Uncanny* (London: Penguin, 2003), pp. 2–22.

Fu, Poshek, *Between Shanghai and Hong Kong: The Politics of Chinese Cinemas* (Stanford, CA: Stanford University Press, 2003).

Fujiki, Hideaki, 'Benshi as stars: the irony of the popularity and respectability of voice performers in Japanese cinema', *Cinema Journal* 45.2 (2006), pp. 68–84.

Galperin, William, '"Bad for the glass": representation and filmic deconstruction in *Chinatown* and *Chan is Missing*', MLN 102.5 (1987), pp. 1151–70.

Galt, Rosalind and Karl Schoonover (eds), *Global Art Cinema: New Theories and Histories* (Oxford: Oxford University Press, 2010).

George, Cherian, *Singapore, the Air-Conditioned Nation: Essays on the Politics of Comfort and Control, 1990–2000* (Singapore: Landmark Books, 2000).

Gilroy, Paul, *After Empire: Melancholia or Convivial Culture?* (London: Routledge, 2004).

Glick Schiller, Nina and Andrew Irving, 'Introduction: what's in a word? What's in a question?', in Nina Glick Schiller and Andrew Irving (eds), *Whose Cosmopolitanism?: Critical Perspectives, Relationalities and Discontents* (New York: Berghahn, 2015), pp. 1–22.

Goodman, Nelson, *Ways of Worldmaking* (Hassocks: Harvester Press, 1978).

Grant, Catherine, 'On "affect" and "emotion" in film and media studies', *Film Studies for Free* blog (4 November 2011). Available at: http://filmstudiesforfree.blogspot.co.uk/2011/11/on-affect-and-emotion-in-film-and-media.html (accessed 31 July 2014).

Green, Eileen, Sandra Hebron and Diana Woodward, *Women's Leisure, What Leisure?* (Basingstoke: Macmillan, 1990).

Gunning, Tom, 'The cinema of attractions: early film, its spectator and the avant-garde', *Wide Angle* 8.3–4 (1986), pp. 63–70.

Gupta, Anthea Fraser, 'Singapore Colloquial English? Or deviant Standard English?', in Jan Tent and France Mugler (eds), *SICOL: Proceedings of the Second International Conference on Oceanic Languages Vol. 1* (Canberra: Pacific Linguistics, 1998), pp. 43–57.

Hansen, Miriam Bratu, 'The mass production of the senses: classical cinema as vernacular modernism', *Modernism/Modernity* 6.2 (1999), pp. 59–77.

Harbord, Janet, *Film Cultures* (London: Sage, 2002).

Herbert, Ian, 'Son's hunt for father exposes betrayal of war heroes', *The Independent* (1 February 2002). Available at www.independent.co.uk/news/uk/this-britain/sons-hunt-for-father-exposes-betrayal-of-war-heroes-9156231.html (accessed 11 June 2015).

Hjort, Mette and Duncan Petrie (eds), *The Cinema of Small Nations* (Bloomington, IN: Indiana University Press, 2007).

Hozic, Aida A., *Hollyworld: Space, Power, and Fantasy in the American Economy* (New York: Cornell University Press, 2001).

Huang, Tsung-Yi, 'Hong Kong blue: *flâneurie* with the camera's eye in a phantasmagoric global city', *Journal of Narrative Theory* 30.3 (2000), pp. 385–402.

Bibliography

Huyssen, Andreas and Natan Sznaider, 'Memory unbound: the Holocaust and the formation of cosmopolitan memory', *European Journal of Social Theory* 5.1 (2002), pp. 87–106.

Iordanova, Dina, 'The film festival circuit', in Dina Iordanova with Ragan Rhyne (eds), *Film Festival Yearbook 1: The Festival Circuit*. (St Andrews: St Andrews Film Studies, 2009), pp. 23–39.

——, 'Mediating diaspora: film festivals and "imagined communities"', in Dina Iordanova with Ruby Cheung (eds), *Film Festival Yearbook 2: Film Festivals and Imagined Communities* (St Andrews: St Andrews Film Studies, 2010), pp. 12–44.

Iordanova, Dina and Leshu Torchin (eds), *Film Festival Yearbook 4: Film Festivals and Activism* (St Andrews: St Andrews Film Studies, 2012).

Ito, Robert, '"A certain slant": a brief history of Hollywood yellowface', *Bright Lights Film Journal* (2 May 2014). Available at brightlightsfilm.com/certain-slant-brief-history-hollywood-yellowface/#.V2qDWY7ccz4 (accessed 10 June 2014).

Iveković, Rada, 'The watershed of modernity: translation and the epistemological revolution', *Inter-Asia Cultural Studies* 11.1 (2010), pp. 45–63.

Jaffee, Valerie, 'Bringing the world to the nation: Jia Zhangke and the legitimation of Chinese underground film', *Senses of Cinema* 32 (2004). Available at http://sensesofcinema.com/2004/feature-articles/chinese_ underground_film/ (accessed 9 July 2014).

Jamieson, Kirstie, 'Edinburgh: the festival gaze and its boundaries,' *Space & Culture* 7.1 (2004), p. 64–75.

Johnson, Brian D., *Brave Films, Wild Nights: 25 Years of Festival Fever* (Toronto: Random House Canada, 2000).

Johnson, G. Allen, 'Review: 24 City', *San Francisco Chronicle* (31 July 2009). Available at www.sfgate.com/movies/article/Review-24-City-3223498.php (accessed 9 July 2014).

Kaplan, E. Ann, 'Melodrama, cinema and trauma', *Screen* 42.2 (2001), pp. 201–205.

Kaplan, E. Ann and Ban Wang (eds), *Trauma and Cinema: Cross-Cultural Explorations* (Hong Kong: Hong Kong University Press, 2004).

Karpovich, Angelina I., 'Theoretical approaches to film-motivated tourism', *Tourism and Hospitality Planning & Development*, 7.1 (2010), pp. 7–20.

Kayman, Martin, 'The state of English as a global language: communicating culture', *Textual Practice* 18.1 (2004), pp. 1–22.

Kirkland, Bruce, 'Ang Lee's a dragon in hiding', canoe.com (3 December 2000). Available at jam.canoe.com/Movies/Artists/L/Lee_Ang/2000/12/03/pf-759755.html (accessed 12 June 2013).

Krishtalka, Sholem, 'Ersatz cinema', *Toronto Standard* (17 September 2012). Available at www.torontostandard.com/culture/ersatz-cinema/ (accessed 10 June 2014).

Bibliography

Lai Chee Kien, 'Imagining Nanyang: the framing of Southeast Asia in Wong Kar-wai's movies', in Lilian Chee and Edna Lim (eds), *Asian Cinema and Space: Interdisciplinary Perspectives* (London: Routledge, 2015), pp. 109–25.

Lamarre, Thomas, 'From animation to *anime*: drawing movements and moving drawings', *Japan Forum* 14.2 (2002), pp. 329–67.

———, 'Introduction: between cinema and *anime*', *Japan Forum* 14.2 (2002), pp. 183–9.

Lee, Leo Ou-fan, 'The urban milieu of Shanghai cinema, 1930–40: some explorations of film audience, film culture, and narrative conventions', in Yingjin Zhang (ed.), *Cinema and Urban Culture in Shanghai, 1922–1943* (Stanford, CA: Stanford University Press, 1999), pp. 74–98.

———, 'Ang Lee's *Lust, Caution* and its reception', *boundary 2* 35 (2008), pp. 223–38.

Lee Weng Choy (ed.), *Space, Spaces and Spacing* (Singapore: The Substation, 1996).

Levin, David Michael (ed.), *Modernity and the Hegemony of Vision* (Berkeley, CA: University of California Press, 1993).

Levy, Daniel and Natan Sznaider, *Human Rights and Memory* (University Park, PA: Pennsylvania State University Press, 2010).

Levy, Emanuel, *All About Oscar: The History and Politics of the Academy Awards* (New York: Continuum, 2003).

Li, Cheuk-to, 'Hong Kong: zest and anguish', in Aruna Vasudev, Latika Padgaonkar and Rashmi Doraiswamy (eds), *Being and Becoming: The Cinemas of Asia* (Delhi: Macmillan, 2002), pp. 92–123.

Liao, Hsien-hao Sebastian, 'Becoming modernized or simply "modern"?: Sex, Chineseness, and diasporic consciousness in *Lust, Caution*', *Concentric: Literary and Cultural Studies* 36.2 (2010), pp. 181–211.

Lim, Edna, 'Displacing Titanic: history, spectacle and Hollywood', *Interdisciplinary Literary Studies* 5.1 (2003), pp. 45–69.

Lim, William Siew Wai, *Architecture, Art, Identity in Singapore: Is There Life After Tabula Rasa?* (Singapore: Asian Urban Lab, 2004).

Lin, Sylvia Li-chun, *Representing Atrocity in Taiwan: The 2/28 Incident and White Terror in Fiction and Film.* (New York: Columbia University Press, 2007).

Ling, Huiping and Allan Austin (eds), *Asian American History and Culture: An Encyclopedia* (Abingdon, Oxon: Routledge, 2015).

Lo, Kwai-cheung, *Chinese Face/Off: The Transnational Popular Culture of Hong Kong* (Urbana and Chicago, IL: University of Illinois Press, 2005).

Lobato, Ramon, *Shadow Economies of Cinema: Mapping Informal Film Distribution* (London: British Film Institute, 2012).

Loh, Sherwin, '15 actor back in school', *The Straits Times, Life!* Section (14 October 2003).

lok, susan pui san, 'A to Y (entries for an inventory of dented "I"s)', in David A. Bailey, Ian Baucom and Sonia Boyce (eds), *Shades of Black: Assembling Black Arts in 1980s Britain* (Durham, NC: Duke University Press, 2005).

Low Beng Kheng. 'Yangtze cinema: guerilla [*sic*] curating to the masses', *Singapore Memory Project* (February 2012). Available at www.singapore-memory.sg/contents/SMA-39cb3836-858b-4ee6-a9df-26c19c6ccb2b (accessed 1 March 2016).

Lowther, Jon, 'Ming Wong re-casts classics to reveal our roles in modern society', *The Japan Times* (8 July 2011).

Lu, Sheldon, 'Dialect and modernity in 21st century Sinophone cinema', *Jump Cut: A Review of Contemporary Media* 49 (2007). Available at www.ejumpcut.org/archive/jc49.2007/Lu/text.html (accessed 13 June 2013).

Lui, John, 'Keep the film festival weird – the way for the rebooted Singapore International Film Festival to go is to stay edgy and creative', *The Straits Times, Life!* Section (11 December 2013).

———, 'Cache of Singapore Malay films recognised by Unesco as part of region's heritage', *The Straits Times* (11 December 2014). Available at www.straitstimes.com/lifestyle/entertainment/cache-of-singapore-malay-films-recognised-by-unesco-as-part-of-regions (accessed 15 June 2015).

Marks, Laura U., *The Skin of the Film: Intercultural Cinema, Embodiment, and the Senses* (Durham, NC: Duke University Press, 2000).

Mathews, Gordon, *Ghetto at the Center of the World: Chungking Mansions, Hong Kong* (Chicago, IL: University of Chicago Press, 2011).

McClintock, Pamela, 'Box office report: Titanic 3D jumps $200 mil in only 12 days', *The Hollywood Reporter* (16 April 2012). Available at www.hollywoodreporter.com/news/titanic-box-office-james-cameron-312497 (accessed 18 June 2014).

Mera, Miguel, 'Read my lips: re-evaluating subtitling and dubbing in Europe', *Links & Letters* 6 (1999), pp. 73–85.

Meskimmon, Marsha, *Contemporary Art and the Cosmopolitan Imagination* (Abingdon, Oxon: Routledge, 2011).

Miller, David, 'Cosmopolitanism', in Garrett Wallace Brown and David Held (eds), *The Cosmopolitanism Reader* (Cambridge: Polity Press, 2010), pp. 377–92.

Millet, Raphaël, *Singapore Cinema* (Singapore: Editions Didier Millet, 2006).

Mitchell, W. J. T., *Picture Theory* (Chicago, IL: University of Chicago Press, 1994).

Moriel, Liora, 'Passing and the performance of gender, race, and class acts: a theoretical framework', *Women & Performance: A Journal of Feminist Theory* 15.1 (2005), pp. 167–210.

Morris, Meaghan, 'Transnational imagination in action cinema: Hong Kong and the making of a global popular culture', *Inter-Asia Cultural Studies* 5.2 (2004), pp. 181–99.

Mowitt, John, *Re-takes: Postcoloniality and Foreign Film Languages* (Minneapolis, MN: University of Minnesota Press, 2005).

Mudge, James, 'The melancholic charm of Tony Leung Chiu Wai', *yesasia.com* (16 January 2007). Available at www.yesasia.com/us/yumcha/the-melancholic-charm-of-tony-leung-chiu-wai/0-0-0-arid.106-en/featured-article.html (accessed 9 May 2014).

Mulvey, Laura, *Death 24x a Second: Stillness and the Moving Image* (London: Reaktion Books, 2006).

Naficy, Hamid, 'Theorizing "third-world" film spectatorship', *Wide Angle* 18.4 (1996), pp. 3–26.

Nafus, Chale, '*Millennium Actress* program notes', Austin Film Society screening (5 December 2006). Available at www.austinfilm.org/page.aspx?pid=2997 (accessed 23 July 2014).

Nagib, Lúcia, Chris Perriam and Rajinder Dudrah (eds), *Theorizing World Cinema* (London: I.B.Tauris, 2012).

Nava, Mica, 'Cosmopolitan modernity: everyday imaginaries and the register of difference', *Theory, Culture & Society* 19.1–2 (2002), pp. 81–99.

——, *Visceral Cosmopolitanism: Gender, Culture and the Normalisation of Difference* (Oxford: Berg, 2007).

Newitz, Annalee, 'Magical girls and atomic bomb sperm: Japanese animation in America', *Film Quarterly* 49.1 (1995), pp. 2–15.

Nichols, Bill, 'Discovering form, inferring meaning: new cinemas and the film festival circuit', *Film Quarterly* 47.3 (1994), pp. 16–30.

Nornes, Abé Mark, *Cinema Babel: Translating Global Cinema* (Minneapolis, MN: University of Minnesota Press, 2007).

Ogihara, Junko, 'The exhibition of films for Japanese Americans in Los Angeles during the silent film era', *Film History* 4.2 (1990), pp. 81–7.

Oon, Clarissa, 'The past is just a memory – heritage issues and conservation causes loomed large in 2011 as Singaporeans reeled from the erosion of personal space', *The Straits Times, Life!* Section (31 December 2011).

Ortabasi, Melek, 'Indexing the past: visual language and translatability in Kon Satoshi's *Millennium Actress*', *Perspectives: Studies in Translatology* 14.4 (2007), pp. 278–91.

O'Sullivan, Carol, *Translating Popular Film* (Basingstoke: Palgrave Macmillan, 2011).

O'Sullivan, Simon, 'The aesthetics of affect', *Angelaki* 6.3 (2001), pp. 125–35.

Pang, Laikwan, 'Walking into and out of the spectacle: China's earliest film scene', *Screen* 47.1 (2006), pp. 66–80.

Papastergiadis, Nikos, *Cosmopolitanism and Culture* (Cambridge: Polity Press, 2012).

Parekh, Bhikhu, *Rethinking Multiculturalism: Cultural Diversity and Political Theory* (Cambridge, MA: Harvard University Press, 2002).

Bibliography

Parker, Andrew and Eve Kosofsky Sedgwick, 'Introduction: performativity and performance', in Andrew Parker and Eve Kosofsky Sedgwick (eds), *Performativity and Performance* (New York: Routledge, 1995), pp. 1–18.

Peary, Gerald, 'Memories of a film festival addict', in Jeffrey Ruoff (ed.), *Coming Soon to a Festival Near You: Programming Film Festivals* (St Andrews: St Andrews Film Studies, 2012), pp. 41–58.

Peng Hsiao-yen and Whitney Crothers Dilley, 'Introduction', in Peng Hsiao-yen and Whitney Crothers Dilley (eds), *From Eileen Chang to Ang Lee: Lust/Caution* (Abingdon, Oxon: Routledge, 2014), pp. 1–12.

Peng Hsiao-yen and Whitney Crothers Dilley (eds), *From Eileen Chang to Ang Lee: Lust/Caution* (Abingdon, Oxon: Routledge, 2014).

Peranson, Mark, 'First you get the power, then you get the money: two models of film festivals', in Richard Porton (ed.), *Dekalog 3: on Film Festivals* (London: Wallflower, 2009), pp. 23–37.

Phillips, Michael, 'Turns out Godard's worldview includes a llama', *Chicago Tribune* (10 June 2011). Available at articles.chicagotribune.com/2011-06-10/entertainment/ct-mov-0610-film-socialisme-20110610_1_godard-llama-film-socialisme (accessed 17 May 2013).

Phillips, Richard, 'Film festival director talks to WSWS about censorship in Singapore', *World Socialist Web Site* (24 April 2000). Available at www.wsws.org/en/articles/2000/04/sff3-a24.html (accessed 14 August 2014).

Pomerance, Murray, 'Introduction', in Murray Pomerance (ed.), *Cinema and Modernity* (New Brunswick, NJ: Rutgers University Press, 2006), pp. 3–15.

Popke, Jeff, 'Geography and ethics: spaces of cosmopolitan responsibility', *Progress in Human Geography* 31.4 (2007), pp. 509–18.

Prakash, Gyan, 'Whose cosmopolitanism? Multiple, globally enmeshed and subaltern', in Nina Glick Schiller and Andrew Irving (eds), *Whose Cosmopolitanism?: Critical Perspectives, Relationalities and Discontents* (New York: Berghahn, 2015), pp. 27–8.

Prieto, Rodrigo, 'The "killer pizza light"', in *Lust, Caution: The Story, the Screenplay and the Making of the Film*, by Eileen Chang, James Schamus and Wang Hui Ling (New York: Pantheon, 2007), pp. 253–4.

PuruShotam, Nirmala Srirekam, *Negotiating, Language, Constructing Race* (Berlin: de Gruyter, 1997).

Radstone, Susannah, 'Cinema and memory', in Susannah Radstone and Bill Schwarz (eds), *Memory: Histories, Theories, Debates* (New York: Fordham University Press, 2010), pp. 325–42.

Radstone, Susannah and Bill Schwarz (eds), *Memory: Histories, Theories, Debates* (New York: Fordham University Press, 2010).

Rapson, Jessica, 'Mobilising Lidice: cosmopolitan memory between theory and practice', *Culture, Theory and Critique* 53.2 (2012), pp. 129–45.

Bibliography

Ravenscroft, Neil, Steven Chua and Lynda Keng Neo Wee, 'Going to the movies: cinema development in Singapore', *Leisure Studies* 20 (2001), pp. 215–32.

REDCAT, 'Ming Wong: making Chinatown', REDCAT website (February–April 2012). Available at www.redcat.org/exhibition/ming-wong-making-chinatown (accessed 10 June 2014).

RemSG, 'A last look at Pearls Centre and its Yangtze Theatre', *Remember Singapore* (20 September 2015). Available at remembersingapore.org/2015/09/20/pearls-centre-yangtze-cinema-closure/ (accessed 1 March 2016).

Rhizome + FACT, 'Five videos: Ming Wong's "Forget it, Jake … it's Chinatown"', *Rhizome* (18 September 2012). Available at rhizome.org/editorial/2012/sep/18/five-videos-ming-wongs-forget-it-jake-its-chinatow/ (accessed 11 June 2015).

Rich, B. Ruby, 'To read or not to read: subtitles, trailers, and monolingualism', in Atom Egoyan and Ian Balfour (eds), *Subtitles: On the Foreignness of Film* (Cambridge, MA: The MIT Press, 2004), pp. 153–69.

——, 'Toronto 2012: haunted by history', *Fandor* (13 September 2012). Available at www.fandor.com/blog/toronto-2012-haunted-by-history (accessed 11 June 2015).

Richie, Donald, *Ozu* (Berkeley, CA: University of California Press, 1974).

Robbins, Bruce, 'Comparative cosmopolitanism', *Social Text* 31–2 (1992), pp. 169–86.

Rohter, Larry, 'Can you say "do it again" in Norwegian?', The *New York Times* (12 April 2013). Available at www.nytimes.com/2013/04/14/movies/two-versions-of-kon-tiki-in-two-different-lanugages.html (accessed 30 June 2014).

Rose, Steve, 'It never gets any easier', interview with Tony Leung, The *Guardian* (23 February 2004). Available at www.theguardian.com/film/2004/feb/23/1 (accessed 9 May 2014).

Ross, Miriam, 'The film festival as producer: Latin American films and Rotterdam's Hubert Bals Fund', *Screen* 52.2 (2011), pp. 261–7.

Ruoff, Jeffrey, 'Introduction: programming film festivals', in Jeffrey Ruoff (ed.), *Coming Soon to a Festival Near You: Programming Film Festivals* (St Andrews: St Andrews Film Studies, 2012), pp. 1–21.

Said, Edward W., *The World, the Text and the Critic* (London: Vintage, 1991).

Sakai, Naoki, 'Translation', *Theory, Culture & Society*, 23.2–3 (2006), pp. 71–86.

Schamus, James, 'Introduction', in *Lust, Caution: The Story, the Screenplay, and the Making of the Film* (New York: Pantheon, 2007), pp. xi–xv.

Schindler, Stephan K. and Lutz Koepnick (eds), *The Cosmopolitan Screen: German Cinema and the Global Imaginary, 1945 to the Present* (Ann Arbor, MI: University of Michigan Press, 2007).

Schoene, Bertolt, *The Cosmopolitan Novel* (Edinburgh: Edinburgh University Press, 2009).

Bibliography

Scott, A. O., 'In Toronto it's all about crowd pleasers and films that get lost in the shuffle', *The New York Times* (7 September 2008). Available at www.nytimes.com/2008/09/08/movies/08toro.html (accessed 29 July 2014).

Seigworth, Gregory J. and Melissa Gregg, 'An inventory of shimmers', in Gregory J. Seigworth and Melissa Gregg (eds), *The Affect Theory Reader* (Durham, NC: Duke University Press, 2010), pp. 1–25.

Seng, Eunice, 'Politics of greening: spatial constructions of the public in Singapore', in William S. W. Lim and Jiat-Hwee Chang (eds), *Non-West Modernist Past: On Architecture and Modernities* (Singapore: World Scientific Publishing, 2012), pp. 143–60.

Sho[c]hat, Ella and Robert Stam, 'The cinema after Babel: language, difference, power', *Screen* 26.3–4 (1985), pp. 35–58.

Sobchack, Vivian, 'What my fingers knew, the cinesthetic subject, or vision in the flesh', *Senses of Cinema* 5 (2000). Available at sensesofcinema.com/2000/conference-special-effects-special-affects/fingers/ (accessed 31 October 2014).

Spencer, Robert, *Cosmopolitan Criticism and Postcolonial Literature* (Basingstoke: Palgrave Macmillan, 2011).

Stacey, Jackie, 'Hollywood memories', in Annette Kuhn and Jackie Stacey (eds), *Screen Histories: A Screen Reader* (Oxford: Clarendon Press, 1999), pp. 22–39.

———, 'The violence of idealizations and the ambivalence of self', in Nina Glick Schiller and Andrew Irving (eds), *Whose Cosmopolitanism?: Critical Perspectives, Relationalities and Discontents* (New York: Berghahn, 2015), pp. 34–6.

Still, Judith and Michael Worton, 'Introduction', in Judith Still and Michael Worton (eds), *Intertextuality: Theories and Practices* (Manchester: Manchester University Press, 1990), pp. 1–44.

Storer, Russell, 'Repeat after me', *Ming Wong: Life of Imitation*, exhibition catalogue (Singapore: Singapore Art Museum, 2010), pp. 57–65.

Stringer, Julian, '"Your tender smiles give me strength": paradigms of masculinity in John Woo's *A Better Tomorrow* and *The Killer*', *Screen* 38.1 (1997), pp. 25–41.

———, 'Global cities and the international film festival economy', in Mark Shiel and Tony Fitzmaurice (eds), *Cinema and the City: Film and Urban Societies in a Global Context* (Oxford: Blackwell, 2001), pp. 134–44.

Szarkowska, Agnieszka, 'The power of film translation', *Translation Journal* 9.2 (2005). Available at translationjournal.net/journal/32film.htm (accessed 29 April 2013).

Talbot, Margaret, 'The auteur of anime', *The New Yorker* (17 January 2005). Available at www.newyorker.com/magazine/2005/01/17/the-auteur-of-anime (accessed 5 May 2014).

Tan, Ern Ser, *Does Class Matter? Social Stratification and Orientations in Singapore* (Singapore: World Scientific Publishing, 2004).

Bibliography

Tan Quancai, Eugene, 'One rule to rule them all: a study of Singapore censorship', *SGNewwave* (10 March 2010). Available at sgnewwave.com/main/2010/03/one-rule-to-rule-them-all-a-study-of-singapore-censorship/comment-page-1/ (accessed 14 August 2014).

Tang Fu Kuen, 'Notes from the curator', *Ming Wong: Life of Imitation*, exhibition catalogue (Singapore Art Museum, 2010), pp. 51–5.

Tay Suan Chiang, 'Theatre Majestic no more – The Majestic's unfriendly design and unattractive surrounds make it tough to find new uses that fit its cultural heritage', *The Straits Times, Life!* Section (19 November 2011).

Taylor, Jeremy E., *Rethinking Transnational Chinese Cinemas: The Amoy-Dialect Film Industry in Cold War Asia* (London: Routledge, 2011).

Teo, Stephen, *Hong Kong Cinema: The Extra Dimensions* (London: British Film Institute, 1997).

——, *Wong Kar-wai: Auteur of Time* (London: British Film Institute, 2005).

Tihanov, Galin, 'Narratives of exile: cosmopolitanism beyond the liberal imagination', in Nina Glick Schiller and Andrew Irving (eds), *Whose Cosmopolitanism?: Critical Perspectives, Relationalities and Discontents* (New York: Berghahn, 2015), pp. 141–59.

Ting, Selina, 'Interview: Ming Wong', *Initiart Magazine* (Summer 2009). Available at www.initiartmagazine.com/interview.php?IVarchive=12 (accessed 21 January 2012).

Turan, Kenneth, *Sundance to Sarajevo: Film Festivals and the World They Made* (Berkeley, CA: University of California Press, 2002).

Turner, Graeme, *Film as Social Practice IV* (Oxon: Routledge, 2006).

Uhde, Jan and Yvonne Ng Uhde, *Latent Images: Film in Singapore* (Singapore: Oxford University Press, 2000).

Venuti, Lawrence, 'Introduction', in Lawrence Venuti (ed.), *Rethinking Translation: Discourse, Subjectivity, Ideology* (London: Routledge, 1992), pp. 1–17.

Vitali, Valentina, 'Hou Hsiao-Hsien reviewed', *Inter-Asia Cultural Studies* 9.2 (2008), pp. 280–9.

Vitali, Valentina and Ashish Rajadhyaksha, 'Introduction to the dossier: Paul Willemen (1944–2012)', *Inter-Asia Cultural Studies* 14.1 (2013), pp. 85–93.

von Flotow, Luise, 'When Hollywood speaks "international French": the sociopolitics of dubbing for Francophone Québec', *Québec Studies* 50 (2010), pp. 27–46.

Wang, Yiman, 'The art of screen passing: Anna May Wong's yellow yellowface performance in the art deco era', *Camera Obscura* 60, 20.3 (2005), pp. 158–91.

Willemen, Paul, 'On realism in the cinema', *Screen* 13.1 (1972), pp. 37–44.

——, 'Pesaro', *Framework* 15/16/17 (1981), p. 96.

——, 'For a comparative film studies', *Inter-Asia Cultural Studies* 6.1 (2005), pp. 98–111.

—, 'Indexicality, fantasy and the digital', *Inter-Asia Cultural Studies* 14.1 (2013), pp. 110–35.
Wollen, Peter, *Paris Hollywood: Writings on Film* (London: Verso, 2002).
Wong, Cindy Hing-Yuk, *Film Festivals: Culture, People, and Power on the Global Screen* (Rutgers, NJ: Rutgers University Press, 2011).
Wu Huating and Joseph Man Chan, 'Globalizing Chinese martial arts cinema: the global–local alliance and the production of *Crouching Tiger, Hidden Dragon*', *Media, Culture & Society* 29.2 (2007), pp. 195–217.
Xiao, Jiwei, 'The quest for memory: documentary and fiction in Jia Zhangke's films', *Senses of Cinema* 59 (2011). Available at http://sensesofcinema.com/2011/feature-articles/the-quest-for-memory-documentary-and-fiction-in-jia-zhangke%e2%80%99s-films/ (accessed 18 August 2016).
Yeoh, Brenda S.A. and Lily Kong, 'Reading landscape meanings: state constructions and lived experiences in Singapore's Chinatown', *Habitat International* 18.4 (1994), pp. 17–35.
Yip Wai Yee, 'Goodbye to softcore cinema Yangtze', *The Straits Times* (1 March 2016). Available at www.straitstimes.com/lifestyle/entertainment/goodbye-to-softcore-cinema-yangtze (accessed 1 March 2016).
Yuen, Belinda, 'Safety and dwelling in Singapore', *Cities* 21.1 (2004), pp. 19–28.
—, 'Searching for place identity in Singapore', *Habitat International* 29 (2005), pp. 197–214.
Zhang Xudong, 'Poetics of vanishing: the cinema of Jia Zhangke', *New Left Review* 63 (2010), pp. 1–18.
Zhang, Yingjin, *Chinese National Cinema* (New York: Routledge, 2004).

Filmography

12 Storeys. 1997. Dir. Eric Khoo. Singapore: Zhao Wei Films.
15. 2003. Dir. Royston Tan. Singapore: Zhao Wei Films.
2046. 2004. Dir. Wong Kar-wai. Hong Kong / China / France / Italy / Germany: Jet Tone Production.
24 City. 2008. Dir. Jia Zhangke. China / Hong Kong / Japan: Xstream Pictures.
Annie Hall. 1977. Dir. Woody Allen. USA: MGM.
Atanarjuat: The Fast Runner. 2001. Dir. Zacharias Kunuk, Canada: National Film Board of Canada.
Be With Me. 2005. Dir. Eric Khoo. Singapore: Zhao Wei Films.
Bullet in the Head. 1990. Dir. John Woo. Hong Kong: Golden Princess Film Production.
Children of a Lesser God. 1986. Dir. Randa Haines. USA: Paramount Pictures.
Chinatown. 1974. Dir. Roman Polanski. USA: Paramount Pictures.
Chungking Express. 1994. Dir. Wong Kar-wai. Hong Kong: Jet Tone Production.
Cinema Paradiso. 1988. Dir. Giuseppe Tornatore. Italy / France: Cristaldifilm.
A City of Sadness. 1989. Dir. Hou Hsiao-Hsien. Hong Kong/Taiwan: 3-H Films, ERA International.
Cold Fever. 1995. Dir. Fridrik Thor Fridriksson. USA / Japan / Iceland / Denmark / Germany: Icelandic Film Corporation, et al.
The Conformist. 1970. Dir. Bernardo Bertolucci. Italy / France / West Germany: Paramount Pictures.
Crouching Tiger, Hidden Dragon. 2000. Dir. Ang Lee. Taiwan / Hong Kong / USA / China: Sony Pictures Classic.
Days of Being Wild. 1990. Dir. Wong Kar-wai. Hong Kong: In-Gear Film.
Death in Venice. 1971. Dir. Luchino Visconti. Italy / France: Alfa Cinematografica.
Doktor Rushdi / Doctor Rushdi. 1970. Dir. P. Ramlee. Malaysia: Merdeka Productions.
Early Summer, 1951. Dir. Yasujiro Ozu. Japan: Shochiku Eiga.
East Palace, West Palace. 1996. Dir. Zhang Yuan. China: Ocean Films.
Fallen Angels. 1995. Dir. Wong Kar-wai. Hong Kong: Jet Tone Production.
Film Socialisme. 2010. Dir. Jean-Luc Godard. Switzerland / France: Wild Bunch.
Ghost in the Shell. 1995. Dir. Mamoru Oshii. Japan: Bandai Visual Company.
The Good Earth. 1937. Dir. Sidney Franklin. USA: MGM.
Goodbye, Dragon Inn. 2003. Dir. Tsai Ming-liang. Taiwan: Homegreen Films.
The Grandmaster. 2013. Dir. Wong Kar-wai. Hong Kong: Jet Tone Production.

Filmography

Happy Together. 1997. Dir. Wong Kar-wai. Hong Kong: Jet Tone Production.
Howl's Moving Castle. 2004. Dir. Hayao Miyazaki. Japan: Studio Ghibli.
Hugo. 2011. Dir. Martin Scorsese. USA: Paramount Pictures.
Ibu Mertua Ku / My Mother-in-Law. 1962. Dir. P. Ramlee. Singapore / Malaysia: Malay Film Productions.
Imitation of Life. 1959. Dir. Douglas Sirk. USA: Universal Pictures.
In the Mood for Love. 2000. Dir. Wong Kar-wai. Hong Kong / France: Jet Tone Production.
In the Realm of the Senses. 1976. Dir. Oshima Nagisa. Japan: Oshima Productions.
Intermezzo: A Love Story. 1939. Dir. Gregory Ratoff. USA: United Artists.
Kimi no nawa. 1991–2. Drama series. Japan: NHK.
Knight Rider. 1982–6. Drama series. USA: NBC.
Kon-Tiki. 2012. Dir. Joachim Ronning and Espen Sandberg. Norway: Nordisk Film.
Labu dan Labi. 1962. Dir. P. Ramlee. Singapore / Malaysia: Malay Film Productions.
The Lady From Shanghai. 1947. Dir. Orson Welles. USA: Columbia Pictures.
The Last Emperor. 1987. Dir. Bernardo Bertolucci. China / Italy / UK /France: Columbia Pictures.
Late Spring, 1949. Dir. Yasujiro Ozu. Japan: Shochiku Eiga.
Le Bal. 1983. Dir. Ettore Scola. Italy/France/Algeria: Massfilm.
The Life of Jesus. 1997. Dir. Bruno Dumont. France: 3B Productions.
Little Flower. 1979. Dir. Chang Tseng. China: Beijing Film Studio.
Lust, Caution. 2007. Dir. Ang Lee. USA / China / Taiwan / Hong Kong: Focus Features.
MacGyver. 1985–92. Drama series. USA: ABC.
Miami Vice. 1984–90. Drama series. USA: NBC.
Mee Pok Man. 1995. Dir. Eric Khoo. Singapore: Zhao Wei Films.
Meshes of the Afternoon. 1943. Dirs. Maya Deren and Alexander Hammid. USA: Mystic Fire.
Millennium Actress. 2001. Dir. Satoshi Kon. Japan: Bandai Visual Company.
Mulan Joins the Army. 1939. Dir. Bu Wancang. China: Xinhua Film Company.
My Geisha. 1962. Dir. Jack Cardiff. USA: Paramount Pictures.
Notorious. 1946. Dir. Alfred Hitchcock. USA: RKO Pictures.
Penny Serenade. 1941. Dir. George Stevens. USA: Columbia Pictures.
Persona. 1966. Dir. Ingmar Bergman. Sweden: AB Svensk Filmindustr.
The Piano. 1993. Dir. Jane Campion. New Zealand / Australia / France: Miramax.
Princess Mononoke. 1997. Dir. Hayao Miyazaki. Japan: Studio Ghibli.
Private. 2004. Dir. Saverio Costanzo. Italy: Istituto Luce.
The Purple Rose of Cairo. 1985. Dir. Woody Allen. USA: Orion Pictures.
Raise the Red Lantern. 1991. Dir. Zhang Yimou. China / Hong Kong / Taiwan: ERA International.
Semerah Padi / The Village of Semerah Padi. 1956. Dir. P. Ramlee. Singapore / Malaysia: Malay Film Productions.

Sex and Zen. 1991. Dir. Michael Mak. Hong Kong: Golden Harvest.
Shrek the Third. 2007. Dirs. Chris Miller and Raman Hui. USA: Dreamworks / Paramount Pictures.
The Silence. 1998. Dir. Mohsen Makhmalbaf. Iran / Tajikistan / France: Makhmalbaf Productions.
South Park. 1997–. Comedy series. USA: Comedy Central.
Spirited Away. 2001. Dir. Hayao Miyazaki. Japan: Studio Ghibli.
Still Life. 2006. Dir. Jia Zhangke. China/Hong Kong: XStream Pictures.
Still Walking. 2008. Dir. Hirokazu Koreeda. Japan: Bandai Visual Company.
Street Angel. 1937. Dir. Yuan Muzhi. China: Mingxing Film Company.
Suspicion. 1941. Dir. Alfred Hitchcock. USA: RKO Radio Pictures.
Tai-Pan. 1986. Dir. Daryl Duke. USA: De Laurentiis Entertainment.
Throne of Blood. 1957. Dir. Akira Kurosawa. Japan: Toho Company / Kurosawa Production Company.
Titanic. 1997. Dir. James Cameron. USA: Paramount Pictures.
Tokyo Story. 1953. Dir. Yasujiro Ozu. Japan: Shochiku Eiga.
Twin Peaks. 1990–91. Drama series. USA: ABC.
What is Your Name? / Always in My Heart / Kimi no nawa. 1953. Dir. Hideo Oba. Japan: Shochiku Eiga.
Whisper of the Heart. 1995. Dir. Yoshifumi Kondo. Japan: Studio Ghibli.
The Wind Rises. 2013. Dir. Hayao Miyazaki. Japan: Studio Ghibli.
Women on the Verge of a Nervous Breakdown. 1988. Dir. Pedro Almadóvar. Spain: Laurenfilm.
Workers Exiting the Lumière Factory. 1895. Dir. Louis Lumière. France: Lumière.
The World. 2004. Dir. Jia Zhangke. China/Japan/France: XStream Pictures.

Index

Note: Page numbers in *italics* refer to images.

2.28 incident, 48
15, 110, *111*
24 City, 59–68
2046, 30, 33, 36, 50

Abbas, Ackbar, 30
affect, 17, 94, 95–6, 97, 101, 118
affective encounter, 94
affirmative criticality, 142
After Chinatown, 130–1
Ahmad, Yasmin, 111
Ahmed, Sara, 123, 136
Allen, Richard, 120–1
Allen, Woody, 10
Almodóvar, Pedro, 39
Always in My Heart / Kimi no nawa, 81, 83
Ampo demonstrations, 83
Andersen, Joseph, 22–3
Anderson, Benedict, 100
Anderson, Kay, 130
animation
　cinematic movement, 86–7
　dubbing and subtitling, 38–47
　history of, 87, 90
　self-reflexivity and (animated) form, 77–91
anime, 40, 77–8, 86–7, 89–90
Annie Hall, 10
Appadurai, Arjun, 2–3
art, 12–13, 142
arthouse cinema, 26, 39, 51, 115, 116
Atanarjuat: The Fast Runner, 25

audiences, 94–5, 122–3, 145
Austin, J. L., 70
Austin, Thomas, 60–1, 63–4
auteur cinema, 8, 40–1, 111
autoethnographer-performer, 133
awards, 25–6

Bachelard, Gaston, 104, 105
Baecker, Angie, 124, 139
Bal, Le, 26
Balfour, Ian, 40, 52
banned films, 58–9, 110
Bauman, Zygmunt, 7–8, 9
Be With Me, 25–6
Béhar, Henri, 39
Behind the Forbidden City, 110
'Bengawan Solo', 32
Benjamin, Walter, 10, 133
benshi narrators, 21–4
Bergfelder, Tim, 11
Bergman, Ingrid, 73, 75, 125
Berlant, Laurent, 109, 118, 143
Berry, Chris, 60
Bertolucci, Bernardo, 65, 74
Better Tomorrow, A, 35
Betz, Mark, 40, 44
bilingualism, 27, 53
Black Arts movement, 127
blackface, 128, 129
Board of Film Censors, 105
bodies
　cosmopolitan body, 136–40
　flâneur/flâneuse, 136

193

Index

bodies *(cont.)*
  gallery bodies and films, 120–3
  see also embodiment
border-crossings, 5, 6–7, 13, 47
Bordwell, David, 14
Bourdieu, Pierre, 24
Breakwell, Ian, 95–6
Bullet in the Head, 50

camera obscura, 66
Cameron, James, 11
Canadian cinema, 25, 111
Cannes Film Festival, 25, 50, 110
Cantonese-language cinema, 10, 27–32, 34–6, 38, 75
Canudo, Ricciotto, 14
carnal encounter, 136
Cathay Organisation, 31, 107
cel animation, 77, 78, 79, 85, 87
censorship, 58–9, 110
Chan, Fruit, 27
Chan, Jackie, 32
Chan, Kenneth, 108–9
Chan, Peter, 27
Chandler, David, 18–19
Chaney, David, 96
Chang, Eileen, 69, 70
Chang Tseng, 65
Chang, Yen-Jung, 85
Chaplin, Charlie, 48
Cheah, Pheng, 1–2, 13
Cheah, Philip, 108, 116
Chen Jianbin, 65
Chen, Joan (Chen Chong), 65, 66, 67, 76
Chen, Leo Chanjen, 48–9, 51
Chengdu, 60, 68
cheongsam (Chinese dress), 74
Cheung, Leslie, 50
Cheung, Mabel, 27
Cheung, Maggie, 28–9, 32, 50, 125
Chew, Matthew, 74
Children of a Lesser God, 48

China
  24 City, 58–9, 60, 61, 63
  After Chinatown, 131
  censorship, 110
  Lust, Caution, 69, 70, 73, 74, 76
  multilingual cinema, 21, 24, 27, 36
  self-reflexive memory and performance, 69, 70, 73, 74, 76
  self-reflexive memory and witness, 58–9, 60, 61, 63
Chinatown, 126–7, 130, 131, 132
Chinatowns, 105–6, 116, 130, 134
Chinese cinema, 4, 8, 10, 21, 24, 26–7, 34–6, 39, 138
Chinese dress, 74, 75
Chinese Exclusion Act, 130
Chinese immigrants, 130–1
Chineseness
  Chinese dress, 75
  embodiment, 127, 131
  Hong Kong cinema, 26–7, 29
  Lust, Caution, 69
  self-reflexive memory and performance, 69, 75
  Singapore Chinatown, 106
Chow, Rey, 17, 29, 30, 37–8, 53
Chua Beng Huat, 36
Chungking Express, 27, 28, 132
cinema
  attraction of, 3–4
  border-crossings, 6–7
  buildings, 4, 136
  cinema of attractions, 21, 101
  cinematic illusion, 66
  cinematic language, 11
  cinematic movement, 86–7
  classical cinema, 12, 14
  comparative cinema, 141–7
  context of film, 92
  as cultural power, 15–16
  cultural proximity/distance, 7–8, 37, 47

Index

cultural translation, 9–10
form, production and
  reception, 16–17
historical origins, 6, 20, 24
and memory, 56–7
politics of the 'foreign film', 8–9
self-reflexive memory, 62–3,
  66, 68, 72
stillness and movement, 62–3
technology, 14–15, 120, 121
temporality, 63
textuality, 7, 14
Cinema Babel, 40
Cinema Paradiso, 105
cinesthesia, 120, 136–7
citizenship, 18, 143, 144
City of Sadness, A, 48–52
city spaces, 103–4
classical cinema, 12, 14
classification systems, 110, 115–16
Cold Fever, 101–2, 103
collective memory, 57, 61
collectivities, 5, 6
colonialism, 3, 29–30, 134
comparative cinema, 141–7
'Concrete Road', 42, 43
Conformist, The, 74
Cooper-Chen, Anne, 41
cosmopolis, 96
cosmopolitan affect, 92–118
  cultural literacy, 111–17
  film festivals, 97, 102, 113
  overview, 117–18
cosmopolitan agency, 12
cosmopolitan body, 136–40
cosmopolitan cinema
  cultural translation, 9–10
  defining, 16–17
  imagined worlds, 12–13
cosmopolitan encounters, 96, 99
cosmopolitan geographies, 129–36
cosmopolitan memory, 57–8, 91

'cosmopolitan paradox', 19
cosmopolitanism
  attraction of, 2–3
  and the cinema, 1–17
  cinema and border-crossings, 6–7
  cinema form, production and
    reception, 16–17
  cinematic language, 11
  critical cosmopolitanism and
    comparative cinema, 141–7
  cultural proximity/distance, 7, 37, 47
  cultural relations, 6
  cultural translation, 9–10
  definitions, 1–3
  imagined worlds, 12–13
  inherent tensions, 4–5
  lure of cinema, 3–4
  and multiculturalism, 18–19
  ontological conflict, 17
  politics of the 'foreign film', 8–9
  self-reflexivity, 2
  textuality of cinema, 7
'Country Roads', 45, 46, 47
critical cosmopolitanism, 141–7
Crothers Dilley, Whitney, 69, 70
Crouching Tiger, Hidden Dragon,
  32, 145
cruel optimism, 118, 143
Cubitt, Sean, 77, 144–5
cultural capital, 6, 103
cultural literacy, 91, 100, 111–17, 145
cultural memory, 65, 91
cultural proximity/distance, 7, 37, 47
cultural relations, 6
Cultural Revolution, 29
cultural translation, 9–10
cultural trauma, 57
cultures, 18, 53, 146
cuts to films, 110, 116

Dargis, Manohla, 61
Days of Being Wild, 29, 33

Index

Death in Venice, 126
Delanty, Gerard, 141, 142
Denver, John, 42, 43, 44, 46, 47
Denzin, Norman, 133
Deren, Maya, 123
Derrida, Jacques, 37, 38
di Caprio, Leonardo, 11
difference, 8, 18, 102, 141, 142
Disney, 77–8, 87
documentary, 61, 64
Doktor Rushdi, 138, 139
Dreamworks, 25
dress, 74, 75
dual-language shooting, 19
dubbing
    cultural translation, 9–10
    Hong Kong cinema, 28, 34, 35, 36
    Japanese animation, 38–47
    multilingual cinema, 24–5, 52
    and subtitling, 44
    Whisper of the Heart, 40–7
Dumont, Bruno, 115
Dunaway, Faye, 126, 127, 128

East Palace, West Palace, 110
Edinburgh Film Festival, 93, 98, 112
Egoyan, Atom, 40, 52
Eisenstein, Sergei, 77, 78
Eleftheriotis, Dimitris, 6, 8
embodiment
    cinema form, production and reception, 17
    cosmopolitan body, 136–40
    cosmopolitan geographies, 129–36
    embodiment and encounter, 123–9
    embodiment as encounter, 119–40
    gallery bodies and films, 120–3
    overview, 119–20
encounters
    cosmopolitan affect, 96, 99
    critical cosmopolitanism, 144
    embodiment and encounter, 123–9

filmic encounters, 100–3
spatial encounters, 103–11
English dubbing, 40, 42, 43
English language, 30, 53
English subtitling, 10, 11, 34, 35, 37, 42, 139
ersatz cinema, 126
Escape to Happiness, 73
Eu Tong Sen, 106
Every Frame a Painting, 86
exile, 5

Fallen Angels, 28
fantasy, 12, 85
festivals *see* film festivals
'fictionalised documentary', 58, 59, 61, 64
Filem-Filem-Filem, 136
film classification, 10, 115–16
film festivals
    and cosmopolitan affect, 92–118
    cultural literacy, 111–17
    cultural memory, 65
    festival circuit, 101, 102
    festival films, 103
    festival gazes, 111, 112
    festival histories, 93
    filmic encounters, 100–3
    historical origins of cinema, 20
    overview, 92–100, 117–18
    spatial encounters, 103–11
Film Four, 40, 41
film-induced tourism, 101
film industry, 8, 15–16
Film Socialisme, 10
filmic encounters, 100–3
flâneur/flâneuse, 132, 133
flashbacks, 56, 64, 79
foreign film
    cultural relations, 6
    cultural translation, 9–10
    multilingual cinema, 20, 25–6, 36, 39, 52, 53

Index

ontological conflict, 17
politics of, 8–9
foreignness, 8–9, 23–4, 36
formalism, 55, 77
Four Malay Stories, 134, 137, 139
Fowler, Catherine, 123, 125
French language, 24–5
Freud, Sigmund, 55–6, 63
Fu, Poshek, 4, 10, 72
Fuji-kan, 24
Fujiki, Hideaki, 22, 23
full animation, 87

gallery bodies, 120–3
gallery films, 120–3
Galperin, William, 126
gaze, 74, 90, 112
geographies, 129–36
Ghibli *see* Studio Ghibli
Ghost in the Shell, 86
Glick Schiller, Nina, 3
'global' cinema, 6, 144
globalisation, 12, 13, 103, 143
Godard, Jean-Luc, 10
Golden Harvest studio, 32
Good Earth, The, 128
Goodbye, Dragon Inn, 108
Goodman, Nelson, 13
Grandmaster, The, 50
Grant, Cary, 73
Great Sichuan Earthquake, 68
Gregg, Melissa, 96, 101, 118, 119

Hammond, Paul, 95–6
Hansen, Miriam, 14
Happy Together, 116
haptic visuality, 122
Hara, Setsuko, 80
Harbord, Janet, 93
Hartley, Hal, 111
Hirasawa, Susumu, 85, 88
history

24 City, 64, 66
cosmopolitan geographies, 129
Lust, Caution, 76
Millennium Actress, 78, 80, 89
self-reflexive memory, 11, 57, 64, 66, 76
self-reflexivity and (animated) form, 78, 80, 89
Hitchcock, Alfred, 73, 74
Hjort, Mette, 100
HKIFF (Hong Kong International Film Festival), 95
Hollywood, 4, 8, 11, 16, 38, 72, 74, 75
Holocaust, 57–8
Hong Kong
cosmopolitan geographies, 132, 133
film festivals, 115
kung fu comedies, 40
multilingual cinema, 24, 26–38, 40, 50
'new wave' cinema, 32
and old Shanghai, 75–6
politics of the 'foreign film', 8
Honna, Youko, 47
Hou Hsiao-Hsien, 49, 50, 51, 52
How to Do Things with Words, 70
Howl's Moving Castle, 41
Hozic, Aida, 16
Hu Die, 75
Hugo, 105
Hunter, Holly, 48
Huston, John, 128

Ibu Mertua Ku / My Mother-in-Law, 137
Iceland, 101–2, 103, 111
imagination, 12–13, 144
imagined communities, 16, 99–100
imitation, 137, 140
Imitation of Life, 124, 140
immigration, 130–1
In Love for the Mood, 125, 139

197

Index

In the Mood for Love, 28, 32–3, *33*, 50, 124, 125
In the Realm of the Senses, 110
Indonesia, 138–9
induced movement, 87
inter-titles, 20
intercultural equivalence, 53
Interdisciplinary Literary Studies, 11
Intermezzo: A Love Story, 73
intertextuality, 61, 72, 85
Iordanova, Dina, 100
Iranian cinema, 102
Irving, Andrew, 3
Ito, Robert, 128
Iveković, Rada, 54

Jaffee, Valerie, 58, 59
Jamieson, Kirstie, 98, 111, 112, 113
Japan, 21–4, 77–8, 80, 85, 87, 89
Japanese animation
  anime, 40, 77–8, 86–7, 89–90
  dubbing and subtitling, 38–47
  history of, 87, 90
  self-reflexivity and (animated) form, 77–8, 86–7
Japanese language, 28
Jia Zhangke, 58, 59, 61, 63, 64, 65, 67
jishizhuyi ('on-the-spot realism'), 60
Johnson, G. Allen, 61, 64

Kabuki, 23
Kaneshiro, Takeshi, 28
Kaplan, E. Ann, 57
Kawase, Naomi, 111
Khoo, Eric, 111, 116
Kiarostami, Abbas, 111
Kim Ki-duk, 111
Kimi no nawa / What Is Your Name?), 81, 83
Kon, Satoshi, 85, 86, 91
Kon-Tiki, 19
Kondo, Yoshifumi, 41

Konfrontasi, 138
Kong, Lily, 106
Koreeda, Hirozaku, 94
Krishtalka, Sholem, 128, 129
Kuala Lumpur, 138, 139
kung fu comedies, 40
Kurosawa, Akira, 80, 81
Kwan, Stanley, 27

La Salle Brothers, 134
Labu dan Labi, 137
Lady From Shanghai, The, 131
Lai Chee Kien, 33, 34
Lamarre, Thomas, 78, 85–6, 87, 89
languages
  cinematic language, 11
  cultural translation, 4, 9–10
  dubbing and subtitling, 25–6, 34–6, 38
  historical origins of cinema, 20, 24
  Hong Kong cinema, 28–32, 34–6, 38
  multilingual cinema, 19, 37–8, 53, 76
  sound and muteness, 48
  vying availability of, 30
Last Emperor, The, 65
Late Spring, 80, *81*
Lau, Andy, 50
Laurel and Hardy films, 19
learning, 141, 142
Lee, Ang, 69, 72, 144
Lee, Bruce, 32
Lee Kang-sheng, 48
Lee, Leo Ou-fan, 69
Leung Chiu-wai, Tony, 30, 32, 48, 50, 69, 125
Levy, Daniel, 57, 58, 68
LGBTQ film festivals, 93
Liao, Hsien-hao Sebastian, 71
Life of Imitation, 123, 124, *124*, 125, 134, 137
Life of Jesus, The, 115
liminal space, 9

Index

liminality of affect, 96
limited animation, 87, 88, 90
Lin Ching-hsia, Brigitte, 132
Lin, Sylvia, 48
linguistic hybridity, 31
literacy, 37
literature, 2, 13
Little Flower / Xioahua, 65, 66–7
Liverpool, 130, 131
Lo, Kwai-cheung, 26, 29, 34–5, 36, 38
Lobato, Ramon, 16
lok, susan pui san, 127
Los Angeles, 24, 130, 132, 133
Lu, Sheldon, 29
Lü Liping, 65
Lumière brothers, 55, 68, 77
Lust, Caution, 69–76
Lynch, David, 66

MacLaine, Shirley, 128
Majestic theatre, 104, 105, 106–9, 110
Makhmalbaf, Mohsen, 111, 114
Making Chinatown, 128, 131
Malay cinema, 138–40
Malay Film Productions, 138
Mandarin-language cinema, 10, 24, 27–32, 34–6, 50, 75
Maoism, 63, 70
Marks, Laura, 122
Marx, Harpo, 48
Mathews, Gordon, 28
Matlin, Marlee, 48
Mee Pok Man, 116
Méliès, Georges, 55, 77
melodrama, 57, 140
memorialisation, 58, 68
memory
   24 City, 61, 63–8
   cinema and memory, 56–7
   comparative cinema, 145
   lure of cinema, 3–4
   memory politics, 57, 58

Millennium Actress, 78, 79, 91
   overview, 55–8
   screen memory, 55
   self-reflexive cinema, 55–91
   self-reflexive memory and performance, 68–76
   self-reflexive memory and witness, 58–68
   self-reflexivity and (animated) form, 77–91
Merdeka Film Productions, 138, 139
Meshes of the Afternoon, 123
Meskimmon, Marsha, 122, 142, 143, 144
methodological individualism, 5, 7
Mifune, Toshiro, 80
Millennium Actress, 78–85, 87, 88–91
Miller, David, 1
Minnan, 48, 50, 51
Mitchell, W. J. T., 91
Miyazaki, Hayao, 41
modernism, 106
modernity, 15, 17
modes of exhibition/reception, 122–3
Monnet, Liva, 86
Moriel, Liora, 137
Morris, Meaghan, 35, 146
movement, 86–7, 88, 90, 144
Mowitt, John, 53
Mulan Joins the Army / Mulan Congjun, 72
multiculturalism, 18, 141
multilingual cinema, 18–54
   advent of synchronised sound, 24
   benshi narrators, 21–4
   cinema form, production and reception, 17
   cosmopolitanism and multiculturalism, 18
   cultural translation, 10
   defining, 19
   dubbing and subtitling, 24–5, 38–47

Index

multilingual cinema *(cont.)*
  historical origins of cinema, 20
  Hong Kong cinema, 26–38
  overview, 18–26, 52–4
  sound and muteness, 47–54
Mulvey, Laura, 4, 62–3, 68
muteness, 48, 49
My Geisha, 128
My Mother-in-Law / Ibu Mertua Ku, 137

narrative storytelling, 3, 11–12
nationalisms, 20, 100
Nava, Mica, 17, 97, 118, 142
Neo Chon Teck, 134
'new wave' cinema, 27, 32, 48
New York Film Festival, 95
Newton-John, Olivia, 47
Nichols, Bill, 100, 101, 102
Nicholson, Jack, 126, 127, 128
nishiki-e (woodblock prints), 85
Nornes, Abé Mark, 36, 39, 40
nostalgia, 3–4, 109, 134
Not Like a Native Speaker, 53
Notorious, 74
Nugroho, Garin, 111

off-screen spaces, 122, 123
Office Kitano, 59
ontological conflict, 17, 30
Ortabasi, Melek, 80, 83
Oshima, Nagisa, 110
O'Sullivan, Carol, 40, 53
Ozu, Yasujiro, 80

Palmer, Belinda, 128
Pan Di-hua, Rebecca, 28, 29, *33*
Pang Laikwan, 21
Papastergiadis, Nikos, 12–13
Parker, Andrew, 70–1
Parker, Trey, 90
passing, 129, 137, 140

Peary, Gerald, 95
peephole cinemas, 134–5
Peng Hsiao-yen, 69, 70
Penny Serenade, 73
performance, 69, 70
performance ethnography, 133
performative utterances, 70
Persona, 125
Petrie, Duncan, 100
Piano, The, 48
plasmaticness, 78, 79
plastic realism, 142
Poetics of Space, The, 104
Polanski, Roman, 126, 130, 131, 132
Pomerance, Murray, 15
Popke, Jeff, 136
pornography, 116, 117, 136
post-colonialism, 2, 12, 143
Prakash, Gyan, 3
Princess Mononoke, 41
Private, 25
Purple Rose of Cairo, The, 105

qipao (traditional Chinese dress), 74, 75
Québecois audiences, 25

R classification, 115–17
racial passing, 129
racism, 130, 131, 132
Radstone, Susannah, 56–7
Rainer, Luise, 128
Raise the Red Lantern, 39
Ramlee, P., 137, 138, 139
Rapson, Jessica, 68
realism, 55, 60, 64, 77
reception, 122–3
REDCAT (Roy and Edna Disney / CalArts Theater), 128
Rendall, Steven, 10
Rich, B. Ruby, 39, 129
Richie, Donald, 22

Index

Robbins, Bruce, 19
Rohmer, Sax, 131
Ronning, Joachim, 19
Ruan Lingyu, 75
Ruoff, Jeffrey, 94

Said, Edward, 14, 16, 127
Sakai, Naoki, 9, 47
San Francisco, 130, 131, 132, 133
Schamus, James, 69–70
Scott, A. O., 94
screen memory, 55–6
Sedgwick, Eve Kosofsky, 70–1
Seeing in the Dark, 95–6
Seigworth, Gregory J., 96, 101, 118, 119
self-reflexive cinema, 55–91
   cinema form, production and reception, 17
   cinematic language, 11
   cosmopolitanism defined, 2
   embodiment, 132
   overview, 55–8, 91
   self-reflexive memory and performance, 68–76
   self-reflexive memory and witness, 58–68
   self-reflexivity and (animated) form, 77–91
Sembene, Ousmane, 111
Semerah Padi, 137
Sex and Zen, 116
Shanghai, 29, 71–6
Shanghai Film Group, 59
Shaw Brothers, 4, 31, 32, 107, 138
Shochiku studio, 83
Shohat, Ella, 52
Shrek the Third, 25
Silence, The, 114
silent cinema, 20, 24
Singapore
   embodiment, 133, 134, 137, 138, 139
   film festivals, 105, 110, 111

multilingual cinema, 25, 36, 37
Singapore International Film Festival, 97, 104, 105, 107, 110–11, 113–17
Sirk, Douglas, 124, 140
Snow, Brittany, 47
Sobchack, Vivian, 64, 119, 136
softcore porn, 116, 117
sound, 20, 23, 24, 48–9
South Park, 90
spatial encounters, 103–11
spectatorship, 4, 10–11, 122–3
Spencer, Robert, 2, 143, 144
Spirited Away, 41, 87
Spivak, Gayatri, 127
Stacey, Jackie, 4, 18
Staiger, Janet, 14
Stam, Robert, 52
Stevens, George, 73
Still Life, 59
Still Walking, 94
Stone, Matt, 90
Storer, Russell, 133, 140
'strangeness', 8–9, 20, 101, 112
'stranger' figure, 7–8, 9
Street, Sarah, 11
Street Angel / Malu Tianshi, 71, 72
Stringer, Julian, 35, 103–4
Studio Ghibli, 40, 41, 44, 87
Subtitles: On the Foreignness of Film, 40, 52
subtitling
   and comprehension, 11
   cosmopolitan body, 139
   cultural translation, 9–10
   dubbing and subtitling practices, 24–5, 44
   film festivals, 105
   Hong Kong cinema, 28, 34–6, 37, 38
   Japanese animation, 38–47
   multilingual cinema, 24–5, 52
   Whisper of the Heart, 42–7
Suspicion, 73

synchronised sound, 20, 23, 24, 48–9
Sznaider, Natan, 57, 58, 68

Tai-Pan, 65
Taiwan, 24, 29, 32, 48–50
'Take Me Home, Country Roads', 42, 44
Tan, Royston, 110, 111
Tan Pin Pin, 111
Tang Fu Kuen, 125, 136
Tang Wei, 69, 72, *73*
techne, 77
technology of cinema, 12, 14–15
temporality of cinema, 63
Teo, Stephen, 27
textuality, 7, 14, 16
Third Cinema conference, 93
Thompson, Kristin, 14
Throne of Blood, 80, *82*, 83
Tihanov, Galin, 5, 6, 7
Titanic, 11–12
To, Johnnie, 8
Tokyo, 42, 78
Toronto International Film Festival, 25, 94, 99, 103, 129
tourism, 101, 102
Translating Popular Film, 40, 53
translation
  and comprehension, 10–11
  cultural translation, 9–10
  dubbing and subtitling, 39–40, 42, 47
  Hong Kong cinema, 28, 38
  Japanese animation, 39–40, 42, 47
  multilingual cinema, 19, 52, 53
  politics of the 'foreign film', 9
trauma, 57, 64
travel, 6, 17, 144
Tribeca, 95
Tsai Ming-liang, 48, 108
Tsung-yi Huang, 133
Turner Classic Movies, 40, 41
Turner, Graeme, 92
Twin Peaks, 66

Ullman, Liv, 126

Venice, 48, 59
Venuti, Lawrence, 39
video installations, 125, 128, 133, 137
visceral cosmopolitanism, 17, 142
Visconti, Luchino, 125
Vitali, Valentina, 51–2
von Flotow, Luise, 25

'Wandering Songstress, The' / 'Tianya Genü', 71–3
Wang, Yiman, 128, 129, 132
Weerasethakul, Apichatpong, 111
Welles, Orson, 131
What Is Your Name? / *Kimi no nawa*, 81, 83
Whisper of the Heart, 41–7
Willemen, Paul, 12, 93, 146
Wind Rises, The, 41
Winslet, Kate, 11
Women on the Verge of a Nervous Breakdown, 39
Wong, Anna May, 132
Wong, Cindy, 93, 94, 95, 103, 112
Wong Kar-wai
  embodiment and encounter, 124, 132
  film festivals, 116
  Hong Kong cinema, 27–9, 32–4, 38
  sound and muteness, 50–1
Wong, Ming
  After Chinatown, 131, 132
  cosmopolitan body, 137, 139, 140
  cosmopolitan geographies, 130, 131, 132, 133, 134
  embodiment and encounter, 123–9
  gallery bodies and films, 123
  Making Chinatown, 128, 131
Woo, John, 35, 50
Workers Exiting the Lumière Factory, 68
'world' cinema, 6, 8, 20

world citizenship, 18, 144
World, The, 58, 59

Xiao, Jiwei, 63, 64
Xiaohua / Little Flower, 65, 66–7
Xinghui Productions, 59

Yangtze cinema, 117
yellowface, 128, 129, 132, 133
Yeoh, Brenda, 106

Yuan Muzhi, 71

Zhang Xudong, 58
Zhang Yimou, 39
Zhang, Yingjin, 31
Zhang Yuan, 110
Zhang Ziyi, 30
Zhao Tao, 65
Zhou, Tony, 86
Zhou Xuan, 71, 75

www.ingramcontent.com/pod-product-compliance
Lightning Source LLC
Chambersburg PA
CBHW062225300426
44115CB00012BA/2228